The Online Teaching Survival Guide

The Online Teaching Survival Guide

Simple and Practical Pedagogical Tips

Judith V. Boettcher
Rita-Marie Conrad

JOSSEY-BASS
A Wiley Imprint
www.josseybass.com

Published by Jossey-Bass
A Wiley Imprint
989 Market Street, San Francisco, CA 94103-1741—www.josseybass.com

Please see page 289 as a continuation of the copyright page.

Readers should be aware that Internet Web sites offered as citations and/or sources for further information may have changed or disappeared between the time this was written and when it is read.

Limit of Liability/Disclaimer of Warranty: While the publisher and author have used their best efforts in preparing this book, they make no representations or warranties with respect to the accuracy or completeness of the contents of this book and specifically disclaim any implied warranties of merchantability or fitness for a particular purpose. No warranty may be created or extended by sales representatives or written sales materials. The advice and strategies contained herein may not be suitable for your situation. You should consult with a professional where appropriate. Neither the publisher nor author shall be liable for any loss of profit or any other commercial damages, including but not limited to special, incidental, consequential, or other damages.

Jossey-Bass books and products are available through most bookstores. To contact Jossey-Bass directly call our Customer Care Department within the U.S. at 800-956-7739, outside the U.S. at 317-572-3986, or fax 317-572-4002.

Jossey-Bass also publishes its books in a variety of electronic formats. Some content that appears in print may not be available in electronic books.

Library of Congress Cataloging-in-Publication Data

Boettcher, Judith V.
   The online teaching survival guide : simple and practical pedagogical tips / Judith V. Boettcher, Rita-Marie Conrad.
       p. cm.
   Includes bibliographical references and index.
   ISBN 978-0-470-42353-0 (pbk.)
  1. Web-based instruction. 2. Computer-assisted instruction. 3. Distance education.
4. Education, Higher–Computer-assisted instruction. I. Conrad, Rita-Marie. II. Title.
   LB1044.87.B63   2010
   371.33′44678—dc22

                                                                          2010003738

Printed in the United States of America
FIRST EDITION
PB Printing   10 9 8 7 6 5 4 3 2 1

The Jossey-Bass Higher and
Adult Education Series

Contents

List of Tables, Figures, and Exhibits   xiii

Foreword   xv
  David McGeehan and Jim Wolford-Ulrich

Preface   xxi

The Authors   xxiii

Introduction   xxv

**PART ONE: CORE PRINCIPLES AND BEST PRACTICES OF ONLINE
              TEACHING AND LEARNING   1**

 1 Teaching Online—the Big Picture   3

        Chapter Overview   3

        Preparing to Teach in the Online Environment   3

        Oh, Oh. What Did I Say I Would Do?   4

        The Definition of a Course   5

        How Are Online Courses Unique?   7

        Three Types of Online Courses   9

        The Four Stages of a Course   9

        Learning Theories and Theorists   12

        How the Chapters in Part One Fit Together   17

        Summary—and What's Next   17

 2 Theoretical Foundations: Ten Core Learning Principles   18

        Chapter Overview   18

        Background of the Ten Core Learning Principles   19

        Ten Core Learning Principles   20

        Summary—and What's Next   35

3 Ten Best Practices for Teaching Online   36

    Chapter Overview   36

    Ten Best Practices for Beginning Online Teaching   36

    Conclusion   47

    Summary—and What's Next   47

PART TWO: SIMPLE, PRACTICAL, AND PEDAGOGICALLY BASED TIPS   49

4 Phase One: What's Happening, Themes, and Tools:
Starting Off on the Right Foot in Course Beginnings   51

    Chapter Overview   51

    What's Happening in Course Beginnings   51

    Course Beginnings Themes   53

    Technology Tools   57

5 Phase One: Tips for Course Beginnings   62

    Chapter Overview   62

    Getting Ready and Getting Acquainted   63

    CB Tip 1: Course Launch Preparations: The Essential
Course Elements of an Online Course   63

    CB Tip 2: Hitting the Road Running: How Not to
Lose the First Week!   70

    CB Tip 3: How an Online Syllabus Is Different   72

    CB Tip 4: Launching Your Social Presence in Your Course   75

    CB Tip 5: Getting to Know Students' Minds Individually:
The Vygotsky Zone of Proximal Development   79

    CB Tip 6: Getting into the Swing of a Course: Is There
an Ideal Weekly Rhythm?   81

    Creating and Designing Discussions   84

    CB Tip 7: The Why and How of Discussion Boards:
Their Role in the Online Course   84

    CB Tip 8: Characteristics of Good Discussion Questions   88

    CB Tip 9: Managing and Evaluating Discussion Postings   93

    CB Tip 10: The Faculty Role in the First Weeks:
Required and Recommended Actions   96

    Summary—and What's Next?   99

6 Phase Two: What's Happening, Themes, and Tools:
Keeping the Ball Rolling in the Early Middle   100

    Chapter Overview   100

What's Happening in the Early Middle Weeks   100

Early Middle: Themes, Best Practices, and Principles   102

Tips for the Early Middle   104

Technology Tools   106

7 Phase Two: Tips for the Early Middle   109

Chapter Overview   109

Managing Your Course   110

EM Tip 1: Tools for Communicating Teaching Presence: E-mails, Announcements, and Discussion Forums   110

EM Tip 2: Learning and Course Management Systems: Making Good Use of the Tools   114

EM Tip 3: Weekly Rhythm: Challenges to the Plan   117

EM Tip 4: Early Feedback Loop from Learners to You   120

EM Tip 5: Early Feedback Tools: Rubrics, Quizzes, and Peer Review   123

EM Tip 6: The Why and How of Group Projects Within Online Courses: Setting Up and Structuring Groups   127

EM Tip 7: Sharing the Teaching and Learning: Working with a Teaching Assistant   130

Strategies and Tools for Building Community   133

EM Tip 8: Promoting Peer Interaction and Community with Learner-to-Learner Dialogue and Teaming   133

EM Tip 9: Online Classrooms and Tools for Synchronous Collaboration   136

EM Tip 10: Using Audio and Video Resources to Create a More Engaging and Effective Course   140

Building the Cognitive Presence   145

EM Tip 11: A Good Discussion Post Has Three Parts   145

EM Tip 12: Discussion Wraps: A Useful Cognitive Pattern or a Collection of Discrete Thought Threads   148

EM Tip 13: Getting an Early Start on Cognitive Presence   151

EM Tip 14: Launching Learner Projects That Matter to the Learner   153

Summary—and What's Next   156

8 Phase Three: What's Happening, Themes, and Tools: Letting Go of Power in the Late Middle   157

Chapter Overview   157

What's Happening in the Late Middle Weeks   157

Late Middle: Themes, Best Practices, and Principles   159

Tips for the Late Middle   162

Technology Tools   162

9 Phase Three: Tips for the Late Middle   165

Chapter Overview   165

Leveraging the Power of Questions   166

LM Tip 1: Questions and Answers: Upside Down
and Inside Out   166

LM Tip 2: Three Techniques for Making Your Students'
Knowledge Visible   169

LM Tip 3: Moving Beyond Knowledge Integration to
Defining Problems and Finding Solutions   170

Assessing Learning as You Go   173

LM Tip 4: "Are You Reading My Postings? Do You Know Who
I Am?" Simple Rules About Feedback in Online Learning   173

LM Tip 5: Feedback on Assignments: Being Timely and Efficient   176

LM Tip 6: Reshaping Learning Habits of Online Students   180

Project Work Practices   183

LM Tip 7: Customizing and Personalizing Learning   183

LM Tip 8: Managing and Facilitating Group Projects   186

LM Tip 9: Assessing Group Projects   190

LM Tip 10: A Rubric for Analyzing Critical Thinking   194

LM Tip 11: Four Effective Practices During Project Time   195

Community Empowerment and Social Networking   199

LM Tip 12: Course Middles and Muddles: Souped-Up
Conversations That Help Build Community   199

LM Tip 13: Using Social Networking Techniques to Build
a Learning Community   201

LM Tip 14: Experts: A Touch of Spice   204

Summary—and What's Next?   208

10 Phase Four: What's Happening, Themes, and Tools: Pruning,
Reflecting, and Wrapping Up in the Closing Weeks   209

Chapter Overview   209

What's Happening in the Closing Weeks   210

Closing Weeks: Themes, Best Practices, and Principles   211

Tips for the Closing Weeks   213

Technology Tools   213

11 Phase Four: Tips for the Closing Weeks   216

Meaningful Projects and Presentations   217

CW Tip 1: Reaching the Heights of Learning:
Authentic Problem Solving   217

CW Tip 2: Using What-If Scenarios: Flexing Our Minds
with Possibilities   221

CW Tip 3: Stage 3 of a Learning Community:
Stimulating and Comfortable Camaraderie   224

CW Tip 4: Learners as Leaders   226

CW Tip 5: Course Wrapping with Concept Mapping:
A Strategy for Capturing Course Content Meaningfully   229

Preparing for the Course Wrap   234

CW Tip 6: Pausing, Reflecting, and Pruning Strategies   234

CW Tip 7: Creating a Closing Experience: Wrapping Up
a Course with Style   236

CW Tip 8: Real-Time Gatherings: Stories and Suggestions for
Closing Experiences   240

CW Tip 9: Debriefing Techniques with Students: What One
Change Would They Recommend?   244

Conclusion—and What's Next?   245

PART THREE: WHAT'S NEXT   **247**

12 Reflecting and Looking Forward   249

Chapter Overview   249

Reflecting and Looking Forward Using the Four Course Phases   249

Reflecting and Looking Forward with the Learning
Experiences Framework   255

Advice from Fellow Online Instructors   257

Rubrics and Best Practices for Quality Online Courses   260

Conclusion: Innovation as a Three-Phase Process   260

Appendix: Resources for Learning More About the Research
and Theory of Teaching Online   261

References   267

Index   277

List of Tables, Figures, and Exhibits

Tables

1.1	Types of Courses	9
1.2	Phase One: Course Beginnings—Starting Off on the Right Foot	10
1.3	Phase Two: Early Middle—Keeping the Ball Rolling	11
1.4	Phase Three: Late Middle—Letting Go of the Power	11
1.5	Phase Four: Closing Weeks—Pruning, Reflecting, and Wrapping Up	12
2.1	Ten Core Learning Principles	20
3.1	Ten Best Practices for Teaching Online	37
4.1	Basic Skills and Tools for Using a Course Management System	57
4.2	Tools in Course Beginnings Tips and Suggested Pedagogical Uses	59
5.1	Elements of an Online Course	68
5.2	Sample Weekly Schedule for an Online Course	83
5.3	Simple Rubric for Evaluating Weekly Postings	95
5.4	Phases of Engagement	97
6.1	Tools in Early Middle Tips and Suggested Pedagogical Uses	107
7.1	Simple Three-Point Rubric	125
7.2	Rubric for Participation and Levels of Thinking	125
8.1	Tools in Late Middle Tips and Suggested Pedagogical Uses	163
9.1	Examples of Critical Thinking Criterion 5: Integrates Issue Using Other Perspectives and Positions	195
10.1	Tools in Closing Weeks Tips and Suggested Pedagogical Uses	214
11.1	Checklist for a Learner-Led Activity	229

Figures

1.1	A Landscape for Teaching and Learning Online	16
2.1	Learning Experience Framework	21
2.2	Customizing Content Resources	27
7.1	Performance Dashboard in Blackboard	115
7.2	Practical Inquiry Model	152
11.1	Concept Map Showing Key Features of Concept Maps	232

Exhibits

7.1	Sample Form for Group Availability and Contact Information	129
9.1	Team Member Evaluation Form	192

Foreword

WE ARE ESPECIALLY pleased to see Judith and Rita-Marie's eminently practical tips for online teaching made available to a wide audience. It has been our privilege to work alongside and learn from these two pioneer distance educators, and we have seen our own online faculty and students benefit from their guidance and practical wisdom now assembled in this book. The tips comprising the heart of this book were crafted to meet the needs of actual faculty, some of them veteran classroom instructors, although many others were novice teachers. All were challenged in one way or another as they sought to embrace and exploit for positive ends the emergent and fluid technologies that have made teaching and learning online over these past ten years or so not only merely possible but also effective and dynamic.

Those whose craft is teaching will rightly want to understand how these teaching tips, viewed as artifacts in the culture of online education, came to be, what purposes they were designed to serve, and how they might best be employed in the user's own context. We aim in this Foreword, then, to describe organizational factors that contributed to their genesis, situate them in the administrative and pedagogical environment in which they first made sense, and suggest ways that readers can leverage them to further advantage.

The School of Leadership and Professional Advancement (SLPA), one of ten schools at Duquesne University in Pittsburgh, serves the educational needs of approximately one thousand nontraditional, working adult students. Our credit and noncredit courses were originally offered only on evenings and weekends in traditional classroom formats. Gradually our student mix has evolved to consist of roughly 50 percent online students: undergraduates and graduates who take online courses comprising nearly half of all their credit hours. Another 25 percent of courses offered now include Web enhancement: the support of a Blackboard (Duquesne's learning management system, LMS) course site for an otherwise classroom-based course, and that percentage is steadily rising.

The instructors who teach SLPA students are either full-time faculty in the other nine Duquesne schools or part-time adjunct professors. We have personal relationships with many part-time faculty who live in the Pittsburgh area and are able to attend faculty events and trainings on campus. Many others are dispersed around North America; some we have never met. We provide technical and pedagogical support to all SLPA instructors, including those who are outside the United States, whether on business or military duty. We have relied heavily on Rita-Marie and Judith for faculty support and professional development, referring to them as e-coaches. By distributing actionable tips, synchronized with the academic calendar and course teaching cycle, by regularly facilitating faculty Webinars open to all SLPA instructors, and by coaching individual faculty on an as needed basis, Judith and Rita-Marie have provided multiple layers of support.

Our partial and ongoing transition to online instruction provided a unique opportunity to influence the teaching practice of faculty. We embedded standardized course site layouts and suggested syllabus elements in the Blackboard template used schoolwide. We provided sample syllabi and rubrics, stock instruction sets for students (for example, on accessing course reserve readings, library electronic databases, or our campus writing center), and context-sensitive help for faculty. Instructors were free to ignore or change such passive guidance, but most built on the platform we provided and leveraged it to strengthen the overall quality of the student learning experience.

As distance learning technology advances and our LMS supports more and more interactive plug-ins, the faculty learning curve steepens. Our part-time instructors, few of whom have teaching backgrounds and most of whom hold full-time professional jobs outside the university, eagerly adopt the instructional and technical aids. This frees us to concentrate on higher-order teaching skills in our faculty development efforts. This is the space that Judith and Rita-Marie have filled, both educating faculty on the use of new and emerging media and challenging assumptions about the nature of teaching and promoting dialogue about the effective integration of technology with teaching and learning.

In a world where innovative communication technologies often drive pedagogical change, we find it refreshing to see online instructional practices rooted in sound pedagogical theory. As an adult and continuing education unit, we needed an approach to helping SLPA faculty develop that was congruent with best practices in teaching adults. Rita-Marie and Judith, tireless advocates for learner-centered, constructivist approaches to teaching, have set the bar for faculty high, and they have provided practical and accessible tips for online teaching. By noting frequent linkages to the theory base, they have filled a much-needed gap in the distance education literature. It is this set of comprehensive and well-grounded tips that you now hold in your hand.

Whether you seek to strengthen your own online teaching practice or to support a local community of online teachers, you will find much value in this book. It has been our privilege to work alongside Judith and Rita-Marie as they have invited our faculty to reflect on and sharpen their online teaching skills. We are pleased that this exchange of teaching practice can now extend, through this book, to the ever growing audience of online educators around the world.

Pittsburgh, Pennsylvania

October 2009

David McGeehan

Director of Technology

Jim Wolford-Ulrich

Associate Professor and Team Leader

School of Leadership and Professional Advancement

Duquesne University

To our families for their constant support and patience
To all faculty striving to do a great job at teaching and learning
wherever they may be

Preface

EVERY BOOK has a beginning, and the seeds of this one were planted in early 2006 with a request from the leadership of the School of Leadership and Professional Advancement at Duquesne University in Pittsburgh, Pennsylvania. The administration wanted to provide more active and ongoing support to online faculty to help ensure the quality of the online teaching and learning experience. The path they chose was to request coaching services tailored to the online faculty. Thus began the creation of a set of tips to guide faculty practices in this new environment. Over time the library of tips grew to almost seventy, and feedback on the usefulness of the tips also increased. And then the idea of organizing these course delivery tips and adding tips on developing online courses in a more permanent and easily referenced format took hold.

We have been colleagues for over fifteen years now, and by the time we launched this project, we had already completed two editions of the *Faculty Guide for Moving Teaching and Learning to the Web* together. We have also worked many years helping faculty integrate pedagogical theory with the generations of new digital tools. We are well versed in the challenges that higher education faces in providing continued professional and teaching support for faculty. A book focusing on the life of a course and the tips for each phase of it seemed a natural choice as a next step to supporting the higher education community.

Acknowledgments

It is never possible to acknowledge everyone who contributed to the ideas, structure, and completion of a book. But we must try. First and foremost, thanks go to Benjamin Hodes, previous dean, and Boris Vilic, previous director of technology services, at Duquesne's School of Leadership and Professional Advancement, who launched the first e-coaching services.

Next, thanks go to the ongoing leadership of dean Dorothy Basset, assistant dean for academic affairs Michael Forlenza, director of technology David McGeehan, and associate professor and team leader of the leadership faculty Jim Wolford-Ulrich.

Thanks also to all the faculty and students whose questions inspired many of the tips and who contributed their ideas and suggestions for making the tips practical, simple, and pedagogically sound. Although the tips were originally for the faculty at Duquesne, faculty from institutions large and small, public and private, graduate and undergraduate, and degree and certificate programs alike inspired the questions. Thanks also go to our colleagues who provided feedback on early drafts of the chapters and to the reviewers for their suggestions and feedback that resulted in an improved guide overall.

Special thanks to our editor Erin Null for her encouragement and support during the sometimes arduous but always satisfying task of completing this book and keeping it focused.

The Authors

JUDITH V. BOETTCHER is a consultant, author, and speaker on online and distance learning. She is affiliated with the University of Florida and a founder of and consultant with Designing for Learning. She is a frequent keynoter at teaching and learning conferences, conducts workshops for faculty in distance and online learning, writes and speaks regularly on these topics, and consults on program designs for online and distance learning. She was the executive director of CREN (Corporation for Research and Educational Networking) from 1997 to 2003 and served as the program director and cohost of the CREN audio Webcast TechTalks for six years. Before joining CREN, Boettcher was the director of the Office of Interactive Distance Learning at Florida State University and the director of Education Technology Services at Penn State University. She served as the project leader for the Educational Uses of Information Technology Joe Wyatt Challenge EDUCOM project, 1990–1992, editing the publication *101 Success Stories of Information Technology in Higher Education: The Joe Wyatt Challenge* (1993). She is the author of many features and columns in higher education magazines and journals, *Campus Technology* (formerly *Syllabus*), *Innovate*, and *EDUCAUSE*. Her columns in *Campus Technology* have been a regular feature for over fifteen years. She is also the editor and coeditor of books addressing planning, design, and implementation issues of higher education technology and distance and online learning. She is the coauthor with Rita-Marie Conrad of two editions of the *Faculty Guide for Moving Teaching and Learning to the Web* (1999, 2004). She is as well one of the editors of the two editions of the four-volume *Encyclopedia of Distance Learning*, 2005/2009 Idea Group. She holds a Ph.D. in education and cognitive psychology from the University of Minnesota and a master's degree in English from Marquette University in Milwaukee, Wisconsin.

• • •

RITA-MARIE CONRAD is an online faculty member at various institutions, including Florida State University, where she has developed and led two online programs: the instructional systems major in performance improvement and human resource development and the instructional systems major in open and distance learning. She has designed and taught online courses on topics such as online collaboration, learning theories, designing online instruction, and developing e-learning strategies for training programs. She has consulted on the design and implementation of online learning courses, evaluated online programs, managed technology-related projects, and provided educational technology consulting and training to K–12 teachers and higher education faculty. She interacts with hundreds of faculty as an online instructor for courses such as Designing Online Instruction and Engaging Online Learners sponsored by the Learning Resources Network. She has presented at conferences sponsored by the International Council for Distance Education, the University of Wisconsin, the Minnesota State Colleges and Universities, League of Innovation, and the Association for Educational Communication and Technology on a variety of online learning topics. She coauthored the *Faculty Guide for Moving Teaching and Learning to the Web* with Judith Boettcher, as well as *Engaging the Online Learner* with J. Ana Donaldson and *Assessing Learners Online* with Albert Oosterhof and Donald Ely. She has a Ph.D. in instructional systems from Florida State University and a master's degree in educational media and computers from Arizona State University.

Introduction

THIS BOOK IS a practical and valuable resource for faculty who want to teach quality online courses. Moving from a face-to-face environment to an environment created by a rich and ever-changing set of technology tools can be intimidating and challenging. Adapting lifelong familiar teaching habits to a technologically immersive environment takes time, energy, patience, and a willingness to try new teaching strategies and new tools. While instructors who are new to online teaching need support of many kinds, from technology to online course design to simple encouragement, they especially appreciate help in the form of simple and practical tips and best practices for teaching in the online environment.

This book meets the needs of online faculty by providing tips for effective pedagogy and technologies in the online environment. It particularly meets the needs of faculty with little support or access to support or information about the unique characteristics of online pedagogy. Often faculty are assigned to take one of their existing courses and teach it online the following term. Faculty may be expected to simply teach the course without any additional time, resources, or support. What happens next is often a frustrating and unsatisfactory teaching experience and a frustrating and unsatisfactory learning experience for learners. This book details not only what faculty must do to offer an online course that is worthy of the name, but how to do it with ease and confidence.

This guide contains a set of simple, practical theory-based instructional strategies mapped to the four phases of a course: Course Beginnings, the Early Middle, the Late Middle, and Closing Weeks. This organization helps new faculty not only survive well their first online teaching experience, but also lays a foundation for many successful and rewarding experiences. This guide provides answers to all-important questions such as, "What is absolutely critical to getting a course online?" "What should I—and my learners—be doing now?" and "What should I—and my learners—be planning on doing next?"

Many resources for assisting faculty in teaching in the online environment address the need for faculty to get to know the new technologies. This guide combines theory-based and practice-based pedagogy in the tips to achieve the twin goals of both effective and efficient teaching and learning experiences. When learning and pedagogical principles guide online teaching practice, experiences in the online environment incorporate the enduring qualities of face-to-face experiences, rich mentor-learner relationships, delight in developing personal competencies, and a richness of community among the learners.

Intended Audience and Uses of the Book

This book can help faculty wherever they might be, on campuses large or small or in areas remote from their home campuses. It can be most helpful for instructors with little access to faculty support services and for faculty with little or no experience in online instructional environments and, likely, little time to prepare for online teaching. This is a useful resource as well for faculty who are planning a gradual transition from the face-to-face environment to online environments, blending campus and online environments. For institutions requiring online faculty to complete a course or program prior to teaching online, this guide can be used as a resource during the training program and as an ongoing resource after the initial training.

Despite the fact that courses have been offered on the Internet for over fifteen years or so, starting in the mid-1990s (docs.moodle.org/en/Online_ Learning_History) structures and processes for supporting faculty for teaching online are still evolving (Sorcinellini, Austin, Eddy, & Beach, 2006). In addition, the use of adjuncts, graduate students, and other less experienced personnel as members of instructional teams is increasing and is projected to increase even more (Bennett, 2009).

Book Overview

Part One provides an overview of the essential online teaching and learning concepts and practices. Chapter One provides the big picture of the organization of a course, from the course beginnings to the early middle, the late middle, and closing weeks of a course. These are the four phases of a course, regardless of the length of the course offering. This chapter also describes how faculty and learner roles change over the term of a course as a community develops and learners assume increasing responsibility for directing their learning. Chapter Two describes a four-element learning experiences framework based on the key elements of learner, mentor, knowledge, and environment. This framework is useful for guiding the design and implementation of any learning experience and simplifies the design and development process of online teaching and learning experiences. This chapter analyzes each of these elements and their pedagogical role in learning experiences. This design framework encourages an analysis of learner characteristics, faculty characteristics, the knowledge and skill structures and competencies desired, and the environment—the where, when, with whom, and with what resources a learning experience happens. With the addition of the management element, this framework provides the basis for the design of new programs and degrees as well. This chapter provides a set of ten core learning principles that serve the purpose of designing and managing effective experiences for the evolving online environments and integrate instructional design, principles of teaching and learning, and principles of technology change and processes. These ten principles serve as the foundational thinking for all the tips in this book. Chapter Three next provides a starter set of effective online teaching practices. The highlights of how to be an effective online instructor are encapsulated in this set of ten practices. This set of best practices is a good starter set for faculty.

Part Two is the core of the book: eight chapters of practical theory-based tips mapped to the four stages of a course. There are two chapters for each of the course stages. The first chapter for each phase summarizes what's happening in that phase and its teaching and learning themes. Each of these chapters also describes some of the tools that are most essential and useful at a particular phase. The second chapter for each phase contains the tips for that phase.

Chapters Four and Five address the first phase of a course. These chapters focus on tips for launching the social dimensions of community and getting to know the initial cognitive states of the learners. Chapters Six and Seven address the early middle phase. They provide strategies and hints for nurturing the growth of the learning community and engaging learners with the core content concepts. Chapters Eight and Nine turn to the late middle phase of the course. They focus on hints for supporting project work and supporting learners' move to independence. Chapters Ten and Eleven address the last phase of a course: closing weeks. They discuss hints and strategies for projects, presentations, and ideas and practices for closing out course experiences.

Part Three looks ahead to how faculty might want to proceed after completing their initial online teaching and learning experiences. Chapter

Twelve reviews some of the recommended ways for reflecting on, analyzing, and then making changes and plans for the next offering of a course. The Appendix sets out resources for continued development as a professional online instructor.

This book provides support for a four-stage structure of courses within a design framework based on traditional pedagogical principles integrated with current memory and brain research, instructional design, and online learning research. In addition, these tips address pedagogical uses of the more recent collaborative and synchronous Web applications such as live classrooms, wikis, blogs, and podcasts and the newer mobile handheld tools. This latest wave of tools makes possible even deeper and more lasting collaboration, communication, and synchronicity online as in the traditional classroom.

How to Use This Guide

Each faculty teaching an online course will find his or her own particular way of using this book. It is intended as a step-by-step guide following the tasks of preparing and teaching a course through the four phases of a course. It is also intended as a reference guide and answers many frequently asked questions. The initial chapters lay the foundation for thinking about pedagogy; the chapters with the tips provide answers to questions that make a difference in the effectiveness and satisfaction of online teaching and learning experiences. These tips help instructors survive and enjoy the challenges of teaching in what is for many a foreign and even intimidating environment. Many faculty will find this book a useful resource as they develop expertise in teaching online, which takes time, energy, and patience.

A faculty member new to teaching online may have time only for reading the initial chapters and then focusing on building assessment plans and creating the posts for the initial set of discussion forums. During the second cycle of a course, a faculty member may be ready to apply many more of the tips. Subsequent to those initial experiences, the faculty member should find the deeper analysis issues of great interest. Most innovative practices take root over a period of these three cycles. The first cycle is survival, the second cycle is a feeling of competency, and the third integrates exploration and innovation.

This is a book that will grow in value as the instructor grows in online experience. The phased nature of the book can be a lifesaver for both faculty and the students they teach.

The Online Teaching Survival Guide

Part One

Core Principles and Best Practices of Online Teaching and Learning

Chapter 1

Teaching Online— the Big Picture

Chapter Overview

This chapter lays out a philosophical landscape for teaching and learning online, introducing some of the core principles and best practices that are characteristic of that philosophy. This chapter also briefly discusses the major differences between an online course and a face-to-face course. It provides an overview of the four phases of a course—course beginnings, the early middle, the late middle, and the closing weeks—and the happenings, themes, and behaviors that normally occur in those stages. It thus serves as an introduction to Chapters Four to Eleven, which provide tips, suggestions, and guidelines on how to create and deliver an efficient, effective, and satisfying course at each stage.

This chapter as well describes the philosophical landscape of the principles, practices, and tips in the later chapters with brief sketches of the key constructivist learning theories and theorists that have shaped and inspired much of the thinking set out in this book.

Preparing to Teach in the Online Environment

As the demand for online programs has increased over the past ten to fifteen years, deans and department chairs have often turned to their faculty and simply assigned them to online courses without much support or training. The expectation is that faculty will use whatever resources are available on campus from technology centers or teaching centers and learn to use online tools: course management systems, synchronous collaborative "live" classrooms, and working with and assessing media of all types, including audio, video, and images. Many institutions do acknowledge the need for time and for assistance, but as the tools are becoming easier to use and more widely dispersed generally, getting time and assistance to learn how to teach online—and to redesign a course for the new online environment—is increasingly difficult. These expectations reflect a belief that teaching online is not much different from teaching in a face-to-face environment. This is not the case. Teachers who are effective in the face-to-face environment will be effective as online teachers, but it is not automatic and it will not happen overnight.

Oh, Oh. What Did I Say I Would Do?

We've all done it at one time or another: agreed to do something and then found ourselves wondering how we were going to do it. Many faculty find themselves in this state of concern and trepidation when they agree to teach a course online. Just minutes later, they often wonder what they have agreed to do and can feel clueless about what the first step might be. Even experienced campus faculty feel a little nervous about teaching online for the first time. And faculty may well have that feeling that everyone else knows exactly how to prepare and teach online, and they don't know what questions or whom to ask.

Well, how hard can it be? A common practice for teaching in the face-to-face environment is to use the syllabus and notes from someone who has taught the course before. This often happens when a mentor hands a new instructor a large binder with his notes and says, "Go forth and teach." For a new course, the strategy is a bit more complex. The instructor must determine the content of the course, search out and review textbooks or resources that map to the learning outcomes, order the resources (probably a textbook), and then plan the class meetings and some assessments and tests around those content resources. Are the steps in preparing a course for the online environment just like this, but with the additional layer of getting to know and use the online environment? This chapter answers these questions.

But to get us started—just what is a course, anyway?

Is This You?

The current cadre of faculty teaching online includes the following major categories of faculty: a tenured faculty member with decades of teaching experience; an assistant professor facing the need to teach, do research, and meet tenure requirements; an untenured faculty member with a heavy teaching load; and a part-time adjunct with content expertise and a touch of teaching experience.

You have been teaching for five, ten, or even twenty to thirty years. You are an expert in your subject area, but not in technology or in the pedagogy of how to ensure learning in different environments. You wish you had someone who could walk you through the steps in preparing a course for online students. You wish you knew which of your classroom teaching strategies and behaviors will work well in the online environment and what new behaviors and strategies you need to learn.

Or you may be a tenure-track faculty member who must focus on meeting tenure requirements.

You do not have the time or the energy to develop all the new skills associated with teaching online. You wish there was a way to reduce the amount of time and energy spent teaching, but you also would like the learners in your online courses to enjoy learning with you. You have been assigned to teach your course online as part of a larger program degree online offering. Are there ways to teach online but within defined time and technology knowledge parameters?

Or you are an adjunct faculty member who will be teaching an occasional course online. In a weak moment, you volunteered. You are excited about the opportunity to teach a course online because you enjoy teaching; you enjoy the dialogue and relationships you build with students, but you don't enjoy the hassles of getting to campus and parking late at night. How can you—with limited time and expertise—create and develop an online course that students will love?

This book can help you achieve your goals.

The Definition of a Course

We often assume that as faculty, we know what a course is and what pedagogy, the study of teaching, is. But do we? Sometimes it is helpful to review the origins of the terms that we use every day. Particularly as we move to new environments, issues of how we structure teaching and learning, purposes of learning, and resources and time for learning are worth a fresh look.

The following definition of *pedagogy* by Basil Bernstein, a British sociologist and linguist, suggests some interesting possibilities as to the means of instruction, particularly in our world of learning objects, tutorials, simulations, and mobile everything:

> *Pedagogy is a sustained process whereby somebody(s) acquires new forms or develops existing forms of conduct, knowledge, practice and criteria from somebody(s) or something deemed to be an appropriate provider and evaluator. Appropriate either from the point of view of the acquirer or by some other body(s) or both [Bernstein, in Daniels, 2007, p. 308].*

This definition highlights three elements of teaching and learning: (1) a learner, (2) someone or something appropriate guiding or directing the learner, and (3) the acquisition of conduct, knowledge, or practice by the learner. The element of "someone or something" leaves open the possibility of learning being guided by a "something," which might include resources such as texts, tutorials, simulations, virtual worlds, or even robots. This will be very common in the online world. Pedagogy, as defined here, requires a sustained process, which needs a context or an environment, that is, a place of learning. In higher education, a course provides that context, and the sustained process is a series of learning experiences in a course. This leads us to a definition of a course that we developed that captures the elements of time, learners and their experiences, mentoring and assessment by an instructor, and earned credit.

A course is a set of learning experiences within a specified time frame, often between six and fifteen weeks, in which learners, mentored by an instructor, are expected to develop a specific set of knowledge, skills, and attitudes. Learners are then assessed as to whether they achieve these goals and are assigned a grade for academic credit.

This description of a course provides the backdrop for a course design that focuses on a learner and his or her learning outcomes.

The definition of a course can vary widely depending on one's perspective. From a student perspective, a course is a set of meetings, requirements, and expectations that result in learning new knowledge, skills, or attitudes and count toward a degree or certificate that certifies a certain level of competency or skill. Students are concerned with the amount of time needed to complete all the course requirements and develop the level of competency required to do well in the course.

From an instructor's viewpoint, teaching a course is generally an assignment for which time and expertise are needed over a specific span of time. A common faculty concern is a question of workload: "How much time does it take to design, develop, and deliver a three-credit online course, and will I have time for my other responsibilities?" Generally a three-credit campus course represents from 20 to 25 percent of a full-time faculty's workload, or about eight to ten hours a week. Thus, after an initial investment of time, learning, resourcing of tools and materials, and course redesign, the goal is that an online course will not require more than eight to ten hours a week of a faculty's time. Is this possible? Yes.

How Are Online Courses Unique?

The major differences between online and campus courses can be summarized in five characteristics:

• • •

1. *The faculty role shifts to coaching and mentoring.* A faculty's role in online courses is primarily coaching, mentoring, guiding, and directing learning rather than lecturing and telling. Online courses are more of a bottom-up development of knowledge that require learners to interact with one another and the content resources to construct their knowledge rather than relying on the trickle-down delivery of content from an instructor. This is actually good, as more research is indicating that lecturing is an inefficient way of learning. In most lectures, learners are too passive for much higher-level learning to occur (McKeachie, Pintrich, Lin, & Smith 1986; Wieman, 2008). This shift means that you as an instructor do not have to spend a great deal of time preparing for live lectures. The time for teaching a course shifts to preparing short mini-lectures and introductions, preparing facilitation and community building experiences, and monitoring and guiding students in their learning experiences.

2. *Meetings are asynchronous.* Online class discussions are primarily asynchronous—at different times—rather than synchronous—at the same time. Since online discussions are asynchronous and require learners' comments and statements, there is an unwritten requirement that learners reflect on what they have learned from the resource assignments before they come to class (online) to participate in the course activities, such as posting their responses in the discussion areas. The online classrooms now provide opportunities for synchronous gatherings, but good online practice uses this time for discussions, question-and-answer sessions, collaborative project work, and presentations.

3. *Learners are more active.* Learners' dialogue and activity are increased in online courses. Learners must do more thinking, writing, doing, sharing, reflecting, and peer reviewing as part of a community of learners. Students often come to a campus class without completing the reading assignment and expect that the instructor will enlighten them, saving themselves time. Learners in an online course cannot hide passively. If they have not prepared and processed the content prior to posting their discussion responses, that shortcoming is evident to

everyone. Learners are therefore motivated to complete the readings to interact well with the others. This change means that faculty must design discussion forums with effective catalyst discussion questions before the course begins.

4. *Learning resources and spaces are more flexible.* Content resources are now increasingly mobile, accessible on smartphones, iPods, and other small, mobile, hand-held devices. This means that learners have many more options than in the past as to when, where, and with whom they work on course goals. Too much flexibility can encourage lax participation, so establishing a weekly rhythm and regular milestones is essential. The world of content resources is also much expanded. In addition to the usual mix of required, highly recommended, and other resources, students will be suggesting and contributing and creating additional content resources.

5. *Assessment is continuous.* Assessment in online courses is continuous, multiphased and often community based rather than concentrated, monitored, and primarily individual (Moallem, 2005). This is pedagogically beneficial and makes cheating and other forms of fraud more difficult. In other words, continuous assessment means that you get to know the students and students get to know other students. Assessment in online courses is also more varied, using low-stakes automated quizzes; frequent, regular postings in discussion forums; short papers; case studies and scenario building; and customizable projects. This means redesigning course assessment plans. Effective assessment in online courses requires getting to know learners as individuals and investing more time in coaching and mentoring. The good news is that most online course assessments are not closed book tests and thus do not require proctoring, eliminating a whole range of potential challenges.

•   •   •

Although these are the primary differences in online courses, campus courses and online courses are still more similar than different. Also, with the growing popularity of blended courses (those that have both online and traditional formats), the courses are actually becoming even more similar. This means that a good way of beginning your own personal development toward being an online instructor is to shift your campus course to a blended environment that combines online activities with classroom-based activities.

TABLE 1.1

Types of Courses

Proportion of Content Delivered Online	Type of Course	Typical Description
None	Traditional face-to-face	Course with no online technology used; content is delivered in writing or orally.
1 to 29 percent	Web facilitated	Course that uses Web-based technology to facilitate what is essentially a face-to-face course. Uses a course management system or Web pages to post the syllabus and assignments, for example.
30 to 79 percent	Blended/hybrid	Course that blends online and face-to-face delivery. A substantial proportion of the content is delivered online; typically uses online discussions and has some face-to face meetings.
80 percent or more	Online	A course where most or all of the content is delivered online. Typically has no face-to-face meetings.

Source: Adapted from Allen and Seaman (2008) and Boettcher and Conrad (2004).

Three Types of Online Courses

Table 1.1 defines three types of online courses. The first type of course listed is the traditional face-to-face course. As you design your online course, you will likely be in the category of an online course, which is defined as a course where most or all of the content is delivered online and that "typically has some face-to-face meetings." The definitions in the table have been adapted somewhat. The table defines an online course as having no face-to-face meetings, but many programs are designed with occasional face-to-face gatherings for introductory, assessment, or celebratory meetings. This is to be preferred if it is at all possible.

The Four Stages of a Course

Each stage of a course is different and depends on how the four elements of the learner, faulty-mentor, content, and environment interact and flow.

More detailed descriptions of what is happening in each of these stages, including the themes and the tools, are in later chapters.

The tables following this section summarize the learner and the faculty behaviors and experiences for each of the four stages. The themes that are common to each stage include learner responsibilities and behavior; faculty responsibilities and behavior, including the content of the three presences: social, teaching, and cognitive; how content knowledge and resources interact with a learner's readiness; and the potential tools for the environment. An overarching theme for the learner and the faculty is the development of a learning community. Chapters Four to Eleven go into detail about how to accomplish the goals of each of these stages.

In the first phase of a course, the goals are to launch the course well, laying the groundwork for a learning community in which learners and faculty support one another in the accomplishment of course goals. Table 1.2 describes some of the behaviors and goals that are characteristic of a good course beginning.

In the second phase of a course, subtitled, "Keeping the Ball Rolling," the primary goal is for the learner to become deeply engaged with the content, laying the basis for more complex learning and course projects in the latter half of the course and for the development of the learning community. Table 1.3 summarizes the behaviors and goals that are characteristic of a good early middle.

TABLE 1.2

Phase One: Course Beginnings—Starting Off on the Right Foot

Learner	Posting background and pictures; getting to know fellow learners; familiarizing self with course goals and setting personal and customized objectives; testing and using the course tools; ensuring access to course resources; understanding the syllabus and course requirements.
Faculty-mentor	Establishing quick trust, promoting social presence; getting acquainted with learners' backgrounds, their points of learning readiness, and personal learning goals; ensuring that all learners are present and engaged; making course expectations clear and explicit; supportive and directed teaching presence so that learners know you and your expertise as well; modeling cognitive framework for course content.
Content knowledge	Access to supplemental content resources in place; learners have acquired core required resources.
Environment	Tools for the designed learning experiences are in place, and learners know how to use them.

TABLE 1.3

Phase Two: Early Middle—Keeping the Ball Rolling

Learner	Settles into a weekly rhythm of readings, postings, collaborating with at least a few fellow learners in the course community; developing a sense of the problem space of the content, engaging with core concepts.
Faculty-mentor	Continuing strong teaching presence, guiding the learning of core concepts and spiraling and connecting ideas and content; supporting community and work in small teams, intense cognitive presence, and supporting learners' exploration and testing of ideas; balancing the need to cover content with the need for understanding.
Content knowledge	Learners are intensely exploring, engaging, and identifying more content resources and bringing them to the community.
Environment	Community has settled into a routine of using a set number of tools for collaboration, teaming, and learning.

TABLE 1.4

Phase Three: Late Middle—Letting Go of the Power

Learner	Engaging well with course concepts and applying core concepts in scenarios, identifying patterns and relationships, supporting and challenging others' ideas and proposals as an accepted member of the community, dealing with complex problems.
Faculty-mentor	Processes are well established; community is mostly working; faculty shifts time from large group teaching presence to more personalized and small group teaching presence; supporting more learners-as-leaders experiences; reviewing, mentoring projects, and providing feedback on assignments.
Content knowledge	Learners are creating content as they learn and sharing with others in wikis, blogs, projects.
Environment	Learners are actively using course tools and may be expanding beyond and personalizing tools and bringing results back to the community.

In the third phase of a course, subtitled, "Letting Go of the Power," the learner begins to focus on particular case studies, scenarios, and other discipline or course issues. Table 1.4 summarizes the behaviors and goals that are characteristic of a stimulating late middle of a course.

In the fourth and last phase of a course, subtitled, "Pruning, Reflecting, and Wrapping Up," the primary goal is for the learner to complete a positive learning experience and identify the knowledge and skills they have

TABLE 1.5

Phase Four: Closing Weeks—Pruning, Reflecting, and Wrapping Up

Learner	Digging deeply into core concepts and resources to support complex project work and complete assignments; learners are actively reviewing, supporting other learners, and may be leading some of the learning experiences; reflecting and identifying their personal outcomes from the course.
Faculty-mentor	Continues a strong cognitive and teaching presence, supporting learners' projects and the course community; supporting and clarifying course wrap-up activities and requirements; managing wrap-up experiences; providing feedback and assessment.
Content knowledge	Content resources used by learners go beyond the basics to support their personalized and customized learning goals and projects.
Environment	Learners are using whatever tools make the most sense for the work and their projects.

developed from the course experiences while supporting the community's goals to accomplish their own personalized, customized learning tasks. Table 1.5 summarizes the behaviors and goals that are characteristic of the reflective and summary phase of a course.

Details about the themes, happenings, and tools for each stages are in the chapters in Part Two.

Learning Theories and Theorists

The principles, practices, and tips in this book are grounded in learning theory and principles. Specifically, this book is grounded in constructivism, the philosophy that holds that learners actively construct and build knowledge structures from the interaction of what they already know with what they pay attention to in their environment, including language, people, and images. The constructivism philosophy reflected in the principles, practices, and tips is broad and expansive, representing a trunk of how we view learning and how our minds work. Much of the work of theories and theorists in the past few decades represents the growth of subsidiary branches of this core philosophy.

Here are a few of the more significant theories and theorists that inspired this inclusive and expansive view of constructivism. These sketches of key learning theorists are in no particular order other than generally chronological. Some of the information in them is loosely adapted from the Theories into Practice database developed and maintained by

Greg Kearsley (http://tip.psychology.org/backgd.html). This database, which contains descriptions of "over 50 theories relevant to human learning and instruction," is a good starting point for digging more deeply into learning theory.

Lev Vygotsky (1896–1934): Theory of Social Development

Vygotsky is a twentieth-century Russian psychologist, linguist, and philosopher whose work became accessible only in the mid-1960s when it was translated into English. His theory is usually called social development theory because a major theme of his theoretical framework is that social interaction plays a fundamental role in the development of cognition. His work also included significant investigations into concept acquisition, which led him into problem solving. His best-known concept is the zone of proximal development, which defines for each individual the state of readiness for learning. The formal definition of the zone is "the distance between the actual development level as determined by independent problem solving and the level of potential development as determined through problem solving under adult guidance or in collaboration with more capable peers" (Vygotsky, 1978, p. 86).

John Dewey (1859–1952): Experiential Learning

John Dewey, an American philosopher, psychologist, and educational reformer, was a major proponent of experiential learning in the first half of the twentieth century. He foresaw an active and collaborative student experience that, almost a hundred years later, we finally have the tools to implement. Dewey emphasized the unique and individualized nature of interaction in the learning experience. He believed, as do many constructivist theorists, that learners construct new knowledge based on previous knowledge and that experiences are unique to each learner. Dewey promoted the active participation of the learner in defining the learning environment, and he conceived of the instructor as a facilitator.

Dewey focused his ideas on developing what he believed to be the aims of education: the development of reflective, creative, responsible thought. In his 1933 treatise, *How We Think,* Dewey said, "We state emphatically that, upon its intellectual side, education consists of the formation of wide-awake, careful, thorough habits of thinking" (p. 78). This single sentence, which captures the essence of Dewey's thinking, sets forth one of the ultimate goals of education. Another key concept in Dewey's work is that interaction and continuity are the two primary characteristics of effective teaching and learning experiences. The characteristic of interaction reinforces the importance of dialogue and communication and engagement in learning; the characteristic of continuity reinforces the perspective that the individual learner must be viewed as the key design element.

Jean Piaget (1896–1980): Genetic Epistemology

A twentieth-century Swiss psychologist and natural scientist, Piaget is best known for his stage theory of child development, culminating in abstract thinking in the formal operations stage (ages twelve to fifteen). Piaget called his general theoretical framework "genetic epistemology" because he was primarily interested in how knowledge developed in human organisms (Kearsley, 2003–2009). In his view, cognitive development consists of a constant effort to adapt to the environment in terms of the processes of assimilation and accommodation. In this sense, Piaget's theory is similar in nature to the constructivist perspectives of Vygotsky and Jerome Bruner (profiled next). Another concept central to Piaget's theory is cognitive structures, which he defined as patterns of physical or mental action that underlie specific acts of intelligence and correspond to stages of child development. These cognitive structures are similar to the schemas of Roger Schank and our current concepts of mental models (Schank & Abelson, 1977).

Jerome Bruner (1915–): Constructivism

Jerome Bruner is an American educational psychologist who is currently a senior research fellow at the New York University School of Law. As a constructivist, Bruner's work has incorporated strong support for discovery learning. He believes that mastery of the fundamental ideas of a field involves not only the grasping of general principles, but also the development of an attitude toward learning and inquiry, toward guessing and hunches, toward the possibility of solving problems on one's own (Bruner, 1963). As a constructivist, Bruner emphasizes the active process of discovery and trial and error through which a student can uncover the interrelationships of concepts and ideas (Clabaugh, 2009).

One of Bruner's best-known statements is that any subject can be taught to any child at any stage of development if it is presented in the proper manner (Bruner, 1963).

Another oft-used quote is about the usefulness of knowledge. Bruner (1963) stated, "The first object of any act of learning, over and beyond the pleasure it may give, is that it should serve us in the future. Learning should not only take us somewhere; it should allow us later to go further more easily" (p. 17). The focus of this thought is twofold. First, Bruner emphasizes that learning should be purposeful, for example, developing skills to serve us in the future. Second, every time we learn something, we add links or nodes to a cognitive structure on which we can build more later; as we build, we are able to learn more and to learn faster. In this view, the more one knows, the more one can know, and know quickly.

John Seely Brown (1940–): Cognitive Apprenticeship

John Seely Brown is best known as the chief scientist at the Xerox Corporation, who directed the company's Palo Alto Research Center, known as PARC, for twelve years up to 2000. He is now a visiting scholar and advisor to the provost at the University of Southern California and independent co-chairman of Deloitte Center for the Edge. As early as 1991 in a *Harvard Business Review* article, Brown envisioned how "advanced multimedia information systems" would make it possible to plug into a "collective social mind" (Brown, 1997), laying the groundwork for our thinking about communities in online learning. Brown explored similar ideas about "learning communities capable of generating, sharing, and deploying highly esoteric knowledge" (p. 127) in his 2000 book, *The Social Life of Information*, written with University of California–Berkeley researcher Paul Duguid. His work on cognitive apprenticeships (Brown, Collins, & Duguid, 1989; Collins, Brown, & Holum, 1991) and learning environments (Brown, 2006) examine how technologies can support problem solving and hands-on learning. A recent article explores how activities within virtual worlds create a "sense of shared space and co-presence which make real-time coordination and interaction not only possible, but a necessary part of the world" (Thomas & Brown, 2009, p. 37).

Roger Schank (1946–): Schema Theory

Schank was one of the influential early contributors to artificial intelligence and cognitive psychology in the 1970s and 1980s. His major innovations in these fields were his concepts of case-based reasoning and dynamic memory. The central focus of Schank's theory has been the structure of knowledge, especially in the context of language understanding. He is well known for his work on schema theory—the concepts of scripts, plans, and themes to handle story-level understanding (Schank & Abelson, 1977). Schema theory is similar to mental models and might be viewed as one way of describing knowledge structures.

Other Theorists and Influencers

We could mention many more leading theorists and researchers who have influenced the tips, but these will be mentioned in context and in the additional references. Before leaving key influencers, however, we want to call attention to the 2000 work of Bransford, Brown, and Cocking and the Committee on Developments in the Science of Learning that resulted in the book, *How People Learn—Brain, Mind, Experience, and School.*

This committee reviewed decades of learning research and identified five themes that are changing our views on the theory of learning:

- Memory and the structure of knowledge

- Problem solving and reasoning

- Early foundations of learning, attempting to answer, "Who knows what, and when?"

- Metacognitive processes and self-regulatory learning processes

- Cultural experience and community participation

These five topics are active research areas that will continue to influence teaching and learning in all environments in the future, and they echo throughout this book.

FIGURE 1.1

A Landscape for Teaching and Learning Online

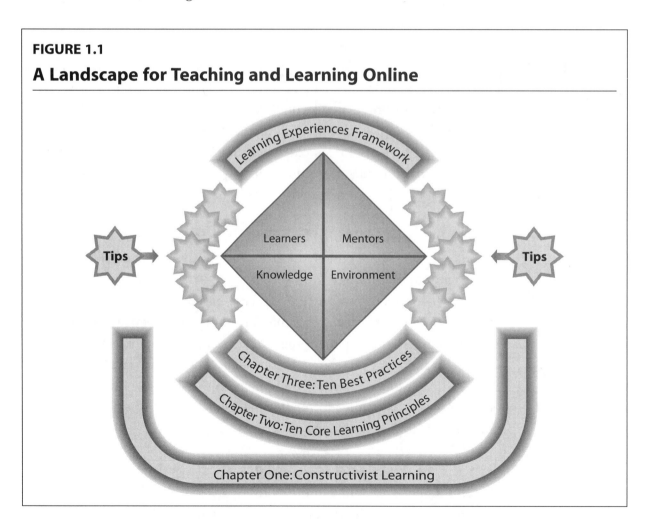

How the Chapters in Part One Fit Together

With the constructivist landscape in place, the next two chapters identify ten core learning principles and ten best practices to guide you as you develop new mental models and skills for teaching in the online environment. Figure 1.1 provides a graphical representation as to how these elements fit together.

Summary—and What's Next

This chapter introduced the key concepts in getting started with online teaching and learning. The big picture of the four stages of a course—course beginnings, early middle, late middle, and closing weeks—helps you envision your course as a series of learning experiences that provide the context for you and your learners to develop a community for learning and developing skills.

Chapter Two discusses a set of ten core learning principles that capture some of the key principles suggested by constructivist theories and related instructional design approaches.

Chapter 2

Theoretical Foundations
Ten Core Learning Principles

Chapter Overview

This chapter lays out the theoretical foundations of pedagogy—the science of teaching and learning. Why is this necessary? It is generally assumed that you as faculty know the fundamentals of teaching and learning theory, but undoubtedly you haven't had a chance to learn the discipline of pedagogy and are generally practitioners rather than theorists. As Derek Bok, a former president of Harvard University, noted, faculty are "rarely exposed to research on teaching during graduate school" (2005). It is also worth noting that faculty hiring and promotion processes generally focus on research and content knowledge, regardless of the practical fact that young faculty generally spend just as much time teaching as conducting research.

The result is that you generally teach the way you have been taught. This has not been overly problematic in the past, but the proliferation of new technologies and new environments such as blended and online learning and the rise of the new wave of digital native students who are comfortable with mobile digital communications are creating new teaching challenges. Rather than wanting to listen to lectures, students want to be doing and creating. This means a change in pedagogical strategies both online and in a traditional campus classroom.

Most campuses that are fortunate enough to have centers that support faculty in the use of technology for teaching and learning recognize this challenge and combine teaching pedagogy with technology in most workshops and teaching and learning sessions. The common belief is that faculty are resistant to change when pushed to teach online or revise traditional teaching methods. Our experience over decades of working with faculty, however, is that they are eager to learn but have great difficulty finding the time, energy, and the easy access to tools they need. The best antidotes to these challenges are support and yet more support, combined with reliable technology institutional infrastructures. The bottom line is that it is important to evaluate what type of support you might need and ask for it. You might not get all that you ask for, but the probability is good that you will get some of it. Deans and administrators, after all, want online programs to succeed.

Studying the science of teaching and learning processes is best done as a lifelong pursuit for those teaching in higher education. For instructors who have the time and inclination to pursue the study of pedagogy, this chapter provides a good foundation and useful starting point for designing effective and efficient learning experiences. Instructors who only want or only have the time now for a simple set of basic learning principles for effective teaching and learning, this chapter provides a pedagogical foundation and the vocabulary for a deeper understanding of the best practices and tips in this book.

Background of the Ten Core Learning Principles

The recent explosion of research on the brain and learning processes combined with the power of the new mobile communications technologies is stimulating a reexamination of traditional approaches to designing teaching and learning experiences. Insights into how the brain works (Bransford, Brown, & Cocking, 2000; Damasio, 1999; Pinker, 1997) and the impact of collaborative and social networking tools on communication and dialogue are not only deepening our understanding of traditional core learning principles; they are also helping to provide practical guidance on how we design and manage learning experiences (Bransford et al., 2000; Gibson & Swan 2006; Richardson & Swan 2003; Swan & Shih 2005). Deriving and integrating a simple set of principles from the large body of research and the body of educational and philosophical theories can be daunting.

These principles have been drawn from and inspired by the work of leading educational theorists of the twentieth century such as John Dewey, Jean Piaget, and Jerome Bruner. However, the most significant inspiration has come from the writings of Lev Vygotsky, whose influence among education continues to grow. Vygotsky's *Thought and Language* (1962) and *Mind in Society: The Development of Higher Psychological Processes* (1978) are now classics and probably the most significant and influential of his writings. Vygotsky is most often described as a social constructivist, emphasizing his belief in learning occurring in the interaction of the learner with the environment and a constructivist from his enlightened description of the concept of a learner's individual zone of proximal development.

The set of ten core learning principles that follows is not necessarily the last word on core learning principles; they are not the result of a survey or any committee process, for example. Rather, it is the set of principles that we have assembled over time in our work with faculty because we feel they particularly help guide the processes of designing and managing effective teaching and learning experiences for online environments. They combine principles from the disciplines of instructional design, teaching and learning theory, and the field of technology change. Each is accompanied by examples of how they can guide the design of teaching and learning processes in online environments.

Ten Core Learning Principles

Table 2.1 sets out the ten core learning principles that can guide the design of your online course and the delivery of your course.

TABLE 2.1

Ten Core Learning Principles

Principle 1	Every structured learning experience has four elements with the learner at the center.
Principle 2	Learners bring their own personalized and customized knowledge, skills, and attitudes to the experience.
Principle 3	Faculty mentors are the directors of the learning experience.
Principle 4	All learners do not need to learn all course content; all learners do need to learn the core concepts.
Principle 5	Every learning experience includes the environment or context in which the learner interacts.
Principle 6	Every learner has a zone of proximal development that defines the space that a learner is ready to develop into useful knowledge.
Principle 7	Concepts are not words but organized and interconnected knowledge clusters.
Principle 8	Different instruction is required for different learning outcomes.
Principle 9	Everything else being equal, more time on task equals more learning.
Principle 10	We shape our tools, and our tools shape us.

Principle 1: Every Structured Learning Experience Has Four Elements with the Learner at the Center

The first core learning principle asserts that all structured learning experiences are created by the interaction of four elements:

- The learner as the center of the teaching and learning process

- The faculty mentor who directs, supports, and assesses the learner

- The content knowledge, skills, and perspectives that the learner is to develop and acquire

- The environment or context within which the learner is experiencing the learning event

This principle is illustrated in the learning experiences framework shown in Figure 2.1. Learning experiences designed with this framework feature the learner "on stage" actively doing something under the direction of the mentor/faculty member using learning resources guiding the acquisition of knowledge, skills, and perspective within an environment of a particular time and place.

This framework simplifies the process of designing and managing instructional experiences. The framework captures a complex set of

---

FIGURE 2.1

Learning Experience Framework

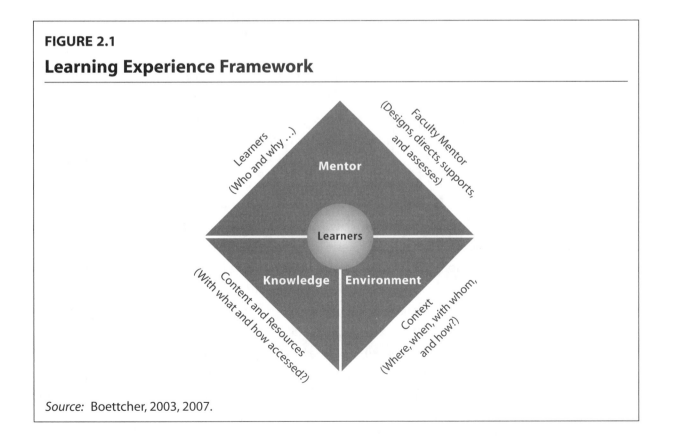

Source: Boettcher, 2003, 2007.

interactions among the four elements in an instructional event and the role those elements play in a learning experience. Faculty can use this framework to analyze planned learning experiences, focusing on learner and faculty behaviors and actions; the knowledge, skill, or attitudes being developed; and the where, when, with whom, and with what resources the event is occurring.

This framework can guide the planning and designing of the sixty to one hundred or more learning experiences that comprise a course. (Of course, these experiences may build on a favorite set of five to eight or more different types of experiences, such as reading or listening assignments, posting and collaborating experiences, and research experiences.)

There are many variations of learning experiences of course, but all structured learning experiences fit this framework. The first element, the learner, may be an individual learner or small or large groups of learners. In collaborative and group learning experiences, for example, multiple learners may well be on stage at the same time, but every learner is experiencing the learning experience somewhat differently.

The second element is the mentor or faculty member who manages instruction and provides support to the learner. The mentor may be physically present on stage or in the classroom, but just as likely may be in the wings directing the learner. The faculty mentor may not be anywhere close to the learning experience, but may be present only implicitly by virtue of having designed the experience.

The faculty or mentor element may also be contained in an inanimate learning object that provides content, instructions, or guidance as suggested by the definition of pedagogy by Bernstein in Chapter One. One futuristic example of an inanimate faculty element is the Holodeck from *Star Trek* that provides an environment for learning without a physical mentor being present (Boettcher, 1998). More likely examples in the near term include simulations, animations, tutorials, and virtual world experiences. In such cases, the mentor is present by virtue of having selected or created the learning object and provided instructions for the use of the object. Note that *mentor* is our preferred term for the instructor or faculty member who is directing the students' learning experiences. *Mentor* captures more accurately the role that the faculty member plays in the learning experience for the learner.

The third element in the learning experiences framework is the knowledge, the content, or the problem that is the focus of the learning experience. In instructional design terms, the knowledge component is the answer to the question, "What is the knowledge, what is the skill, and what is the attitude that the instructional experience is intended to facilitate in each of the students?" In a geology course, for example, the knowledge or skill may involve student proficiency in identifying distinctive rock formations in order to reconstruct the natural history of a particular setting.

The fourth element is that of the environment. Mobile handheld communications technologies make it possible to learn anytime, anywhere, and even as learners are exercising, driving, or while doing other tasks, but learners need to determine exactly when and where learning will occur for them. The fourth element, the environment, answers this question: "When will the learning experience take place, with whom, where, and with what resources?" For example, the result of an instructional experience might be for a student to accurately identify the different types of sedimentary rocks, the locations where they might be found, and the processes required to find them. This might be done in a virtual environment where the student can examine a rock in three dimensions or the student may be tasked to collect real specimens in the field, photograph them, and contribute these specimens and photographs to a collection using mobile handheld photography technology. Another example of a context may be a group of students gathering in a study group, either in the same physical space or a virtual space.

Whatever the scenario, the core of this first principle is that the learner is at the center of his or her individual learning experience. The learner is on stage, guided by the experience designed by the mentor, accessing whatever resources might be needed, and acquiring useful knowledge, skill, or perspectives from the experience within a particular and specific context. Learning does not just happen in our heads in a "sometime" manner. It happens somewhere at a particular time and place. This fact echoes Vygotsky's insistence on learning being a sociocultural activity.

Principle 2: Learners Bring Their Own Personalized and Customized Knowledge, Skills, and Attitudes to the Experience

This core learning principle focuses on the learner as an individual. The goal of any learning experience is for learners to grow their knowledge bases. Every course has a set of core concepts and knowledge for the students to learn, and if learners and their faculty mentors work together well, the students integrate core concepts into their unique knowledge structures. Each learner's brain is as unique as his or her fingerprints and DNA. Our students' knowledge bases thus become more different rather than less different over time. Students may share experiences and concepts, but how these experiences and concepts are encoded, linked, and structured in their individual brains will be different. Our goal is not standardized brains, but richly differentiated, creative brains with shared experiences.

In designing learning experiences, faculty mentors generally are working from general expectations of their learners' zones of proximal development. This concept from Vygotsky has so much impact on the design of learning experiences that it is described as another core learning principle. In brief, it is similar to the traditional readiness principle—the knowledge and concepts that a learner is ready to learn.

Getting to know learners in a course means getting to know the existing knowledge structure of their brains. Some students probably arrive at the course with a "jungle" brain, replete with intricate patterns of knowledge about art, biology, electricity, and communications; other students may arrive with a brain characterized by isolated, unrelated bits and pieces of information resembling scraggly weeds, scrawny bushes, or a sparse, bare tundra (Kandel, 2006; Boettcher, 2007). It's important to know how well developed our students' networks of neurons and dendrites are and how detailed and flush are the patterns and images in their brains.

Learners who are encountering not just one concept but perhaps a confluence of new terms and concepts naturally work to make sense of this new information by attaching this incoming knowledge to existing nodes and patterns. A traditional educational principle asserts, "Build on what students already know." Memory research is confirming the significance of this principle by demonstrating the impact of students' existing mental models on incoming knowledge (Damasio, 1999). Damasio explains that the process of learning might be defined as that of our brain's finding receptor nodes for bits of new information and then arranging that information into a useful mental model. A simple rule of thumb is, "The more you know, the more you can know." The more concepts, the more patterns, and the more interconnectedness in the brain structure, the more receptor nodes exist.

By knowing what students already know, faculty can design experiences to ensure an accurate knowledge structure and growth of that structure. One of the ways faculty can tap into students' existing knowledge is to begin a learning experience by asking them what they already know or think they know about the topic. Some of the tools that can be used for this are the discussion boards or forums, simple inquiries, and sample problems and case studies to assess their current problem-solving skills.

Principle 3: Faculty Mentors Are the Directors of the Learning Experience

Recent trends have encouraged a focus on learners and learner-centered experiences. The learning experiences framework reaffirms the importance of learners by placing them center stage; however, the framework also affirms the critical role of the faculty mentor in the learning experience. The faculty mentor provides direction and purpose to learning experiences by doing the following:

- Designing and structuring the course experiences

- Directing and supporting learners through the instructional experiences

- Assessing learner outcomes

To continue the theater metaphor, the faculty mentor is the director of learning experience, not a sage on the stage transmitting knowledge or a guide on the side with minimal input into the learning experience. When the faculty member steps out in front of learners as a sage, the learner tends to retreat and be more passive unless the faculty is encouraging interaction and engagement with the content every few minutes and providing time for reflection and integration. When a faculty is preparing mini-lectures, demonstrations, and summaries of content discussion, it is he or she who is reaping the benefits from working with the content, structuring the content, and then communicating the content. One important goal in designing learning is to get the students engaged with the content at that intense level. Strategies that support this shift in responsibilities include assigning students roles in moderating forums; preparing concept explanations, summaries, and examples for other students; and even occasionally assuming responsibility for being the frontline moderator. A faculty member need not be present at 2:00 A.M. or 2:00 P.M. on a Saturday for monitoring questions and discussions; students can support other students, either formally or informally at almost any time. Students tend to be working and learning at the same time as each other. The role of the faculty member in this learning experiences framework is to mentor, monitor, examine, and challenge the thinking of students doing these types of teaching and learning activities.

The learning experiences framework assumes that the designing, managing, and assessing functions are the responsibilities of the faculty. This does not mean that all teaching functions need to be embodied in one person. Many distance and online education administrative models technologies unbundle these responsibilities, so that a faculty member can concentrate on the best use of his or her expertise. For example, the design and development of online courses might be done by an instructional designer collaborating with a faculty member. In this case, a faculty new to online teaching and learning will be teaching a course that is already designed and already has a significant portion of the teaching facilitation and direction materials prepared. The faculty member is then responsible for course delivery, including the functions of directing, supporting, and assessing the learning of students.

The need for some level of technical support at all times is accelerating a shift away from the "lone ranger" faculty member to the model of learning supported by an instructional team. A larger instructional team means that the faculty member has more time to mentor the learning processes of students. Less time is spent on addressing technological, administrative, and content access issues and more time on the formation of thought and knowledge.

Mobile and collaborative technologies also free a faculty mentor from the need to be physically in any particular place at any particular time. New synchronous collaborative tools are accelerating this flexibility. A faculty mentor can monitor student learning and facilitate discussions from anywhere that has a high-bandwidth connection: a home office, a coffee shop, or a hotel or office on the other side of the world. Members of the extended instructional team can also support students for the faculty member for selected periods of time as well if schedule or emergencies occur.

Principle 4: All Learners Do Not Need to Learn All Course Content; All Learners Do Need to Learn the Core Concepts

This core learning principle focuses on content and the knowledge, skill, attitude, or perspective to be learned, acquired, or developed. All content is not equal. Only a portion of the content of any course is core concept knowledge; the bulk of course content is the application and use of core concepts in various scenarios and contexts.

Imagine the usual set of course content resources arrayed as a set of concentric circles similar to a pie (Figure 2.2). The innermost circle represents the core concepts; the next circle represents the content resources that learners use in initial practice experiences as they apply the core concepts to relatively straightforward problems where the answers are known. The third circle represents content resources that learners use to solve more complex problems that are novel to them. The fourth circle represents the content used in experiences of students' own choosing in applying con-

FIGURE 2.2

Customizing Content Resources

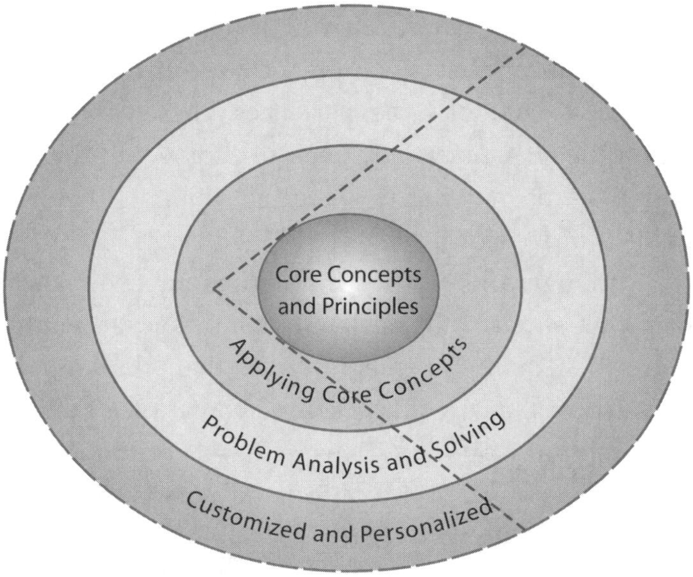

Core Concepts and Principles

Applying Core Concepts

Problem Analysis and Solving

Customized and Personalized

Source: Boettcher, 2003, 2007.

cepts to difficult and complex problems where the answer may or may not be known.

The goal for each student is to master a slice of the pie, but to be sure that the slice includes the whole of the center with the core concepts and principles. The slice of the course content that the student would master is shown by these dotted lines. The next layer is experience at applying the core concepts, then moving to the third layer, that focuses on using those core concepts in ever more complex and novel scenarios, and the fourth layer is the student choice in terms of students' selecting and directing much of their own experience with the content. As students develop expertise in the content experiences, they increasingly direct and customize their learning according to their own needs, interests, and priorities.

A key element of design for effective learning is designing for the set of resources that students will use for each of these layers of content. In this content model, the faculty member is not responsible for defining and making all the content accessible. It is a team effort, that includes the campus resource infrastructure: the library team and information technology team and the student.

The most obvious answer of how to provide this level of content flexibility and customization is the Web. No longer is the choice and availability of content necessarily circumscribed by the size or cost of a textbook. If mentored well, students will naturally gravitate to the content resources and experiences that match their zones of personal proximal development. This does mean that designing a course includes providing access to a rich database of content and experiences. These databases and their integration into course resources may need to evolve, but the principle of a wide and varied set of materials to meet all students' needs and interests should guide our decisions.

Although a bounty of content resources is readily accessible, faculty members should still designate core required content that students will make their own and integrate into their thinking. This required content will also be the core of the shared content for the experiences in common for community building. This required core content should be digital, if at all possible, and also in various formats, such as video, audio, and text. Students need to be required to have access to this core content. Another set of content resources contains those that are highly recommended. These are content resources that may well be the favorites of the faculty member as well as traditional classics or seminal articles within the discipline that professionals regularly make reference to. In the third set of resources are those that support customized and personalized learning and thus can come from almost anywhere. Learners may be required to justify their selection, however.

Web applications are enabling content creation at an amazing rate, and these new content resources, along with the steady daily increase in news from all over the world, mean unlimited resources for teaching and learning. Both learners and faculty are energized with the ability to quickly and easily become producers and creators of content resources as they think about them. Here are just two brief examples. By the time this book is in print, there will no doubt be many more. Be sure to watch for them and plan on using them. These tools and suggestions for how to use them for teaching and learning are in some of the tips:

- Small videocams, such as Flip Video, have flip-out USB connectors making it possible to connect the videocam to a laptop or mobile phone and upload shareable videos to YouTube, the video-sharing site, in minutes.

- Blog and Twitter applications bring today's (in fact, this minute's) happenings and thoughts to what are becoming shared daily journals, making it possible to keep up with what's happening in selected communities of interest.

- VoiceThread, an asynchronous Web place for incorporating mixed media, such as video, graphics, pictures, voice, and text into student projects and discussions, is a good tool for short, interactive presentations.

A good rule of thumb for faculty is to select required course content focusing on the core concepts that is available both digitally and able to be printed or purchased in print if desired. Having the core content in multiple packaged digital formats increases the likelihood that students will use and learn the content. Because students will be playing an active role in identifying and evaluating content resources, faculty mentors should design courses so that students develop metacognitive awareness of how they learn and the strategies and materials that work for them and why.

Principle 5: Every Learning Experience Includes the Environment or Context in Which the Learner Interacts

This core learning principle completes the four key elements of any learning experience: every learning experience occurs in an environment in which the learner interacts with the content, knowledge, skill, or an expert. The environment might be simple, as in a learner using one resource independently, possibly at home, or out and about while jogging or driving, or working in a popular "third place" (Oldenburg, 1999). Or the environment might be complex. Several learners may be gathered together working on problems or a project in a face-to-face study group, or several may be on a conference call or in a collaborative virtual setting. Or the environment might be a synchronous virtual meeting place, such as one of the live classroom areas or collaborating wirelessly with word documents or spreadsheets or presentations while on their cell phones. Again, the faculty member may or may not be physically present.

The types of questions to be anticipated by a faculty member when designing a set of course experiences include the following:

- Where, when, with whom, and with what resources will any particular instructional experience be likely to occur?

- What are the expected learning outcomes or interim points of learning?

- Will the learning experience be a small group meeting planning a team project using one of the new synchronous meeting tools or synchronous collaborative tools?

- Will this event be a real-life experience such as one in which one or two students interview restaurant workers about their knowledge of public health regulations?

- Will this experience be an individual experience where the student is working through a complex and lengthy simulation?

A well-planned course balances the three dialogues of faculty to learner, learner to learner, and learner to resources (Moore, 1997). A well-planned course also balances individual, small, and large group activities. These different groupings and dialogues bring stimulating and varied interactions with people and with content resources.

Principle 6: Every Learner Has a Zone of Proximal Development That Defines the Space That a Learner Is Ready to Develop into Useful Knowledge

Vygotsky's concept of the zone of proximal development (ZPD) is one of the foundation concepts within the theories of constructivism. It is a concept that significantly influences the design of teaching and learning experiences. According to Vygotsky (1978), a student's ZPD is "the distance between the actual developmental level as determined by independent problem solving and the level of potential development as determined through problem solving under the adult guidance or in collaboration with more capable peers" (p. 86).

This generally means that the goal of learning experiences is growth, echoing the familiar dictum of John Dewey as well. The concept of the ZPD emphasizes that all learning experiences need to pull learners forward and "that the 'only good learning' is in advance of development" (p. 89). It means that students should be encountering problems and concepts beyond that which they already know, which is their actual developmental level and helping them to work on their "potential development." So the ZPD is quite literally the space between what students can do independently and what they can do successfully with the help or guidance of a person who might be an expert or simply a more capable peer.

Vygotsky's concept of the ZPD is similar to the familiar concept of readiness that is often used in instructional design processes thinking about the probable level of readiness of a group. The concept narrows the focus to the individual and suggests that a learner's zone or openness to a particular learning experience might be fairly narrow. In other words, the window of learning opportunity may be smaller than we think. When students say they are "totally lost," they are probably expressing the feeling of being outside their effective ZPD. When they sit back and obviously disengage, they have probably lost the link—the relationship of one idea to the other. When this happens in a group situation or a discussion board, the teaching and learning community, or the culture, needs to support the student in asking a question and having someone "back up" to where the student got lost so that he can get "linked" again. Otherwise the time will probably be lost to the learner; the learner will disengage and have difficulty catching up to what might be called the "group zone."

The concept of the ZPD is simultaneously comforting and overwhelming. What are the elements of the learning community that support students' comfort level in asking questions or in the mentor truly checking in with each learner? How do faculty mentors determine a learner's ZPD, and how do they determine what kinds of problems students can solve now?

This ZPD principle emphasizes the need to be alert to students' state of understanding and capabilities on a continuing basis. This principle encourages embedding feedback and demonstrations from students earlier and more consistently throughout a course experience. Student questions, comments, participation, and outputs are means of determining more precisely the progress or state of concept development in students.

Principle 7: Concepts Are Not Words But Organized and Interconnected Knowledge Clusters

This principle, also inspired by and drawn from Vygotsky's work, is simple but profound. Concept formation is not a one-time event. Vygotsky, for example, describes concept formation as a series of intellectual operations including the centering of attention, abstracting, synthesizing, and symbolizing (1962). Similarly, noted neuroscientist Walter Freeman observes that meanings are assimilated as a process of "successive approximations in conversation" (2000, p. 15). Freeman's work focuses on how the brain puts a priority on meaning rather than data and notes that meanings reside only in observers, not in objects. His work thus affirms the role of interaction and dialogue in the creation of meanings.

What does this mean for designing learning experiences and courses? Students who are facing a new field or discipline often focus on learning the vocabulary of that discipline, but it is often done in isolation from the concepts that give the words meaning. Without the underlying concepts, words are akin to isolated weeds and seeds likely to be blown away by the winds of time, usually mere hours after an exam. Students can in fact become quite proficient at using vocabulary while not having the ability to really think with the words. They have the words but not the underlying rich concepts.

Discussion forums, blogs, wikis, journals, and small group work are all excellent strategies for engaging learners in clarifying and enriching their mental models and concepts and identifying and establishing meaningful links and relationships. Online tools are particularly useful for building concepts because they provide a public forum in which the cumulative, step-by-step process of concept formation, refinement, application, and revision is fully visible to student peers as well as their mentors. By providing a comprehensive record of how concepts take form as multiple clusters of knowledge, such tools can promote the development of more complex and lasting knowledge and competencies in students.

Principle 8: Different Instruction Is Required for Different Learning Outcomes

Gagné, widely considered the father of instructional design, observed that all instruction is not equal and that different types of instruction are required for different learning outcomes. This is not a groundbreaking concept today, but the idea was quite novel when he wrote *The Conditions of Learning* in 1965.

This principle means that what a faculty mentor does makes a difference in what students do—that is, in what students learn and in what concepts and skills students may or may not develop. This principle also reinforces the instructional design practice of planning student assessments simultaneously with the planning of instructional experiences, and then embedding and integrating assessments within instructional experiences. This principle encourages beginning all program and course planning with the well-known instructional design question: "What knowledge and set of skills, attitudes, and perspectives do you want your students to develop competence in by means of the instructional experiences of a particular course or program?" Once that question is answered, the task of the designer or faculty member is to design and develop the teaching and learning events to accomplish those goals.

A simple and effective example of this principle is the apprenticeship model. If the desired outcome is for students to be great chefs, they need to cook; if the desired set of skills is to become an entrepreneur, students probably need to apprentice themselves into an internship environment or at least practice entrepreneurial activities. This principle is also at work with pilots training on simulators and students practicing lab techniques in a model environment. The types of learning experiences do affect what is learned and what students feel competent in doing. In short, courses designed to transmit knowledge do just that; courses designed to develop competencies design experiences using the knowledge. Knowledge can sometimes be transmitted, but experience and competence must be developed.

Principle 9: Everything Else Being Equal, More Time on Task Equals More Learning

This principle has traditional roots and is probably the best known of all the principles. It is basically the time-on-task principle: as students spend more time interacting with, creating, and manipulating information and applying concepts and skills, the more facile, accomplished, and confident they will be. Time on task helps students to make the knowledge their own and create the linkages and relationships within their own data knowledge structures. Learning and developing new ideas and skills is intrinsically rewarding and enjoyable. (Imagine the delight of a one year old at repeatedly pushing light switches on and off or a sixteen year old with a driver's permit and her excitement at driving and driving and more driving.) If we design great experiences, students will spend more time interacting with and developing more complex, better-structured knowledge bases and efficient automatic behaviors.

Faculty mentors, as directors of instructional events, can encourage time on task by searching out and identifying well-structured materials that assist in concept formation, practice, and problem solving. This includes identifying engaging, inviting, and stimulating content at the right ZPD. Matching content and practice to each student's ZPD is still inexact, so the best way of ensuring a match is for the set of course materials and experiences to be rich and diverse. Another way of ensuring a match is to teach students to be metacognitively aware and be part of the process in identifying and using resources that work for them.

A corollary of the time-on-task principle is that learning can be more efficient if we chunk information. In today's environments, simulators, animations, and "living worlds" such as SimCity and Second Life are powerful learning chunkers. Chunking is just one reason games and role-playing scenarios are popular and valuable. Other valuable features of games and simulations are their unpredictability and infinite variety. These are the kinds of challenges students enjoy working to master. Canned, predictable, and static learning resources are less interesting and less engaging and, dare we say, tiring and boring.

Principle 10: We Shape Our Tools, and Our Tools Shape Us

The fact that we are shaped by our tools and that we shape our tools may appear at first to be a strange design and learning principle. Yet this principle emphasizes that learning occurs only within a context and is influenced by the environment. Simply put, learning tools make a difference. This contextual aspect of learning—that it occurs only through a process of a person interacting with the environment—is a key conceptual element of the traditional theories of Dewey (1933) and Vygotsky (1978) and the more recent work of Damasio (1999) and the How People Learn work (Bransford et al., 2000). The environment as envisioned in these theories includes all the tools, resources, and people who are part of any particular learning experience (Daniels, 2001).

Learning tools are part of our environment and part of how our brains engage with the content. A learning environment in which all students and all faculty have their own personal laptop computer or its equivalent in smaller devices such as smartphones makes a difference in the kinds of teaching and learning experiences that are possible. These tools create an environment that is transformed and infused with powerful psychological learning tools. The first wave of laptop universities rolled out in the mid-1990s, followed quickly by a second wave of wireless and Web-enabled cell phones, followed by another wave of mobile and handheld digital tools, such as smartphones and Web 2.0 applications such as Twitter and location-based services that help you find your buddies and the coffee shop where you may be meeting. These tools have dramatically changed the traditional communication patterns and relationships between learners and faculty.

Faculty were initially unprepared for the shift in learning dynamics and relationships created by these tools, and many are still struggling to adapt. In an environment infused with these tools, the faculty member moves from the center of the class communication pattern, as was common in the traditional transmission mode of learning, to the periphery or, in the stage model, to the wings.

A second far-reaching impact of these tools is the ease by which students can customize their own learning experiences because courses no longer have content boundaries. Students now live and move within the community-building and networking power of Twittering, instant messaging, and generally always being connected. The anywhere, anytime, anywhile access to communication tools makes it easy for students to go outside the organized course structure.

Readily available mobile tools now support information access and flow in real time, enabling current events, global perspectives, and far-flung resources to be brought into immediate and fresh relief. Every statement by a faculty member is subject to challenge or confirmation from a student using a search engine. This means that faculty need to adapt the course and the content to students who bring in ideas and content that might be quite unfamiliar to them and to defend and support their own mental models. Lifelong learning certainly has a new meaning now.

Summary—and What's Next

The research on how we learn is illuminating in new and significant ways the processes involved in teaching and learning. These insights, integrated with core learning principles, can help guide our design of learning so that both teaching and learning can be efficient and effective. One major insight is the uniqueness of each brain in its structure and its accumulated experiences. We each experience and remember events just a little differently from everyone else. This richness of perspective is a challenge as well as a potent creative force. The combination of the uniqueness of each learner and the richness of perspective argues persuasively for much more emphasis on teaching and experiencing community, culture, and ethics in combination with knowledge and content and skills.

Finally, our learning environments, whether on campus or online or somewhere in between, are the places where structured teaching and learning take place. Just as we evaluate and redesign the teaching and learning processes between faculty and learners, so too we must keep a watch on the environments in which the teaching and learning occur, ensuring that the design of the environment and the tools that we select support our teaching and the learning processes and the unique brains we are responsible for nurturing.

These ten core learning principles provide the theoretical context and inspiration for the many tips that follow in the next chapters. You may want to refer back to these frequently.

The next chapter is designed as a companion chapter to this one in that it describes ten best practices that together apply many of the ten core learning principles from this chapter. Instructors who use these ten practices can significantly increase the probabilities of an initial satisfactory teaching and learning outcome. However, following these practices without a deep appreciation and use of the core principles and many of the tips in the book is a bit like students knowing the words but not the concepts of new knowledge. So aim for the deep understanding and lifelong learning of teaching and learning. Aim high, and enjoy our new world of teaching and learning.

Chapter 3

Ten Best Practices for Teaching Online

Chapter Overview

Teaching online and within a course management system for the first time can feel like exploring a new and unfamiliar space: the individual components look familiar, but the overall feeling is quite different.

Although research into teaching online is still in its infancy, it has affirmed a number of online practices that contribute to an effective, efficient, and satisfying teaching and learning experience for faculty and students. This chapter provides a set of ten best practices to help you on your journey in developing expertise in online teaching. We selected these ten from teaching and learning research studies and best practices that have been developed over the past fifteen to twenty years of online teaching and learning. Instructors who follow these practices will increase the probabilities of providing an effective, efficient, and satisfying teaching and learning experience.

Just as the ten core learning principles in Chapter Two are not necessarily "the" best set of core learning principles, this set of practices is not necessarily "the" best set; rather, it is a set of practices that captures much of what we now know about effective and efficient teaching online. These practices will likely continue to evolve with continuing research and practice.

Ten Best Practices for Beginning Online Teaching

Table 3.1 sets out ten best practices to guide your initial online teaching experiences.

TABLE 3.1

Ten Best Practices for Teaching Online

Best practice 1	Be present at the course site.
Best practice 2	Create a supportive online course community.
Best practice 3	Develop a set of explicit expectations for your learners and yourself as to how you will communicate and how much time students should be working on the course each week.
Best practice 4	Use a variety of large group, small group, and individual work experiences.
Best practice 5	Use synchronous and asynchronous activities.
Best practice 6	Ask for informal feedback early in the term.
Best practice 7	Prepare discussion posts that invite responses, questions, discussions, and reflections.
Best practice 8	Search out and use content resources that are available in digital format if possible.
Best practice 9	Combine core concept learning with customized and personalized learning.
Best practice 10	Plan a good closing and wrap activity for the course.

Use a variety of tch. strategies/activities to reach diverse learning styles
— audio   — text
— video
— visuals (pict, photo)
— mvmt,
— song
— art

Best Practice 1: Be Present at the Course Site

Being present at the course site is the most fundamental and important of all the practices. Over time, we have learned to quantify what it means to "be present." The best online faculty, according to students, are faculty who are present multiple times a week, and at best daily. No matter how expectations are communicated regarding faculty availability, the default mode is twenty-four hours a day, seven days a week. Students expect online faculty to be present when they are there, no matter the day or the time, unless explicitly told otherwise.

Thus, one of the most important expectations for online faculty is—if at all possible—to be present in some way every day. These expectations can be modified, and students will be very accepting if their faculty clearly states personal policies on presence and provides notice if family or professional events cause deviation from these policies.

Liberal use of tools, such as announcements, discussion board postings, and faculty blogs, lets students know just when the faculty member will likely be present for fast turnaround on questions and potentially available for live interaction by phone or collaborative online tools. These same tools can communicate when the faculty member may be away for an extended time—say, two days or more. Strategies such as assigning a student or a team of two students to monitor question forums or blogs can also be a good stand-in for the faculty presence for a day or two and create community support and networking connections.

Why is presence so important in the online environment? When faculty actively interact and engage students in a face-to-face classroom, the class evolves as a group and develops intellectual and personal bonds. The same type of community bonding happens in an online setting if the faculty presence is felt consistently. Regular, thoughtful, daily presence shows the students that the faculty member cares about who they are, cares about their questions and concerns, and is generally present for them to do the mentoring, guiding, and challenging that teaching is all about. In other words, text and audio presence compensate for the physical remoteness of online learning and the lack of face-to-face presence.

One posted message from students that you do not want on your site is the question, "Is anybody there?" Such a posting would be made only by a student who is feeling abandoned, alone, and isolated—a clear and unambiguous signal that not all is well.

The concept of daily presence may be alarming to you as it might fuel the widely reported perception that online courses take significantly more faculty time than classroom-based courses. One way to create a sense of presence without it consuming too much time is to focus discussions on the course site and avoid one-to-one e-mails. Time-released announcements that remind learners of assignment due dates and prepared audio containing additional content that can be swiftly uploaded midweek are other ways to let the learners know you are there.

Of course, there is the danger that too much faculty presence will stunt the discussions as well as delay the development of learner self-direction. So while you may check in to the Web site daily for a few minutes to see if there are questions, by no means feel that you have to add significant daily comments to the course site.

Research on faculty presence suggests that there are three types of presence: social presence, teaching presence, and cognitive presence. (Garrison, Anderson, & Archer, 2000). More about these types of presence are in the tips in Part Two.

Best Practice 2: Create a Supportive Online Course Community

Nurturing a learning community as part of an online course is almost as important as being a significant presence. A learning community in a face-to-face environment often develops spontaneously as students generally have more opportunities to get to know one another and develop friendships outside a particular course. More explicit nurturing and planning is required in the online environment for a learning community to develop.

Community building is the focus of much research in online learning (Brown, 2001; Rovai, 2002; Shea, 2006). Some of the research seeks to define a community; other research examines the stages of a community and the faculty and student behaviors that facilitate community building at these different stages.

Here's how to get started with designing community into an online course. (Many more ideas are in the chapters with tips in Part Two.) A good strategy for developing a supportive online course community is to design a course with a balanced set of dialogues. This means designing a course so that the three dialogues of faculty to learner (F-L), learner to learner (L-L), and learner to resource (L-R) are about equal (Pelikan, 1992). In one online course, the F-L dialogue might be accomplished with three types of communications: short mini-concept introductions, twice-weekly announcements, and interactions with the student postings. In another course, this dialogue might be accomplished with a combination of announcements, discussion postings and monitoring, written mini-lectures, or audio/video podcasts.

Encouraging the L-L dialogue can be done with one or more of these strategies:

- Launch the class with a personal introduction posting so that students get to know one another and you get to know about the students and their interests. The types of information often shared by faculty and students at the beginning of a course touch on professional experiences and personal data such as family, friends, pets, or hobbies, often supported by a photograph or two. It is not uncommon to see pictures of learners with their dog or car or engaged in a hiking, kayaking, skiing, or another activity. Faculty also often include information about their teaching philosophy and current work or research projects.

- Encourage the use of a general open student forum for students to post and request help and assistance from each other through the various peer-to-peer tools, such as discussions and help areas. Learners can use this type of space as a first place to go for help from each other. Think of this place as a student union or coffee shop where students can collaborate, brainstorm, and support one another.

- Divide a larger class into small groups of four to six, similar to a study group, that students can depend on for supportive networking or mentoring, including help in identifying resources or clarifying key points of a class assignment.

- Set up problem-solving forums or discussion boards, and assign students or student teams to monitor and support direct questions.

Not all learners will respond to these strategies for encouraging the building of a learning community. Learning within the setting of an online course community will work better for some students than for others. Some students may choose not to participate very actively at all; others find it is the best way for them to learn. The point is that for students who need it, it is an essential part of how they learn. Vygotsky's theories remind us of how much we learn as social beings within a social context. The online community is part of what makes this happen for many students.

Best Practice 3: Develop a Set of Explicit Expectations for Your Learners and for Yourself as to How You Will Communicate and How Much Time Students Should Be Working on the Course Each Week

This best practice cannot be overemphasized. It clarifies, specifies expectations, and reduces uncertainty. Develop and post prominently on your course site a set of explicit expectations for how students are expected to communicate online and how you expect them to communicate with you. For example, some faculty have a rule that they do not answer content-focused e-mails. This is a good practice because content-focused queries belong in one of the many public spaces of the course site. Queries and responses posted in open course spaces benefit all the learners, as students see both the questions and the responses, and you can develop expectations that students can answer each other's questions. Of course, e-mail remains a good choice for personal and confidential communications.

What about a policy on response time for questions posted on a course site or to e-mail? Institutions have varying policies on this question. Some institutions with large online programs have a policy that faculty are expected to respond to learners within twenty-four hours during the week. Expectations for responses during the weekend can vary, but as most working professionals work on their online courses during the weekend, faculty should establish a general rule as to weekend windows of opportunity.

Another common effective practice is for online faculty to schedule special virtual office hours, being available by chat or live classroom, e-mail, or phone, particularly when learners are likely to be working on an important assignment. In the interests of time and community, it is best to use a communication tool where responses and content can be shared with everyone and archived for flexibility in access and review.

This basic expectation of response time can easily be modified as long as the change is communicated to the students. It is easy to develop your own policies or rules of thumb if the institution does not have them in place. Think about the students as family for the duration of a course or program. Students are very accepting of a faculty member's time and life requirements if they know what is going on. And students often step in and help each other even more when they know a faculty member is sick, traveling, or engaged in significant professional or family obligations. Often students can agree to monitor course questions posted in the open forum or in the discussion boards, for example.

Online learning is just as intensive as learning face-to-face, and time to do the work needs to be scheduled and planned for, just as if one were attending face-to-face classes. Being clear as to how much effort and time will be required on a weekly basis keeps surprises to a minimum.

How much time should learners be expected to dedicate on a weekly basis to an online course? A good rule of thumb is six hours of productive learning time that is used for activities such as reading and processing content, as well as participating in online discussions. For many learners, it can take ten hours to achieve the six productive hours.

Best Practice 4: Use a Variety of Large Group, Small Group, and Individual Work Experiences

A learning community works better when a variety of activities and experiences is offered. Online courses can be more enjoyable and effective when students have the opportunity to brainstorm and work through concepts and assignments with one or two or more fellow students. Of course, some students work and learn best on their own. Building in options and opportunities for students to work together and individually is highly recommended.

Teams are particularly effective when students are working on complex case studies or scenarios for the first time. Early in a course, students may like to get to know one another by working with just one or two other students in teams of two or three. Later in the course, with more complex projects, groups of three or four can work well. It is also important to build in whole class activities such as discussion boards or events with invited experts.

Best Practice 5: Use Synchronous and Asynchronous Activities

When online courses were introduced, they were almost totally asynchronous—an updated version of the correspondence distance learning courses so widespread in the middle of the twentieth century. Now we have course management systems, virtual live classrooms, spontaneous collaboration tools, and an almost infinite number of Web tools and smartphones that support synchronous chat, video messaging, and more. These tools make it possible to do almost everything that we do in face-to-face classrooms. In addition, we can often engage learners in more extensive collaborative and reflective activities.

Sometimes there is nothing better than a real-time interactive brainstorming and sharing discussion; at other times, the requirement to think, plan, write, and reflect is what makes learning most effective for an individual. The variety of activities now possible online makes it easy to create many types of effective learning environments. For example, in financial and statistical courses, real-time problem-solving and question-and-answer review sessions can be effective learning strategies. While working professionals often choose to complete advanced degrees online so that they can make use of the asynchronous, anytime, anywhere features of a program, these same learners enjoy getting together at a specific time to interact in real time.

Best Practice 6: Ask for Informal Feedback Early in the Term

Course evaluations have been called postmortem evaluations because they are done after the fact, and nothing can be changed to increase the satisfaction of the students making the comments. Early feedback surveys or informal discussions are effective in getting students to provide feedback on what is working well in a course and solicit suggestions and ideas on what might help them have a better course experience. This early feedback is done in about week 3 of a fifteen-week course so time is available to make corrections and modifications while the course is ongoing. A request for informal feedback is an easy opening for students who might have comments, suggestions, or questions. A simple e-mail or discussion forum asking one or two of these questions works well:

- What's working thus far?
- How could your learning experience be improved?
- What do you want or need help with?

- What are the top three to five understandings you have learned thus far?

Best Practice 7: Prepare Discussion Posts That Invite Responses, Questions, Discussions, and Reflections

One of the primary differences between the online teaching classroom and the classroom of the campus-based course is how students and faculty communicate and the range of tools that they use to do so. After all, we don't see the students; rather, we get to know them by what they write and say in the discussion boards and their assignments and, to a lesser degree, in e-mail, phone, and collaborative online classrooms.

The communication tool that is the heart and soul of the online course community is the discussion board. This is the primary place where faculty talk to students and students talk to other students. This is also the place where students and faculty get to know one another and the tool that helps a widely dispersed group of students and faculty become a learning community.

Discussions in an online course are the equivalent of class discussions in a face-to-face class. A key difference, of course, is that these discussions are asynchronous, meaning that students have time for thought and reflection. Another key difference is that discussions, blogs, and other tools require written or audio comments that are captured and become part of a course archive.

Discussions are often designed for one of the following learning purposes (Painter, Coffin, & Hewings, 2003; Goodyear et al., 2003, cited in Grogan, 2005):

- Providing an open question-and-answer forum
- Encouraging critical or creative thinking
- Reinforcing domain or procedural processes
- Achieving social interaction and community building so that students get to know each other personally and intellectually
- Validating experiences
- Supporting students in their own reflections and inquiries

Here are a few hints for discussion postings culled from many conversations with experienced online faculty:

- Create open-ended questions that learners can explore and apply the concepts that they are learning.

- Model Socratic-type probing and follow-up questions. "Why do you think that?" "What is your reasoning?" "Is there an alternative strategy?"

- Ask clarifying questions that encourage students to think about what they know and don't know.

- Stagger due dates of the responses, and consider a midpoint summary or encouraging comments.

- Provide guidelines and instruction on responding to other students. For example, suggest a two-part response: (1) "Say what you liked or agreed with or what resonated with you," and (2) "Conclude with a follow-up question such as what you are wondering about or curious about."

- Provide choices and options. Providing choices for students in questioning follows the recommended design principle of encouraging personalized and customized learning. Working professionals are often grappling with many issues; providing choices and options makes it possible to link the learning more directly with their work experiences, interests, and needs.

- Don't post questions soliciting basic facts or questions for which there is an obvious yes-or-no response. The reason for this is obvious: once one student responds, there is not much more to say. Specific fact-based questions that you want to be sure that your students know are good items for automated quizzes or for students to record in blogs.

- Log on to your course a minimum of four days a week to answer e-mail, monitor discussions, post reminders, and hold online office hours. For higher satisfaction for you and your students, log in every day.

Best Practice 8: Search Out and Use Content Resources That Are Available in Digital Format If Possible

If content is not digital, it is as if it does not exist for most students. This means that students will more likely use content, resources, and applications that are online, digital, and readily available. They want to be learning anywhere, anytime, and often while they are doing other things, such as driving, taking care of children, or exercising. Carrying around large, heavy textbooks feels like an anachronism to them.

Book publishers are now making more of their content available digitally. Some institutions are running pilot programs with students using the new larger-screen Kindle from Amazon or one of the Apple iPod series. Selecting a textbook available in multiple formats can be a boon to students, particularly working professionals who may have heavy travel schedules. For many courses, however, textbooks are not yet available in digital form, but publishers are responding. This best practice can be applied to supplementary resources and library resources. A reference document with instructions on remotely accessing library resources is a must for online courses. In addition, a key member of the instructional team is the library reference person assigned to support online learners.

Students enjoy seeing how what they are learning links to current events. Thus, building links to current events into discussions, blogs, and announcements supports the exploration stage of early grappling with core course concepts. So this best practice includes encouraging students to make good use of Internet resources. You might want to consider enlisting student assistance in identifying high-quality content that is available online. This can include tutorials, simulations, and supplementary material. The number and quality of tutorials in complex concepts in physics, chemistry, engineering, and business continue to grow. Students enjoy searching and testing these resources and often engage more deeply as they use resources that they may have found themselves.

Best Practice 9: Combine Core Concept Learning with Customized and Personalized Learning

This best practice combines a number of basic learning principles, many of them addressed in more depth in the tips in Part Two. Briefly, this principle means that faculty need to identify the core concepts to be learned in a course—the performance goals and learning outcomes—and then guide and mentor learners through a set of increasingly complex, personalized, and customized learning activities to help learners apply these core concepts and develop their own knowledge structures. Vygotsky's principle of the zone of proximal development includes the concept that the learning experiences ought to pull students' learning forward, always in advance of development (Del Rio & Alvarez, 2007).

In practical terms for online courses, it means designing options and choices within learning experiences, assignments, and special projects. Supporting learners with their personal and professional goals that are closely linked to the performance goals of a course and even beyond the course parameters is a win-win situation for the learners individually and as a group. It enhances the meaningfulness of the learning and infuses learner enthusiasm in completing the assignments.

Another key principle that aids in concept learning is also inspired by Vygotsky (1962, 1978). He noted that concepts are not words, but rather organized and intricate knowledge clusters. This simple but profound principle means that while we must teach in a linear fashion, presenting concepts individually and in small clusters, we need to continually reapply core concepts within a context, such as those in case studies, problems, and analyses.

Effectively learning concepts, as we know from studies of novice and expert learners, requires a focus on patterns and relationships, not only on individual facts or vocabulary.

A popular new teaching and learning suggestion advocates making students' thinking visible (Collins, Brown, & Holum, 1991). Making our thinking visible requires students to create, talk, write, explain, analyze, judge, report, and inquire. These types of activities make it clear to students themselves, the faculty, and fellow learners what they know or don't know, what they are puzzled about, and about what they might be curious. Such activities stimulate students' growth from concept awareness to concept acquisition, building in that series of intellectual operations that Vygotsky believes is required for concept acquisition.

Discussion forums, blogging, journals, wikis, and similar social networking type tools provide excellent communication channels for engaging learners in clarifying and enlarging their mental models or concepts and building links and identifying relationships.

Best Practice 10: Plan a Good Closing and Wrap Activity for the Course

As courses start coming to a close and winding down, it is easy to focus on assessing and grading students and forget the value of a good closing experience. In the final weeks of a course, students are likely to be stressed and somewhat overwhelmed by the remaining work. In this state, they often do not pause to make the lists and do the planning that can help reduce stress and provide a calming atmosphere. A useful image for reducing stress is in David Allen's book, *Getting Things Done* (2002). Allen notes that making a list helps us to clear the "psychic RAM" of our brains so that we feel more relaxed and more in control. Once we have made lists and prepared our schedule, we don't have to continually remind ourselves of what needs to be done and when.

End-of-course experiences often include student presentations, summaries, and analyses. These reports and presentations provide insights into what useful knowledge students are taking away from a course.

At the same time, these learning events can provide a final opportunity for faculty to remind students of core concepts and fundamental principles. These end-of-course experiences are a good time to use live classrooms, YouTube, and other synchronous collaborative tools.

Conclusion

Traditional courses have long focused on tools and techniques for presenting content. Traditional concerns of faculty focused on covering the material, getting through the book, and meeting expectations so that faculty in other courses wouldn't muse and wonder, "Didn't you learn these concepts from faculty X? And didn't you study the work and contributions of [fill in your favorite who]?"

A major drawback with course designs that have content as a priority is that it often focuses attention on what the faculty member is doing, thinking, and talking about and not on the interaction and engagement of students with the core concepts and skills of a course. Recent trends in higher education are encouraging a focus on learners as a priority, resulting in many publications such as *Launching a Learning-Centered College* (O'Banion, 1999). This movement refocuses instruction on the learner and away from the content, a shift that encourages faculty to develop a habit of asking questions such as, "What is going on inside the learner's head?" "How much of the content and the tools can he or she actually use?" "What are learners thinking, and how did they arrive at their respective positions?"

We have much to learn about teaching and learning, and specifically about teaching and learning in the online environment. The good news is that we now know much more than what we did when online learning started in the early 1990s.

Summary—and What's Next

This set of ten best practices is really the tip of the iceberg in developing expertise in teaching online, but we hope you find it a useful set of practices as you get started. The next eight chapters provide many tips and examples for teaching online, as well as summaries and themes for what is happening in the four phases of a course.

Part Two

Simple, Practical, and Pedagogically Based Tips

Chapter 4

Phase One: What's Happening, Themes, and Tools

Starting Off on the Right Foot in Course Beginnings

Chapter Overview

If you have only a week or two to get ready for teaching an online course, this is a good place to start. This chapter describes the types of interactions and experiences common in the first part of any course, including the faculty and learner behaviors common to Phase One. We also summarize the themes underlying these initial experiences and describe the tasks essential for an effective online course launch and the beginnings of building a course community. This chapter provides an introduction to and description of the essential tools that are basic to teaching online. The next chapter presents the tips for the course beginnings.

What's Happening in Course Beginnings

One of the best ways to start an online course on the right foot is to focus on social presence activities for both learners and faculty. Social presence, that is, getting to know each other as three-dimensional people, is the foundation of building trust and presence for the teaching and learning experiences. Getting acquainted at the social level creates a trusting and understanding environment for reaching out and risking beliefs in the content discussions. Think of the social gatherings you've been required to attend. You enter the room, introduce yourself to various people, and find connections with one another before discussing any of your life beliefs in depth. A similar process happens in the online environment. If we expect learners to be open and vulnerable in expressing what they do or do not know without seeing one another, encouraging social interaction first is a must. Only then can learners shift to a content focus. One of the most important social presence actions is in the getting-acquainted postings by faculty and learners.

A good second question shifts from the social presence interaction to thinking and discussing the course content and personal learning goals. After the getting-acquainted posting in the first week of the course, ask the students to identify their learning goals for the course. This is the early launching of cognitive presence. This question about goals helps to provide insights as to the state of the learners' knowledge, confidence, and experience with the content. It is also a way of gaining insight into learners' individual zones of proximal development—their point of readiness for learning.

During the course beginnings, part of the instructor's responsibilities is to take action to ensure that all learners are engaged, present, and participating. The role of the faculty member at this time is sometimes referred to as a "social and cognitive negotiator" (Conrad & Donaldson, 2004). The faculty member focuses on providing positive, supportive, and encouraging comments about the overall course process and clarifies course expectations and the types of learning experiences in the course requirements. The instructor also introduces other members of the instructional support team.

Another major goal of the course beginnings is launching the course community. This means ensuring that students are engaging in the core concepts of the course and "thinking and talking out loud" about the course concepts. One of the characteristics of community is identifying and sharing common values and being respectful of others' ideas, even if they are quite divergent from our own. The instructor helps to guide this process with a combination of social, teaching, and cognitive presence.

In summary, in the first part of a course, this is what is happening:

- Learners are getting acquainted with each other, reviewing course requirements, getting an overview of the course content and resources, and setting personal and working learning goals.

- In the week or two prior to the course launch, the instructor is finalizing the course and ensuring that all is ready for the learners. Once the course begins, the instructor focuses on creating a comfortable and trusting learning environment and begins implementing the course plan for the first weeks. The faculty member models thinking behavior by making connections among the learners, the content, and the desired learning outcomes. Other important actions for the faculty member are making course requirements clear and processes for communicating explicit, leading the launch of the course learning community, and ensuring that all students are engaged.

- The content resources are in place, and students have acquired the required content resources. If there are problems with access to these resources, the community comes together with ways to address the problems.

- The tools for the online environment are in place. Learners know how to use the applications and tools that are required or know how to access the help that they might need.

Course Beginnings Themes

The themes for course beginnings are presence, community, patience, and clear expectations. These themes capture the basics of the teaching and learning dialogue goals and relationships that are essential features of any online course. They are good to post on your computer, cell phone, watch, or calendar.

Keeping an eye on these themes during course beginnings can help you feel confident about your teaching in the first weeks of an online course. And in fact, these themes are of continuing importance throughout any online course.

Presence

Presence is the most important best practice for an online course. This is the first of the set of ten best practices described in Chapter Three. The tips in this chapter describe specific actions and behaviors for achieving social, teaching, and cognitive presence in a course. These three types of presence were described in a community of inquiry model generated in 2000 by Garrison, Anderson, and Archer at the University of Calgary. The simplest description of presence is "being there." Research links presence most closely to student satisfaction and a related belief that a course is effective. Here are descriptions of the three presences and how they interact and work within the teaching and learning experiences of a course.

Social Presence

One of the best ways to get an online course off on the right foot is to ensure the social presence of the instructor and all the learners. Social presence is "achieved in the community of inquiry model by faculty and students projecting their personal characteristics into the discussion so they become 'real people'" (Garrison, Anderson, & Archer, 2001). It is imperative that the trust-building process is established at the social level so that content discussions can be open and substantive. One of the first tips focuses on strategies for getting acquainted at the social level, sharing personal favorites such as drinks, food, ideas, books, or movies in the first week. This encourages expression of feelings, perspectives, and openness.

Cognitive Presence

A good follow-up question in the first week of the course is to ask the student to identify their learning goals for the course, shifting from the social presence interaction to thinking and discussing the course content and personal learning goals. This question about goals helps an instructor gain insights into the state of the learners' knowledge, confidence, and experience with the content. It is a way of gaining insight into learners' individual zones of proximal development. This question also encourages relatedness and connections as learners discover shared and complementary experiences and goals.

Cognitive presence is defined as the "extent to which the professor and the students are able to construct and confirm meaning through sustained discourse (discussion) in a community of inquiry" (Garrison, Anderson, & Archer, 2000, p. 89). Cognitive presence is cultivated by students' expressing a desire to understand ideas more deeply and by dialogue that discerns patterns, connects ideas, and identifies relationships. Getting a sense of what students know and how they know it lays the foundation for the learning experiences that follow.

Teaching Presence

Teaching presence in an online course consists of at least two major categories of teaching direction. The first category consists of all the course materials that are prepared before the course begins: the syllabus, concept introductions, discussions, assessment plans, and lists of required and recommended resources. The second category consists of all the monitoring, mentoring, questioning, and shaping of the growing knowledge of particular learners in a course. The first category of teaching presence is developed on the assumptions of what students probably know and understand—the "mythical" student for design purposes. The second category of teaching direction is customized to the particular set of students. Garrison (2009) further categorizes this teaching presence into facilitation and the work of direct instruction of focusing and resolving any issues with individual students.

Community

Building a sense of shared understanding, knowledge of one another, and mutual support, even if values are not shared, are elements of community. The goal of community in an online course is twofold: building knowledge and competencies within learners and building a network of mutual respect and sharing of ideas and perspectives.

Patience

Be patient with yourself as you develop online teachings skills. Also be patient with your students as they develop online learning skills that often mean that they must become more active learners and take more responsibility for what they know and the skills and values they want to develop.

Clarity of Expectations

Clear and unambiguous guidelines about what is expected of learners and what they should expect from an instructor make a significant contribution to ensuring understanding and satisfaction in an online course. Watch for how this theme of clear expectations surfaces in many of the tips. Teaching and learning at a distance and sometimes over time zones, plus using a set of tools and systems that might not always work quite right or be available carry the potential for many sundry misunderstandings. Clarifying how all this will work and sometimes might not work can help create a smooth and trusting learning environment.

Course Beginnings Tips

There is much to do before your students arrive at your course. But this work is manageable. The first set of tips in Chapter Five describes the basic tasks in preparing and launching an online course and how the syllabus of an online course is different from that of a face-to-face course. The basic tasks generally require a minimum of twenty to thirty hours if you are familiar with the tools and if you have taught the course before in a face-to-face mode. If the tools are new to you, this preparation time is usually a little longer because you will be learning new habits and processes. If you are learning while preparing, it is not uncommon for this preparation to take closer to forty or even fifty hours over two or three or more weeks. And if you like to feel *very* ready, it can take even longer. During the first cycle of an online course, the time in preparation and delivery is similar to the first time teaching a new course in the face-to-face environment. The primary difference is that more planning must be done before the students arrive at your course site: excited, curious, and a little nervous, but nevertheless expecting to see a full course plan.

The tips for phase one of your course summarize what you must do to get ready for the course launch, including the week or two just prior to the official launch of the course. The first phase is generally from two to four weeks, depending on the total length of your course term. If you are teaching short courses, you will want to adjust these phases to your particular course structure.

The first set of tips in Chapter Five, on Getting Ready and Getting Acquainted focus on beginning well. These are the steps and actions in preparing the essential course elements of an online course, the actions for launching an online course well, and faculty actions to be completed immediately prior to the launching of a course. The most important initial goals to achieve in the first weeks are getting acquainted with the learners, establishing trust, and launching the learning community. These getting-acquainted experiences lay the trust groundwork for the teaching and learning relationship and the social presence (Garrison et al., 2000).

A second set of tips for the course beginnings, Creating and Designing Discussions, focuses on designing and organizing the essential content and knowledge pieces of an online course. This includes creating engaging and challenging discussion questions with clear rubrics for assessing the online discussions. Creating engaging discussions is one of the highest priorities for a new course. Discussions are the core of online teaching and learning and critical for effective online socialization and cognitive engagement. The threaded discussions and other dialogue spaces, including informal interactions among learners, create the sense of an inviting gathering place and spaces for sharing experiences that are part of a community. The difference is that these are online virtual classroom spaces rather than a face-to-face classroom.

Entering into the world of online teaching and learning can create uncertainty and trepidation, and even a feeling of being overwhelmed as you venture into a world of unfamiliar tools and students at a distance. However, if you have been an effective instructor in the face-to-face environment, you will soon adapt to the new environment with a little time and practice. Your first step is to work on the preparations and establish a goal of creating a set of learning experiences that engages and challenges your students. For a new online instructor, this is the most work-intensive time.

Technology Tools

You may not be feeling quite ready to tackle all the tools that are available for your online course. This is actually wise. The best approach for teaching a first online course is to keep it simple. Focus on the essential tools, and build your first course around those tools. You can branch out later as you teach the course a second or third time and gain experience, confidence, and a sense of exploration. Students can also be a source of help and advice. Don't be shy about accepting their help. They will feel part of the process and proud to be part of your learning too.

Essential Tools and Features of a Course Management System

Some of the basics that you will need to know are uploading text documents, setting up and creating discussion forums, and setting up and using the grade book (Table 4.1). You may want to put learning how to assign members to teams at the top of your list of learning goals if you have a larger class and to have separate discussion areas for some discussions.

The primary tool that you will need to become familiar with is the course management system (CMS) that your institution uses. Some of the most used systems in higher education are Blackboard, Desire2Learn, Moodle, WebStudy, and Sakai. Reviews of these systems and many others including details of their features and tools are at WCET Edu Tools site (http://www.edutools.info). WCET is a nonprofit, membership-based organization.

Most institutions offering online programs also have workshops and tutorials introducing faculty to the particular CMS at their institution.

TABLE 4.1

Basic Skills and Tools for Using a Course Management System

1. Requesting or arranging for a course template
2. Uploading documents and pictures
3. Updating and revising documents
4. Setting up and creating discussion forums
5. Setting up and using the grade book
6. Setting up teams and groups

Many tutorials and hints are widely available from the CMS sites such as www.blackboard.com and www.moodle.com and also from faculty support sites at other universities. A search often will reveal many useful resources on any of these topics.

If your institution is not set up with a CMS, you may wish to consider a system such as Moodle, which is available free of charge from www. moodle.com. Of course, policies and access privileges always change, but this is a good place to start.

The tips in each phase of the course suggest a number of tools for you to consider. But it is vital that you add tools only as you are ready. If a tip suggests a tool that is not available to you or you are not quite ready for, simply adapt the tip as makes sense to you and come back to it for further consideration the next time you are teaching the course. Some faculty identify one or two tools to learn and use with each course offering as a way of expanding their expertise. Of course, if your students are familiar with tools and want to continue using them for their projects or for communication purposes, that usually works out just fine. For now, we are talking about the tools required for teaching and learning experiences.

Tools and Applications for Teaching and Learning Online

Many tools mentioned in the course beginnings tips are not necessarily part of the CMS at your institution. These tools make it possible to design almost any learning experience that you have designed for your face-to-face environment. Learning how to use them will keep you busy for some time to come. However, it's important not to get overwhelmed. Just pick one to three that are best suited for your learning goals and discipline and learn those. Remember, too, that tools are constantly changing, but usually they are also getting much easier and many of them are free. The tools that you will want to develop an awareness of over time are listed in Table 4.2. More description of the tools and which tip mentions the tool follows the table.

More Background on the Tools

Audio and video lectures can be accomplished with many different tools. The audio tools that are generally available include the latest version of PowerPoint; online classroom or other collaborative meeting tools; many of the current generation of audio players, such as the iPod, iPod touch, and iPhone series; and free software such as Audacity. All that is needed is a microphone and, in the case of video lectures, a Webcam. Many computers now have those media and camera elements built in, making audio and video lectures even easier to create. All you need to do is find

TABLE 4.2

Tools in Course Beginnings Tips and Suggested Pedagogical Uses

Tools and Applications in Course Beginnings Tips	Course Beginning Tip Number	Suggested Pedagogical Uses and Purposes
E-mail, announcements, and discussion forums	CB 1	Basic and essential communication tools for guiding learning and building a learning community
Audio and video lectures and resources	CB 1	Creating a media-rich learning environment
Audacity audio software (free at www.audacity.com)	CB 1	Creating announcements, short mini-lectures, or concept introductions
Blogs: Online journals, either part of a CMS or separate applications	CB 1, CB 6, CB 7	Capturing students' thinking as they learn and a place for others to comment and suggest if desired
Wikis: Collaborative project tool, part of a CMS or separate application	CB 1, CB 6, CB 7	Supporting student collaboration and teamwork on projects
YouTube: A Web site for posting short videos	CB 1	A place for posting videos and early concept introductions or for process demonstrations
Course management system, such as Blackboard, Desire2Learn, Sakai, Moodle, and WebStudy	CB 1	Providing a virtual place to gather, meet, think out loud, learn, and practice; these systems are like virtual classrooms and campuses
Text messaging, instant messaging, and Twittering	CB 2, CB 6	Good nearly synchronous tools that faculty can use to be available for quick information checks, for example, before an assignment is due
Turnitin software	CB 3	Software for detecting plagiarism; many institutions have a site license for this and it is linked to the CMS
Social networking sites: Facebook, MySpace, Ning, and LinkedIn	CB 4	Internet sites for social networking and extended community that can supplement course places and carry networking beyond courses and programs
Synchronous collaboration tools and online classrooms: Elluminate, Wimba, and Acrobat Connect	CB 4	Synchronous tools that generally need to be part of the online teaching and learning infrastructure linked to the institution's CMS; can be used for scheduled or spontaneous group meetings

TABLE 4.2

(Continued)

Tools and Applications in Course Beginnings Tips	Course Beginning Tip Number	Suggested Pedagogical Uses and Purposes
Quizzes: testing subsystems within a CMS	CB 5	Timed, open-book quizzes good for testing automaticity of lower-level learning objectives such as vocabulary and initial understanding of core concepts
Discussion board for learners	CB 6, CB 7	A place where learners can ask general questions of the instructor or other students; good to have one discussion cybercafé/student union forum for social student interaction and another for general course questions

a relatively quiet office space. Do this when you are ready and feeling adventuresome and can take a little time with it. You might even encourage your students to try it first and then learn from them.

YouTube is a social networking site that makes it easy to upload and share videos. To find out how to do this, visit the help area of the site and type in the question, "How do I get started?" The instructions include using digital recorders that you probably already have on hand and may have used to record videos of family and friends. You can use these same tools for creating short audio and video content. This is also a tool that your students probably have already used. A very easy way of capturing video is with your own camera or the Flip Video recorder. If you travel to a conference during the middle of a course and want to stay in touch with your students, you can capture a three-minute interview with an expert or colleague and send it back to your students.

Some course management systems have Wimba voice tools built in that make it even easier to record audio announcements, provide audio feedback, and have asynchronous audio discussions. When you are ready or prefer not to have to type so much, look into using the Wimba voice tools or the free audacity software or even the Flip Video camera.

Blogs and wikis, media-rich Web applications, are mentioned in a number of course beginning tips. Blogs are online journals or logs that are organized with the latest postings appearing first. They can be used as reflective or outreach documents by individuals or groups. Blogs often have many levels of access with opportunities for commenting and review so that you can customize the blogs to your teaching style. Free blogging tools are widely available and many CMSs have built-in blogs.

Wikis are particularly well suited for organizing and storing information that might be helpful for managing and producing collaborative group projects. The most famous example of a wiki is the modern encyclopedia project Wikipedia. More information about blogs and wiki is contained in later tips.

Instant messaging, mentioned in CB Tips 2 and 6, is a text-based communications method that enables real-time conversation by pop-up windows on mobile devices such as cell phones and BlackBerry. The language of instant messaging can sometimes appear in discussion boards, such as LOL for "laugh out loud" or ?4U as in "I have a question for you." Most online courses have a policy of discouraging instant messaging vocabulary for obvious reasons.

Second Life, mentioned in CB Tip 3, is a free three-dimensional virtual reality world that is imagined and created by the residents of Second Life. Many higher education institutions have created virtual campuses and are using this online space for synchronous lectures and demonstration of projects and collaborations. You can explore Second Life through its Educator Get Started Program (http://secondlifegrid.net/slfe/education-use-virtual-world).

Facebook, MySpace, Ning, and LinkedIn are mentioned in CB Tip 4. These are social networking sites where users find and communicate with friends using pictures, blogs, videos, profiles, and "what I am doing now" messages. Many of your learners will be very familiar with these sites and can probably suggest ways for how to use some of the techniques from these sites in your course.

Elluminate, Wimba, and Adobe Connect are mentioned in CB Tip 4. These are just a few of the real-time synchronous Web conferencing tools that are being used for a wide range of teaching and learning interactions. Some of the most popular uses are live discussions, presentations by faculty and students, question-and-answer sessions, and general collaboration. These tools make it easy to prepare short lectures or concept demonstrations as well.

Be sure to relax and just focus on the tools that you need to teach the course for the first cycle. You will have plenty of time and probably help in learning new tools as you go. Table 4.2 will serve as a reference or glossary tool as you journey on your way to being an accomplished online instructor.

Chapter 5

Phase One: Tips for Course Beginnings

Chapter Overview

This chapter provides ten tips for course beginnings. Six of the tips in this phase, Getting Ready and Getting Acquainted, describe the tasks to be completed to ensure a smooth launch of the course and the initial experiences that help to create a social learning community. Three focus on effective use of discussion boards, with tips on developing good questions, and the final tip describes how your role as an instructor changes over the four phases of the course.

Each of the tips begins with the questions commonly asked by online faculty and addressed by the tip. The tip then suggests practical steps and actions supported by theory, practice, and research.

This is the list of the course beginnings (CB) tips in this chapter:

- CB Tip 1: Course Launch Preparations: The Essential Course Elements of an Online Course

- CB Tip 2: Hitting the Road Running: How Not to Lose the First Week!

- CB Tip 3: How an Online Syllabus Is Different

- CB Tip 4: Launching Social Presence in Your Course

- CB Tip 5: Getting to Know Students' Minds Individually: The Vygotsky Zone of Proximal Development

- CB Tip 6: Getting into the Swing of a Course: Is There an Ideal Weekly Rhythm?

- CB Tip 7: The Why and How of Discussion Boards: Their Role in the Online Course

- CB Tip 8: Characteristics of Good Discussion Questions

- CB Tip 9: Managing and Evaluating Discussion Postings
- CB Tip 10: The Faculty Role in the First Weeks: Required and Recommended Actions

GETTING READY AND GETTING ACQUAINTED

The first set of tips in this chapter describes the tasks to be completed to ensure a smooth launch of the course and the initial experiences that help to create a social learning community. One of the tips describes how an online syllabus differs from a campus syllabus; other tips describe ways to support the development of social and cognitive presence so that students and faculty get to know one another as a person and as a learner.

CB Tip 1: Course Launch Preparations: The Essential Course Elements of an Online Course

This tip answers questions such as these:

- What course elements, such as a syllabus and assessment plans, are essential to have ready for students before the start of a course?
- What course elements should be ready for an instructor to feel comfortable at the start of an online course?
- Is there a checklist that I can use to review my course?

One way of describing a course is that it is a set of learning experiences designed to guide learners as they acquire and are assessed on a specific set of knowledge, skills, and attitudes. The set of experiences and the processes for assessing learners need to be designed, which leads us to the question, "What course elements are essential to be designed and developed before launching a course?" This tip identifies those essential course elements and the steps in getting them ready.

Essential Course Pieces

The course elements that must be completed for an online course are the syllabus, the weekly plans and discussion postings for the first weeks, and the course site. The syllabus is a familiar part of the teaching process for a faculty. Building the other online course components is less familiar, but almost all have an analogue in the face-to-face class. Just as a new face-to-face course goes through a gradual process of refinement, faculty can anticipate that it generally takes about three cycles of teaching a course for it to be fully developed. During the initial three cycles, faculty develop a new set of teaching behaviors for guiding, mentoring, and assessing students in an online environment. Here is a brief description of each of these critical course pieces.

Syllabus

The syllabus for an online course performs the same functions as for a face-to-face class, but even more so. Providing a bird's-eye picture of the whole course so that learners can plan their lives is essential to learners' having a sense of control and optimism.

The online syllabus sets out the overall course plan with performance goals, learning outcomes, and requirements. It includes a description of the core content resources (textbook, readings, audio and video resources, and so forth), the course schedule, the assessment plan, and policies and procedures. A syllabus may also contain the boilerplate information on library access, technical support, and contact information for noncourse-specific questions. More detail on building a syllabus and how the various components differ in an online course is in CB Tip 3.

Weekly Teaching Guides

In planning a face-to-face course, many faculty devote significant time to creating and developing lectures. For online teaching, the time spent in preparing lectures transforms into preparing short text, audio or video introductions or mini-lectures, developing and managing threaded discussions, and monitoring other student spaces, such as forums on the course site. Lectures in the face-to-face class are the primary channel for faculty-to-student dialogue. This is important to the teaching presence (Garrison, Anderson, & Archer, 2000) as these lectures convey the special expertise and personality of the instructor. In the online classroom, the equivalent teaching presence is expressed in the weekly plans, teaching guides, discussions, and faculty comments and observations.

Weekly teaching guides are short text, audio, or video pieces that introduce the goals and purposes and activities for the week. They often provide the rationale for the choice and design of the learning experiences and a brief introduction to the core concepts. Creating short personal videos is so easy now that some faculty are preparing short mini-lecture videos and posting them on YouTube. For example, the short video introductions at http://www.youtube.com/watch?v=jAj5uBKyqv8, prepared by Tony Picciano of Hunter College for graduate programs in education, are generally about two to six minutes long. Part of the high value of these videos is the opportunity to hear as well as see the instructor.

However, video weekly teaching guides are not critical. Some faculty use some forms of video, including live classrooms, when visual graphs or pictures are necessary to better convey the particular content being discussed. In your first cycle of teaching, just use whatever tool feels best to you. It may be text introductions, and that is fine.

Discussions and Rubrics

The discussion board in an online course is the equivalent of a whole class or small group discussion in a campus class. The discussion board is the primary place where dialogue, discussion, and peer-to-peer interaction take place. The student postings in discussion boards and in other Web tools such as blogs and wikis are where faculty "see" their students. Rather than seeing their students' eyes and faces, the discussion postings are even more revealing of what the students know or think they know and may be about to think.

Investing time in developing good questions for the discussion boards and planning out the scoring rubrics and evaluation of the discussion boards makes a real difference in how quickly a learning community starts to form in a course. Experienced online faculty will plan out all of the discussions before a course begins. This is absolutely recommended for your first online course as a faculty mentor. You may find that you will want to make changes as you get to know your students, but having the discussions planned raises your confidence and lowers your stress. Since you may decide to make changes in the specifics of the discussions, counsel students not to work too far ahead of the group as a whole. It is possible that you would like to know more about rubrics as you are developing your discussion questions. (For more about rubrics, see CB Tip 9 and Early Middle [EM] Tip 5.)

Course Site

The campus classroom serves as a gathering place for interactions, sharing learning experiences and small and large class activities. In an online course, these gatherings take place online, often in a learning management system (LMS) or course management system (CMS) such as Blackboard, Moodle, or Sakai. A course site is the "physical space" for the online classroom. This is where the instructor and students gather, share thinking, ideas, and complete the course requirements. You as the faculty mentor serve as the hub, the host, the glue of the learning community.

In getting a course site ready, your first step is to complete the administrative paperwork with the information technology services group at your institution to request that a course site be set up. At some institutions, this may be done automatically, but a good rule is to leave nothing to chance. Textbooks are often ordered many months before a course launches. For online programs, this might be done by a departmental administrative staff member in the middle of the previous term. If textbooks haven't been ordered and it is time for the course to begin, work with the support staff to offer alternatives such as online bookstores or even arrange with publishers for permission to scan a chapter or two to keep students moving forward in the course until they receive their textbooks.

This is a good time to check on the details of what might be needed to get a course site up. If you have enough time prior to the first offering of a course, you may find it helpful to have a practice site set up months in advance or to use an online course site with a campus class.

The other items that a faculty member is responsible for becoming familiar with is the institution's information on library access, technical support, and contact information for noncourse-specific questions for online students. One rule of thumb that is a time saver is making certain this information is prominent, so that the students know whom they should contact for noncontent questions. This is a highly effective way of building loyalty to the institution as the students develop relationships with a broader instructional team.

To-Do List for Preparing an Online Course

You may find this summary to-do list useful as you develop your online course. Note this assumes that someone else is in charge of finding and recruiting students for your class, just as for a regular campus class:

1. Find out who is responsible for setting up the course site. If you don't know where to start, start with the person who assigned you the task of teaching online.

2. Make a request for a course site. While that is under way, work on the syllabus.

3. If you have this course designed for a face-to-face course, start with your existing syllabus. Review your course performance goals and learning outcomes, and consider how realistic and appropriate they are for an online course. If you can, review the course goals prior to and following your course.

4. Review and select textbooks. If you have a choice between a textbook with digital content and one without, choose the textbook with a set of rich expanded materials online and one that offers an option of formats.

5. Order the textbooks.

6. Prepare the syllabus, using this and other syllabus tips. Part of preparing your syllabus will be to identify the eight to ten modules or chapters for your course.

7. Check to see if there is a standard course template for your online course for your college or institution. These templates often contain the standard boilerplate information as well as the standard set of tools that are available to you.

8. Be sure you can access your course site and that the template for your institution and program is in place for your site, or request it.

9. Prepare a draft of your assessment plan, being sure to have multiple points of assessment and including points for discussion, assignments, quizzes, and projects.

10. Plan out the full course schedule, being sure to take note of universal holidays and events particular to your institution. Plan assignments so you can get feedback to your students in a reasonable time. Think in terms of a regular weekly rhythm.

11. Prepare discussion postings, and post them in the course site. Prepare the rubrics for posting.

12. Review actions and plans for the week before the course starts and the next three weeks.

13. Ask for feedback from another instructor or use the Quality Matters rubric. Check standards of quality for an online course. (More on these quality checks follow.)

In the midst of getting ready, it is easy to forget how important it is to complete your own getting-acquainted posting. For this introductory posting, be sure to include a picture of yourself, your favorite food, current book that you are reading or perhaps writing, research interests, or other introductory information.

Table 5.1 summarizes the critical course elements and shows their relationship to one another.

Quality Standards for an Online Course

This section is not absolutely required for launching an online course, but it is a good reference to use for checking the quality of a course. It is definitely a resource to use before the second delivery of a course. How do you evaluate your course? If you would like to do a quick check, a useful checklist is available at the Quality Matters Institute. This rubric

TABLE 5.1

Elements of an Online Course

Course Elements	Description
Syllabus	The overall plan for the course with performance goals and requirements. It usually includes an overview of the course goals, a description of the core content resources (textbook, readings, other resources), the course schedule, and the assessment plan. A syllabus may also contain boilerplate information on policies and procedures, library access, technical support, and contact information for noncourse-specific questions. Check to see if your institution has a syllabus template and use it.
Content resources, including textbook (often a section of the syllabus)	Required and recommended resources for core content and initial application of core concepts, plus starting points for resources for more complex customized and personalized learning experiences.
Assessment plan (often a section of the syllabus)	Summarizes the assessment activities for assessing student learning and ideally maps the assessment experiences to performance goals and requirements. Online assessment plans include multiple assessment experiences, including low-stakes quizzes, peer responses and reviews, concept integration papers, and high-stake projects.
Papers, projects, and quizzes	The usual components of an assessment plan. These are the products of students' learning. The requirements for each of these are in the assessment plan. The directions and specifications for projects and papers are often separate documents; the quizzes, if any, are within the quiz section of the course management system.
Schedule of class activities and events	The overall course calendar that summarizes the course activities. This course calendar usually needs fine-tuning to ensure a balanced course design: balanced dialogue, a range of individual and group activities, and synchronous and asynchronous events. Learners use this course calendar to integrate their life events over the term of a course.
Online classroom: The course site	Where learners and faculty gather for the course experiences and activities. Getting a course site ready for an online class means getting the syllabus ready and preparing the resources and activities. The resources include the teaching guides, the discussions, and planned individual work.
Teaching guides	A set of introductions and guides for each of the course topics and modules and setting out the requirements and specifications for student action and learning. These teaching guides are part of the prepared teaching presence.

TABLE 5.1

(Continued)

Course Elements	Description
Discussions and interactions	A set of catalyst discussion questions, usually a set for each week, that focus on the course core concepts and performance goals. These discussions are the means by which community grows, develops, and flourishes.
Individual work and reflection	The learning work that students complete more or less on their own: reading, writing, researching, or collaborating with another learner or a study group. The resources, learning outcomes, and goals of these activities are designed in broad terms by the instructor, but the instructor is generally not present while the learner is doing the work.

was developed as part of the Quality Matters (QM) project funded by the Fund for the Improvement of Postsecondary Education. The goal of the project is to provide tools for assessing and ensuring the quality of online courses. The rubric has eight sections that address the key elements of online courses.

- Course overview and introduction
- Learning objectives and outcomes
- Assessment and measurement
- Resources and materials
- Learner interaction
- Course technology
- Learner support
- Accessibility

This rubric is now part of a for-profit entity that certifies online courses with the Quality Matters rubric. However, use of the FY 05/06 Quality Matters Rubric (webbasedinstruction.googlepages.com/C7_QMRubric.pdf) is not constrained and is a good checklist as you are getting started. A research paper (Legon, 2006) comparing the Quality Matters rubric to other online standards and accreditation guidelines from the Council for Higher Education Accreditation affirms that the QM rubric is fully consistent with published accreditation standards for online education.

CB Tip 2: Hitting the Road Running: How Not to Lose the First Week!

This tip answers questions such as these:

- Should I contact students prior to the course start date?

- How should I interact with the technical support staff and other members of the instructional team?

- How do I ensure that students have the right set of tools and know how to access their courses, the library, or technical help?

Students new to a campus generally arrive a few days early to settle in and become familiar with their physical surroundings. The same recommendation applies to online learning; the difference is that students sign in and explore their course a few days before the start date to make certain that they have what they need for the first weeks of the course. Once learners are accepted into an online course or program, they usually are directed to a Web site with information specific to their program of study. This information generally includes data on the required and recommended learning tools, such as a computer, a browser, and the bandwidth required for the online course. Alternatively, these requirements can be stated elsewhere on an institution's Web site for online learning courses and programs. This information might also have a list of the types of learning skills and technical skills expected of students in online courses. But again, it is not good to leave these expectations to chance. Find the site at your institution with this information, and reference it in your syllabus or repeat it.

The week before a course begins is also the time to check the basic online skills of students and remind them of the other members of the instructional team who support online learners. Unlike campus courses where faculty often feel like the Lone Ranger handling everything that comes up, online faculty are part of a designated instructional support team. Personnel are usually in place to help students in the areas of technical support, student services, and library resources. Faculty find it useful to provide a list of contact numbers and descriptions of the people and resources available to online students. This information is usually available on a general informational site, but the closer it is to the students when they need it, the more likely they are to contact the support personnel rather than you. This is definitely to be encouraged. Online learning is a 24/7 activity, but faculty need to sleep, and they have a profusion of other professional and personal responsibilities. One of the principles for online faculty is to focus on their particular role of guiding and mentoring of students in learning content knowledge and achieving the performance goals of a course.

Students can generally access a course site a few days to a week before the course begins, so have some preliminary activities ready for them. Some institutions have instituted an official "preweek": the time that students access the course site, review the course requirements, and even post their getting-acquainted note. Also have activities that check the following:

- Are the students able to get their passwords and access the course site? Are they able to navigate their way through the university portal to the course site?

- Do the students know how to access the library resources?

- Do the students have the textbook and other required resources? Do they need any help with accessing or obtaining these resources?

- Do the learners know how to post on the discussion board? Have they posted their getting-acquainted posting? Students are more relaxed at this time and often explore their abilities to post audio or pictures.

- Will the course schedule work for students? Check on dates and times for any planned synchronous experiences.

Some experienced online faculty contact their students by e-mail a week prior to the course start date and invite them to the course site during the preweek to check out access, complete the getting-acquainted posting, and generally ensure that they are ready for the course. If any student doesn't have a getting-acquainted post up by the end of the preweek, send an e-mail to that student, or post an announcement reminding all students to do so, call the student, or send an instant message (IM) to the student.

The first week is also the time to ensure or refresh students' familiarity of the communication processes and resources. Remind them of the resources and times of the help desk and that their fellow students are resources for questions in the open discussion forum or cybercafé. Many faculty set up a special open discussion area that they call the Cybercafé, Learner Corner, or Cyberbits (or something similar) for informal interactions among students. Of course, the policies and procedures section of the syllabus includes your personal schedule for when you are going to be online and available for phone, e-mail, or chat on other course-related questions. Post this information prominently in your course site, either in a general posting area or in a couple of announcements.

CB Tip 3: How an Online Syllabus Is Different

This tip answers questions such as these:

- Which areas of my syllabus need to be changed for an online course? What about strategies for assessing learning, for discussions and dialogue, and for weekly pacing?

- Should information and policies about netiquette and plagiarism tools be included?

If you are modifying an existing campus course for the online learning environment, many of the core components of a course can remain the same—for example:

- Course description

- Performance goals and learning outcomes

- Content resources such as textbooks and access to supplementary recommended resources. This section may be expanded to include more online resources. Instructions about where to purchase a textbook or other required resources are essential. Online courses generally move quickly, and students must have required resources on hand when the course begins.

- Assignments. You might add instructions on how to turn in the assignment online if this hasn't been covered in other orientation material.

The sections in a syllabus that will be different for an online course include policies, procedures, and the mechanics about how to communicate and learn in an online environment. Just as there are effective practices for faculty, there are effective practices for learners that they may need to learn.

Instructors usually do not have to remind students how to behave in a classroom: students generally know the script for a campus classroom. They come in, find a seat, and begin to take notes and ask questions once the lecture starts (although sometimes we have to remind them not to sleep, play computer games, or text their friends). In an online learning environment, we cannot assume that learners know how to communicate effectively with an instructor or their fellow students. They may have extensive experience in online chatrooms and virtual environments, such as Second Life, but they may need to learn how to communicate well in the more structured course environments. Here are sections to consider including in a syllabus for an online course:

- *Netiquette guidelines, or how to communicate effectively and courteously online.* There are many good sites for netiquette, so don't feel you have to make up a set of these rules on your own. Here are a couple of starting points:

- *The Core Rules of Netiquette* by Virginia Shea (http://www.albion.com/netiquette/corerules.html).

- *Top 26 Most Important Rules of Email Etiquette.* These are also applicable to discussion posts (http://email.about.com/od/emailnetiquette/tp/core_netiquette.htm).

  - *Emoticons.* These are symbols that are used to add emotion to text. The one that is most used is "colon-dash-right parenthesis," which becomes a happy face. Here are a couple of sites describing emoticons and their meanings: http://messenger.msn.com/Resource/Emoticons.aspx and http://en.wikipedia.org/wiki/Emoticon. Some faculty discourage the use of emoticons, but as long as they are used tastefully, they convey some invisible body language.

  - *Communication patterns.* Remind students that communication patterns in an online course are different from those in the face-to-face environment. In face-to-face environments, the instructor is in front of the students, and most questions are directed to him or her, so communication patterns flow predominantly between faculty and students. In the online course site content, questions are posted in the question forum and not in a private e-mail to the instructor. The purpose of the online question forum, or questions within a threaded discussion, is to encourage whole class or group participation in content discussions. All content comments are public to the class members and the instructor, unless exceptions seem prudent. This communication pattern of one to many and many to one, regardless of role, encourages community, course discussion, brainstorming, and mutual help. A separate space, such as an open forum area, can be established strictly for socializing. Other communication patterns can be used in wikis or blogs.

  - *Plagiarism.* A section on plagiarism, particularly what it is and how to avoid it, can be helpful. If your syllabus already includes an institutional academic honor policy, it may not address the ease of plagiarism today and how to avoid inadvertent plagiarism. Here are some sites to consider directing your students to on this topic:

- Definition of plagiarism: http://en.wikipedia.org/wiki/Plagiarism.

- Self-detection and checking: http://plagiarism.com/self.detect.htm and http://turnitin.com/static/index.html. Many institutions have a site license for the Turnitin application.

- Another self-detection and checking tool: http://www.essayrater. com/?gclid=CKHcr_b6s5cCFQKfnAodmwRqig.

- *Expectations:* You may currently have a section on expectations, but it's a good idea to make sure this section includes information on communication turnaround time—for example, "I'll reply to most e-mails and discussion posts within twenty-four to forty-eight hours during the work-week. I'll check for urgent messages on the weekend." In addition, participation guidelines provide specifics on how often to log in to the course, how often to post in the discussions, length of posts, and depth of posts. These can be specific to assignments and activities.

- *Assessment:* Assessing participation in a campus face-to-face course is often based on memory or a few notes about what you, the instructor, remember about each student's participation in the class discussions. Often if a student is listening intently and offers a few thoughtful comments during the semester, that is deemed satisfactory. In an online course, participation in discussion boards and forums is a more significant source of getting to know a student and his or her understanding of course content. This means that participation points should be part of the assessment plan.

In the early days of online courses, a colleague of ours conducted a small action research project in which the instructor did not say anything about the value of participation and just let the learners participate as they felt moved to do so. Only 20 percent of the class posted anything in the discussions. The next time the course was offered, the instructor wrote guidelines and based about 30 percent of the course grade on participation. Participation in this course jumped to 80 percent of the class posting in the discussions. So if you are thinking that "if you post it, they will participate," we suggest rethinking that strategy. A scoring system or rubric can let learners know the difference between superficial and meaningful participation.

- *Troubleshooting:* In the event something goes wrong in a course, learners need to know whom to contact. If you do not specify whom to call for what, students will contact you in a panic when any technical glitch occurs. This information can be in a separate troubleshooting section or a subset of the policies and procedures section of your syllabus. Stating ahead of time the contact information for the help desk and what to do in the event the course site is down and an assignment is due helps the students and helps you. Remind students to post in the question forum if something is going wrong.

• • •

Adding these sections will not ensure a trouble-free course, but it will prepare students to participate fully and effectively in the course and be able to resolve problems without involving you every step of the way.

CB Tip 4: Launching Your Social Presence in Your Course

This tip answers questions such as these:

- Why is presence so important? What is social presence? Teaching presence? Cognitive presence?

- What do I do to establish social, teaching, and cognitive presence?

- What is a good example of how to request a getting-acquainted posting?

- What is a good example of a getting-acquainted response posting?

Interaction and Presence as a Key Point of Satisfaction for Learners

Regular and timely interaction of faculty with students is one of the key quality indicators of online courses. A number of studies (Richardson & Swan, 2003; Burnett, Bonnici, Miksa, & Joonmin, 2007; Gould & Padavano, 2006; Young & Norgard, 2006) suggest that learner satisfaction with their online learning courses is directly related to the social or virtual presence of their faculty member. The research on the community of inquiry model identified three types of presence: social, teaching, and cognitive. Just as the three most important things in real estate are location, location, location, the three most important things in online learning are presence, presence, and more presence. Here are some ways to be present for your students.

A Getting-Acquainted Posting Before the Course Begins

This posting a week or so before the course begins helps to build social presence and launch the feeling of community. It also helps to build the quick trust between faculty and students because of knowing "where you are coming from" (Coppola, Hiltz, & Rotter, 2004). Not only do students want to know you, but they also want to know something about their fellow students. The getting-acquainted discussion post is an opportunity to tell a story or a general something about yourself and encourage students to share something personal about themselves. This can be done by simply asking students to complete a statement, such as, "My favorite movie, or book, or learning place is …" You can also ask students to share or post one or two of their favorite pictures. Students often share pictures of themselves on vacation, with pets, with family, or even a hobby, such as refurbishing an antique car. Simple sharing at this level elicits a wealth of information, so that everyone connects on several levels with each other.

Many faculty forget how important it is for them to post a rich and substantive getting-acquainted posting about themselves. You may wish to share with your learners the many places you've traveled or lived in order to connect in that manner. For example, I (Judith) grew up in Minneapolis and lived in Milwaukee for six years while doing undergraduate and master's work at Marquette University. Then I had brief sojourns in Huntsville, Alabama, and Birmingham, Alabama, where my four children were born. I later lived in Orlando, Florida, and State College, Pennsylvania, and then landed in Tallahassee, Florida, because of my association with Florida State University. Rita grew up in Chicago and also landed in Tallahassee at Florida State University by way of Arizona and California and at this writing lives in North Carolina.

What is fun about sharing this personal information is that you can almost visually see and feel the connecting threads that you and your students are weaving among the group as you discover common points of life experiences. Part of the power of Facebook, MySpace, Ning, and LinkedIn and the phenomenon of Twitter is derived from this feeling of closeness that comes from sharing personal, often inconsequential information that builds social links and an ongoing social ambience between people. Part of the challenge of understanding people from other cultures is that we do not share some of those common data points, and thus links between minds can be more difficult. Online courses that are international in character want to be sure to recognize this and find ways of bridging those gaps and creating those connections.

Here are elements of getting-acquainted postings that you might use:

- Picture
- Short biography
- Link to your favorite professional publication
- Other personal picture or favorites
- Hobbies

This initial posting focuses on creating social presence in your course, that is, the "ability of learners to project their personal characteristics into the community of inquiry, thereby presenting themselves as 'real people'" (http://communitiesofinquiry.com/socialpresence).

A Getting-Acquainted-Cognitively Posting

Another good practice is to follow a getting-acquainted-socially posting with a getting-acquainted-cognitively posting. This posting helps to get to know your students' minds. This posting focuses on the state of knowing what is in a learner's mind at the beginning of a term. The first week is a good time to discuss and process the course goals, objectives, and projects. Details about this posting are in the CB Tip 5.

The Announcements Tool and Being on the Course Site

Using the Announcements tool (or equivalent) of your course Web site three to four times a week, for a quick hello, a reminder of a discussion posting due, an insight about the relevance of a current event, or a quick-check quiz is another useful technique for staying in touch with your students.

Faculty often ask, "How often and for how long should I be on my course site?" Although there are no hard-and-fast rules, the best practice is to start "being present" every day, including one of the weekend days. Most online learners do much of their learning work during the weekend, and thus your dropping in to check on how things are going can make a huge difference to them. Usually this weekend dropping in can be done in fifteen or twenty minutes primarily to check if any new questions are posted in your online office. You might also consider giving students your cell phone number for any assignment-related emergencies.

Being there every day is most important in the preweek and the first two weeks, when everyone is getting settled and learners tend to panic if no one answers their questions in what to them is a timely manner. In other words, let your students know you are available and interested in how they are doing with their assignments and general progress. Your presence serves to encourage the students to think aloud so that they can process information and link ideas and concepts. Students often just need to hear an occasional "uh-huh" to keep going and feel as if their efforts are being recognized. Postings are also a way to link current events and issues to the course content.

For faculty accustomed to teaching a face-to-face class and meeting students one, two, or three days a week, the demands of teaching an online course can be shocking. Students often expect faculty to be there all the time. This is why setting policies and expectations for feedback and presence is essential to student satisfaction. This is also why it is effective to set up a question forum space. This means that all questions are posted there and that all members of the course community can post and answer questions. The faculty mentor then communicates ideas, suggestions, and comments in a public space to increase presence while minimizing, and even eliminating, all e-mail associated with content questions.

Some online faculty find that a useful practice is to schedule a virtual meeting time with themselves to be on the course site, for example, on Tuesdays, Thursdays, and Saturdays, so the days don't get away from them. In the first week or two, it is good to schedule these times every day either early or late.

Faculty presence and involvement change over the weeks of a course. In the phases of engagement (Conrad & Donaldson, 2004) in a course, your role in the first phase is that of a social negotiator. Later you shift to being a structural engineer, designing opportunities for students to form teams of two or three and having the students engage in critical thinking and sharing of ideas.

Using the Discussion Board

Regularly post substantive comments related to assignments or discussions on the discussion board. The discussion board is the online gathering place for the course, and faculty's presence there is essential to the overall teaching and learning context. Much more about the faculty role is detailed in the next set of tips on discussion boards.

Live Collaborative Time

Plan a live collaborative time early in the term with your students. This can be an informal question-and-answer session about the course and what the class as a group will be doing. If your students are located in widely varying time zones, such as military serving in Iraq and Afghanistan or elsewhere, this can be an optional activity that is archived. The many live collaborative tools include Elluminate, Wimba, and Adobe Connect.

Background

Many sets of principles for effective online teaching and learning have been developed over the past fifteen to twenty years. An early set of guiding principles for distance learning was developed by the Working Group of the Indiana Partnership for Statewide Education (2008). This set of guiding principles is now archived, but the statement about communication and collaboration is particularly clear, focusing on how important communication is in the beginning of the course and reaffirming the importance of *presence* and *structure*. This principle recommends using multiple communication channels and regular interactions early.

Communication and collaboration foster strong learning communities, counteracting the often isolating nature of distance learning. Providing a variety of communications channels—e-mail, telephone, video, discussion forums, online chats—encourages student-to-teacher and student-to-student interaction, particularly if that communication is integrated well into assignments and begun early in the semester.

CB Tip 5: Getting to Know Students' Minds Individually: The Vygotsky Zone of Proximal Development

This tip answers questions such as these:

- How do I get to know my students individually when I can't physically see them?

- What are some strategies for having students set their own learning goals?

- What is an example of a getting-acquainted-cognitively posting and sample responders?

One of the core learning principles in Chapter Two states, "Learners bring their own personalized and customized knowledge, skills, and attitudes to the experience." In CB Tip 4 on getting acquainted socially, we recommend that the immediate second posting in a course should focus on getting acquainted cognitively. Teaching and learning are all about relationships and nurturing the growth of a learner's knowledge base. So in addition to getting to know your students in the social context of their lives, you want to know what they know now and what more they would like to know at the end of a term. In other words, you want to know what is in their minds now and what they think they know.

When the concept of the zone of proximal development was introduced earlier, you may have been asking yourself, "Just how do I get to know my students' zones of proximal development? How do I find out what they know now?" An initial cognitive posting is a good starting place. One example of a getting-acquainted-cognitively post is to ask the students to review the course performance goals and learning outcomes that you have developed for the course and have them prepare a posting about their performance goals and the contexts in which they hope to use the knowledge, skills, and perspectives from the course. You might also ask students to share why they are taking the course and what skills or competencies they expect or hope to learn. The directions should be quite specific, asking the learner to state in 250 to 400 words or so why they are taking the course and what their goals and purposes are. The discussion post may be as simple as asking the students to complete this sentence: "What I hope to be able to do as a result of taking this course is ..." The responses might be "be a better leader" or "read and understand a balance sheet" or "solve differential equations and recognize when I need them." Or the posting directions can be even more informal, asking students what they know about the course topic now and what they intend to do with the knowledge they hope to acquire or the skill that they hope to develop.

The syllabus states the expected learning outcomes or, as we like to call them, performance goals. The purpose of this posting is to ensure that students examine those goals, and personalize and internalize them, opening a window to their minds to the instructor and fellow students. As faculty, we often develop an ambitious syllabus assuming that students will read and digest it. But a specific post or assignment that requires students to review the course objectives and develop some personal and customizable objectives helps to focus students on performance goals as well as knowledge goals. You may want to ask students to select the most important objective for them in their current or future plans, or ask them to identify the section that they believe is most fundamental, difficult, or easy for them. These getting-acquainted posts help us learn more about the students and make it easier and more natural to build associations and relationships, developing core concepts based on what students already know.

Keeping the Students Straight in Your Mind

The tricks of the memory trade work online as well as in the physical face-to-face classroom. The best strategy is linking something personal, unique, and unusual about the learner to the learner's name, personal goals, or something else. Learners can be encouraged to post something that will help you individualize them by asking them something that will likely result in a memorable posting.

Here are a few suggestions for questions to include in the getting-acquainted postings:

- What do you think is particularly unique about how you think?
- What is your most memorable "aha!" learning moment?
- What is your highest-priority goal for the course, and why?
- What's your best secret for being a successful online learner?

- What do you have in common with at least one other learner here?

- What do you think is particularly unique about how you think?

And remember that learners individualize themselves to you and others through their writings.

Background and Summary

The concept of cognitive presence, also part of the community of inquiry model (Garrison, Anderson, & Archer, 2000), evolved gradually and now is often described as the extent to which the professor and the students are able to construct and confirm meaning through sustained discourse (discussion) in a community of inquiry.

A posting early in a course is one tool for getting to know a student's zone of proximal development. Reading a student's postings on how he or she thinks provides baseline information for the faculty mentor in shaping comments and teaching directions based on what students already have in their heads. How do we know what they know? And how do students even know what they know or don't know? We ask them to tell us in various ways.

CB Tip 6: Getting into the Swing of a Course: Is There an Ideal Weekly Rhythm?

This tip answers questions such as these:

- Should I have a weekly rhythm for my course?

- What are the different types of activities that need to be scheduled and planned for?

- How much time should I estimate for monitoring and responding to discussion posts in the first weeks?

- When should learner-to-learner engagement be started?

The weekly schedule for campus classes usually revolves around scheduled classes. These classes serve well as pacing events and reminders for students. Regular weekly assignments and activities keep students engaged with the course content. Students find that a weekly rhythm for an online course provides similar benefits in keeping learners on track with the program. Is there an ideal weekly rhythm? Not really, but a weekly schedule makes expectations clear and helps students plan their daily personal and work lives. It also helps to set clear expectations that an online course requires regular commitments and interaction.

Online students have schedules from many competing responsibilities, such as working, parenting, and travel. So running your online course with a predictable weekly schedule is a tremendous aid for everyone. Many faculty like to use the class discussion board activity as one of these pacing activities. For example, the discussion board might open with a problem, question, or challenge on Monday and require an initial posting or response by Wednesday and comments on other students' postings by Friday or Saturday. The faculty member then commits to commenting on the posts by the following Monday. Readings, assignments, projects, and other content assignments can orbit around these class discussions.

Table 5.2 provides a sample weekly schedule for students in an online class based on a six-day schedule. This schedule anticipates that most online learners will be using one of the two weekend days for their learning. It also assumes about five to seven hours a week for one online course, or about an hour a day. Although it is not necessary for students to work on an online class every day, learners should plan on logging in to their online course at least two or three times a week. This sample schedule encourages this level of participation.

This schedule may well change in the second half of the course when more project and team and group work is more common. When group work is required, it is useful in the first phase of a team project for learners to identify a time that works for synchronous or almost synchronous collaborative activity.

Note that the schedule categorizes activities into individual and group activities and also suggests weekly collaborative times when the instructor might be available by phone, e-mail, instant message, or live classroom time. Of course you determine the days and times for your monitoring and scanning of students' work, responding to students' questions, and providing feedback to students. Note the insertion on the schedule of Tuesday as "special availability hours." This might be a time for you to schedule an audio or audio and video question-and-answer time. Remember that these can be recorded and archived for students who are not able to participate in a synchronous event. Faculty using synchronous online classrooms often schedule these events on different days, alternating Tuesdays and Thursdays, for example, or even offering them twice a week, but always in consideration of their own schedule and the perhaps special considerations of students' family and work schedules.

The tasks and activities for an online course are primarily of three types, each corresponding to the three types of dialogue in a course (Moore, 1997). One dialogue type is the tasks and assignments that students do by themselves at any time when they are engaging in a dyad of learner to

TABLE 5.2

Sample Weekly Schedule for an Online Course

	Monday	Tuesday	Wednesday	Thursday	Friday	Saturday
Individual activity I (L–R dialogue)	Assignment: Listening, reading, creating (1.0 hour)		Assignment: Listening, reading, creating (1.0 hour)		Assignment: Listening, reading, creating (1.0 hour)	
Individual activity II (L–F and L-L dialogue)	Discussion board opens	Discussion board readings and postings (1.5 hours)		Discussion board readings and postings (1.5 hours)		
Individual activity III (L–R dialogue)			Self-test quiz review (30 minutes)		Occasional survey/ feedback	
Individual activity IV (L-L dialogue)	Instant messaging, social networking, e-mail (20 minutes)	Instant messaging, social networking, e-mail (20 minutes)		Instant messaging, social networking, e-mail (20 minutes)		Instant messaging, social networking, e-mail (20 minutes)
Group or team activity (L-L dialogue)		Possible group activity day		Possible group activity day		Possible group activity day
Faculty activity	Feedback to students on previous week discussions	Special availability hours	Monitoring and scanning student interactions plus possible audio/video Q&A session	Special availability hours	Monitoring and scanning student interactions plus possible audio/video Q&A session	

Note: L–R dialogue: learner-to-resource dialogue. L-L dialogue: learner-to-learner dialogue. F–L dialogue: faculty-to-learner dialogue.

resource. Examples of these dialogues are reading assignments, watching or listening to streaming lectures or presentations, analyzing and solving problems, reading and responding to online discussion forums, online postings in blogs or wikis, online quizzes, sending or receiving instant messages, e-mail, and general research or thinking. Although these activities can be done at any time, a time to do them needs to be scheduled. Experience has taught us that if something can be done anywhere and anytime, it usually never gets done.

Other types of learning activities are learning events that students do with other students or with the instructor. The dialogue between students is expressed as learner-to-learner (L-L) or peer-to-peer dialogue; dialogue between students and faculty is expressed as faculty to learner (F-L) dialogue. Examples of L-L activities include participation in team or group meetings and study or review sessions. Examples of F-L dialogue include participation in review or presentation sessions as well as all the asynchronous monitoring and commenting. Thus, it is important to set aside specific times for these kinds of activities.

CREATING AND DESIGNING DISCUSSIONS

The second set of tips for the course beginnings focuses on the purpose and effective use of discussion boards. One of the tips describes the characteristics of questions that elicit engagement, reflection, and community, followed by a tip on strategies for managing and evaluating discussion postings as one tool in assessing student learning. The last tip in the chapter focuses on the faculty role in the threaded discussions and how the faculty role changes over the phases of a course.

CB Tip 7: The Why and How of Discussion Boards: Their Role in the Online Course

This tip answers questions such as these:

- Why are discussion boards so important in an online course? Are there any other tools, such as wikis and blogs, that can be used for similar purposes?

- What types of learning goals are discussion boards good for?

- How are questions for online discussions different from questions in class discussions?

- How many discussion questions should be posted in a course each week?

- Are there guidelines or requirements for student responses to discussion questions?

The purpose of discussion boards or forums in an online course is similar to planned discussions in a classroom-based course, only much more so. We like to think of discussion boards as the "campfire" around which course community and bonding occur at the same time that content processing and knowledge development are happening. Discussion boards are designed so that the discussions are threaded, meaning that learners post their comments and respond to one another asynchronously. New discussions or threads are started for new topics.

Discussion activities provide an expressive space for learners to process, analyze, and make connections among ideas. Sometimes a large percentage of course activities are receptive or passive: learners are reading, listening, watching, and paying attention. In a classroom-based course, active or expressive activities such as quizzes and short presentations are often used only to provide data for assessing a student's learning.

In the online classroom space, discussions play a much larger role. Discussion activities give all learners a chance, and in fact they generally require learners to reflect on the ideas in the content resources or the ideas expressed by other students, and then to write about what they think, know, and reason from those ideas. It is this cycle of reading, reflecting, considering, and making connections that actually changes the knowledge structure inside the learner's brain. Often it is only when students are responding to a question or to another student's ideas that they begin to know what they think or know or, sometimes more important, what they don't know. (We know what we know only when we actually write or state it in some way.) Discussion activities give students a way to describe how they are integrating incoming knowledge with their existing knowledge structures. The discussion boards provide time and opportunity to explore and develop ideas collaboratively and recognize and build shared values. These expressive activities often help crystallize students' thoughts and increase confidence in what they think and why. (See Bonk & Zhang, 2008, for a similar cycle: read, reflect, display, and do.)

Best Learning Goals for Discussion Boards

One distinction between online discussion questions and class discussion questions is that the instructor generally plans the online discussion in more detail with more specific goals in mind. One reason this is important is that it is difficult to modify the posted questions and the posted assessment rubrics once a discussion has begun. Planning questions in advance also helps the course to have more internal integrity and coherence with the desired performance goals, skills, and behaviors. A good design approach is to concentrate the weekly discussion questions on core concept topics. Rather than asking questions for which answers are readily discovered, questions can direct students to the application of concepts in various contexts. Research (Bransford, Brown, & Cocking, 2000; Haskell, 2000; Byrnes, 1996) suggests that learners do not easily transfer knowledge from one setting to another. In other words, they can be incredibly literal, so problem solving, particularly for novice learners, within particular contexts is valuable. Discussions targeting core concepts help students build knowledge frameworks around the core concepts and link this new knowledge to existing knowledge. In the process, they can also personalize and customize their learning. Recall how unique learners are and how each builds his or her own knowledge structures.

The Number of Discussion Questions Each Week

The answer to how many discussion questions to put up each week is, "It depends." It depends on whether questions are short answer essay questions that require students to apply core concepts in relatively simple problem situations; or if the questions are complex, requiring students to think deeply about what they can confirm; or problem-solving questions that require students to search out new information and develop or work with scenarios. Also some discussions will require students to respond to and evaluate postings from the other students.

Another consideration is the number of other assignments and activities due in a particular week. For short-answer essay questions, a general rule of thumb is no more than two or three discussion questions each week if there are no other assignments due at that time. For more complex questions, one or two discussion questions per week is probably realistic. For weeks when major projects or exams are scheduled, there may be no discussion questions requiring reading or research. In those weeks, students may use the general class posting areas for giving and receiving help on their projects.

Requirements for Student Responses to Discussion Questions

Faculty also have questions about requirements for students' responses to discussion questions, particularly when learners should post responses and how often. In general, learners should be encouraged to post as early in the week as possible in order to maximize the opportunity for peer and faculty response and dialogue. For example, one strategy for short answer essay questions is for learners to be required to post a response to the question and then respond to the posts of one or two peers. In this scenario, it is often useful to require students to post their initial personal responses by midweek, providing time in the latter part of the week for other students to respond to postings.

Here are additional guidelines that some faculty have found useful for guiding student responses to discussion questions. These guidelines can be posted to the discussion area as reminders to students:

- Postings should continue a conversation and provide hooks for additional continuous dialogue. For more ideas on encouraging substantive postings, see the Early Middle (EM) Tip 11, which encourages learners to respond with answers to "What?" "Why?" and "What I wish I knew."

- Postings should be evenly distributed during the discussion period rather than concentrated on one day or at the beginning or end of the discussion time.

- Postings should be a minimum of one short paragraph and a maximum of two to three paragraphs. (This applies to short-answer essay questions.)

- Avoid postings that are limited to "I agree," or "Great idea," and similar other comments. If you agree or disagree with a posting, say why by supporting your statement with concepts from the readings or by bringing in a related example or experience.

- Address the question or topic as much as possible, keeping on topic and not letting the discussion stray.

- Incorporate where possible quotations from the articles that support your statements in the postings, and include the reference and page numbers.

- Recognize and respond to others' responses to create threads of thought in a discussion, showing how ideas are related and linked.

- Weave into your posting, where possible, related prior personal knowledge gained from experience, prior course work or work experience, discussions, and readings.

- When posting, use proper language, spelling, and grammar, similar to the tone and manner of expression that you would use within a professional environment. Refer to netiquette resources.

A Rule of Thumb for the Length of Discussions

One week is the most common length of time for discussions, although a discussion board or conference involving an external expert may be shorter. Discussion boards with complex topics might be open or run for longer, up to two weeks.

CB Tip 8: Characteristics of Good Discussion Questions

This tip answers questions such as these:

- What are some of the basic types of questions, and which work best for discussion boards?

- Is using Bloom's taxonomy of questions as a guide a good idea?

- Is it practical to use problem-solving questions in discussion boards, or are those better used in written assignments?

- What types of questions should be avoided on discussion boards?

Developing Great and Effective Questions

This tip describes the characteristics and topics of good questions and questions that don't work. Here are some starting guidelines:

- Good discussion questions are open-ended and exploratory. They require learners to "inquire within" about what they currently believe and know and then to provide evidence to support their beliefs.

- Avoid objective, factual questions that have a single answer. Once one student answers a question, there is not much left for anyone else to contribute.

- Good discussion questions require understanding and use of core concepts while applying this knowledge to varied scenarios, preferably researched and customized to learners' interests.

- Factual questions can be used in quick check quizzes; important fundamental factual data can be incorporated into the stem of a question to remind students of core concepts. For example, factual knowledge in a course on organizational development might be knowing that, according to Peter Senge, systems thinking is the fifth discipline that integrates the other four disciplines of any learning organization: personal mastery, mental models, building a shared vision, and team learning (Senge, 1990). Factual knowledge in a math course would be the formulae; factual knowledge in a physics course would be the laws of thermodynamics.

Core Assumption of Constructivism

In developing questions, keep in mind a core foundational assumption of the constructivist educational philosophy: that we know the world through our existing mental framework and bring in, transform, and interpret new information as it fits into this framework. An aha! insight experience can shift and reshape areas of this knowledge base. This assumption highlights how important it is for us and for students to think deeply about what we know or believe we know because new knowledge is built on and integrated with what is already in our heads. (For more on the constructivist model of education in online courses, see Muirhead, 2006.)

Getting Started on Questions

Developing good questions for discussion boards takes practice. Often the most important thing to do is to start and then work to refine questions over time. Students themselves are good sources of feedback and questions.

Good discussion board questions are open-ended and exploratory in nature, often requiring learners to apply and integrate information from multiple resources, including their own work or life environments. Questions to be posed early in the course might focus on how core concepts can be discerned within one's particular work or life experiences. A course on conflict scenarios, for example, can be quite revealing. In a public health course, questions might direct students to research water or air quality for their region. This requires learners to develop skills on how to find the information they need and understand the measures used to evaluate the air or water quality. The results of these mini-research questions can be shared with other students and used to create a regional or national map with those specific data points. In a course on leadership, learners can be asked to state their personal leadership philosophy with the story of how it has evolved. Or learners can work in teams to develop an ideal philosophy statement with teams commenting on one another's final statements.

Types of Questions

A common question from faculty goes something like this: "I have tried to use a range of questions, from those that are very objective such as definitions and core processes to those that are more complex, following the well-known Bloom's Taxonomy (Bloom, 1956) and the revised taxonomy by Krathwohl (2002). But I am still struggling to find the best balance for a question: one that elicits thoughtful and substantive discussion without overwhelming the students. Is there a set of guidelines somewhere?" Here is one way of thinking about questions that we have found effective in mapping to the online environment. We like to think about questions in these three large categories:

- Factual content questions that often represent the enablers and data elements required for developing core concepts
- Questions using the Socratic method requiring students to inquire within themselves
- Problem-solving questions that intersect three areas: a learner's zone of proximal development, core concept development and complex, and customized learning

Factual Questions

Factual questions are generally those with a known answer. This includes short-answer essay questions, such as the pros and cons of different leadership types. These are often straightforward questions and facts that are part of more complex concepts. Students can sometimes apply these straightforward questions to their own experiences. These questions can include basic principles, guidelines, and accepted practice. For these types of questions, students can also be asked to identify or find ideas from relevant topic resources. A good way to ensure the learner's attention to these fundamental enablers is to use the quiz function within CMS systems and simply provide a low point value to a completion requirement.

Socratic Questions

Questions based on the Socratic method encourage students to go within themselves and clarify what is known to them and then to provide the assumptions behind their reasoning and the data behind those assumptions (Paul & Elder, 2008). Here are some typical clarifying questions that can be incorporated into discussion questions and into question debriefings:

- What is your main point? And how is it related to X?
- What do you think is the main issue here?
- How does this relate to our discussion, problem, or issue?
- What do you think John meant by his remark? What did you take John to mean? Jane, would you summarize in your own words what Roberto has said? Roberto, is that what you meant?
- Could you give me an example?

With these types of Socratic questions, learners often shift easily into the roles of questioner, summarizer, and encourager. Much more on Socratic questioning and the analysis and assessment of thinking is at the

Center for Critical Thinking and Moral Critique at Sonoma State University, California.

Problem-Solving Questions

Problem-solving experiences are generally good for the following situations:

- Serious thinking about complex issues
- Customizing learning and making it relevant and meaningful to adults
- Incorporating challenges from current events and multidimensional issues
- Getting learners engaged and involved in real-world issues
- Working on learner projects, either individual or group
- Encouraging critical thinking

Problem-solving questions can range from relatively straightforward scenarios in which the recommended strategies and solutions might be known or well accepted, to very complex scenarios in which answers and solutions are not known and in need of truly creative and innovative thinking. As faculty, we also get inspired and enthusiastic when we challenge our students to work on questions for which there are not known answers or strategies.

Discussion Questions on Core Concepts in a Course

A good design approach for creating discussion questions is to develop questions that incorporate or use one or more core concepts. These discussion questions can map directly back to the general and personal performance goals and learning outcomes of a course. These concept-focused questions can provide opportunities for students to see how the core concepts reveal themselves in very different scenarios, researching and citing examples from real life. The goal is to structure questions that lead students to think through the applications of those core concepts, resulting in more transferable knowledge.

The following are some brief examples of discussion questions focusing on core concepts.

Business Case Studies

- What types of marketing programs work best for small businesses? For technology innovation companies?
- What are the different ways of translating a good idea into a company?

Biology and Genetics

- What if your doctor could choose medical treatments based on your genetic makeup that are guaranteed to be effective?

History/Environment/Anatomy

- Students assume the role of an osteologist and are tasked with identifying the bones a farmer found in a field.

Many additional examples of discipline problem solving are at the Virtual Resource Site for Teaching with Technology at the University of Maryland, University College (http://www.umuc.edu/virtualteaching/disciplines.html).

More Resources for Discussion Questions

One of the modern classics in using discussions for both campus and distance learning is *Discussion as a Way of Teaching* (Brookfield & Preskill, 2005). Brookfield and Preskill have found the following categorization of questions to be useful for starting and maintaining momentum in discussions:

- Questions that ask for more evidence
- Questions that ask for clarification
- Open questions
- Linking or extension questions
- Hypothetical questions
- Cause-and-effect questions
- Summary and synthesis questions

They also address the special types of discussions that occur due to gender and cultural differences.

Here are more ideas on all levels of questioning selected from a much larger set developed for encouraging Reasoning Across the Curriculum (Peirce, 2004):

- *Conduct brief opinion or thought polls related to course readings to arouse interest in topics and assess and estimate students' prior knowledge.*

- *Create cognitive dissonance. Provoke discomfort, unsettle confirmed notions, uncover misconceptions, inspire curiosity, and pose problems.*

- *Present activities that require considering opposing views.*

- *Assign a mediatory argument promoting a resolution acceptable to both sides.*

- *Ask students to evaluate Internet resources.*

- *Ask students to reflect on their responses to the course content and on their learning processes in private journals.*

One of these strategies might be particularly well suited to your content and desired skills and behaviors and knowledge of your students.

CB Tip 9: Managing and Evaluating Discussion Postings

This tip answers questions such as these:

- How do I manage discussion postings so that everyone responds in a timely manner with substantive comments?

- How do I support the students without squelching brainstorming ideas?

- How do I grade or evaluate discussions?

- How many points for a course should be allocated for discussion postings?

Managing and Evaluating Discussion Postings

This tip focuses on managing and evaluating discussion board postings. One of the primary benefits of the discussion board space being asynchronous and requiring every learner to post is that it encourages more learner-to-learner dialogue and encourages the instructor to "talk and tell" less. This means that discussion boards support the creation of a new set of communication patterns in which the instructor's voice is more in the background, guiding, observing, challenging, and monitoring the discussions. Reading and evaluating student postings provide a window into a student's knowledge structure. The state of a student's conceptual development becomes very clear, sometimes wonderfully so and sometimes painfully so. But it is a way of seeing "mind-to-mind" rather than simply "eyeball-to-eyeball." Thus, discussions in this asynchronous and thought-captured space can be many times more effective than a classroom discussion.

Three basic communication models built on the transactional distance theory (Moore, 1997) are seen in discussion boards in courses.

The first model is basic and quite straightforward: student-to-faculty and faculty-to-student communication. In this basic model, students respond to one or more related questions, and the instructor reviews and analyzes the responses and writes a summary of them. This model can seem quite familiar to an experienced classroom instructor who is coming from the lecture model.

The second model creates another communication pattern: that of learner-to-learner or peer-to-peer communications. In this model, students read, respond, and post responses to other students. This establishes communication strands in which the faculty member is more of a coach and observer, ensuring that students are on track and confirming what is going on, but not being in the forefront. To maintain the teaching presence, the faculty member might question, comment, suggest links in wrapping up the discussion at the end of the week, or make comments on the discussion summary if students prepared it.

The third model is often reserved for students who are experienced and mature online learners. In this model, students might work in teams to review, analyze, and stimulate thinking. In this model, students often act as surrogate faculty, summarizing, monitoring, and tracking responses.

Monitoring Discussion Boards

The design of discussion boards makes managing multiple themes and ideas easy. The subject lines (topics or themes) of the discussions drive the postings by the students and encourage exchange, analysis, and synthesis of ideas. The design encourages a thought product, which can be text as well as audio enriched with pictures, including links to other resources. If a student wants to start a new conversation, or "thread" as these conversations are called, it is a matter of making the decision and clicking a button. Then all comments related to that topic flow under that topic heading. This threaded feature makes sustained conversations over time possible and makes tracking, monitoring, and engaging in multiple conversation threads quite easy. The visual layout of the discussion board is also helpful in providing a quick visual look at how many students are participating and when. These features encourage topic-driven, multivoice discussions. Other tools such as blogs and wikis share some of the characteristics of discussion boards, but these tools may be better suited to individual or group reflection and in-depth thinking over a longer period of time (Newberry, 2008). (For more about blogs and wikis, see the Late Middle Tip 13.)

How to Ensure Lively Participation

You can ensure that students do not participate in discussions by not allocating any assessment points to discussions. How you grade discussions and how many points are allocated to discussion postings and participation is something that needs to be part of your overall assessment and grading plan. If you are reluctant to assign points to the discussions, start by providing bonus points for the discussions, but we highly recommend that you move quickly to the required mode. The minimum number of points for discussion board participation is about 15 percent, increasing to 35 percent, depending on the complexity and requirements of the postings.

Allocating Points and Using Rubrics for Evaluating Postings

Table 5.3 presents a rubric to get started on a model for evaluating postings that fits your style of teaching and your content. A rubric is a scoring system that is usually set up as a matrix with the two or three desired

---

TABLE 5.3

Simple Rubric for Evaluating Weekly Postings

Desired Characteristics	Poor: 1 point	Good: 2 points	Excellent: 3 points
Timely and quantitative discussion contributions	One to two postings per discussion; somewhat distributed, with first posting occurring on the weekend.	Two to three postings per discussion; postings distributed throughout the week, with first posting occurring before the weekend.	Three to four postings per discussion; well distributed throughout the week, with first posting occurring midweek.
Responsiveness to discussion; demonstration of knowledge; understanding gained from assigned reading	Postings had questionable relationship to reading material or topic under discussion, with little or no evidence of understanding.	Clear that readings were understood and that concepts and insights were incorporated into responses.	Very clear that readings were understood and ideas were incorporated well into responses; postings continued the comments and insights of other learners.
Followed online protocols for clear communications; correct grammar, spelling, and understandable statement flow	Two to three online protocols were not followed; organization unclear.	Most online protocols were followed; statements were mostly organized and clear.	All online protocols were followed; statements were well organized and clear.

characteristics in the left-most column and a three-point scale for each of those desired characteristics in the next set of three columns. In the example here, the rubric includes measures of time (when and how often postings are posted), quantity (a length appropriate to the discussion topic), and content (resource related, thoughtful, and substantive) that factor into the points earned. Another measure often used in rubrics is format, which includes adherence to appropriate written English. Instructors often invite or assign students to take a supportive monitoring role for some discussions, such as the role of evaluator or summarizer with additional points.

• • •

For more ideas and hints about building rubrics, you might explore a site created by the Teaching and Learning Technology group at Penn State University, in particular, the topic Managing Learner-Instructor Interaction and Feedback (http://tlt.psu.edu/suggestions/research/interaction.shtml). You may also find the resources in the Guide to Rating Critical and Integrative Thinking at the Washington State University Web site useful for customizing your course rubrics when you are ready.

CB Tip 10: The Faculty Role in the First Weeks: Required and Recommended Actions

This tip answers questions such as these:

- What is the role of an instructor in an online course? How do I convey content without lecturing? How do I cover content?

- What is my role in the first weeks of a course, and how does it evolve over the phases of a course?

The Role of Faculty in Discussion Boards

A common question from new online faculty is how to balance presence without taking over the conversation. Some faculty find it helpful to think about how faculty and students communicate as a series of stages from more involved to less involved. This means that as a course progresses, the roles of faculty and students change. The teaching and cognitive presence of the faculty member is just as important in the later phases of a course as in the beginning, but the emphasis is different. In the initial stages of a course, the focus from the faculty member is often on the core content, ensuring that students are reading and thinking about and exploring the core content and facilitating interaction so that a learning community develops that is engaged in the content. In the later stages of a course, when it is likely that students have substantive content questions and insights, the role of the faculty member is to comment, clarify, support, and challenge students.

A framework described by Conrad and Donaldson (2004) that defines four possible stages of faculty and learner roles throughout a course is set out in Table 5.4. Notice that as learners become more active, the instructor moves from more directive interaction to participating and facilitating in activities as needed. As students assume more independent and collaborative roles and responsibilities, a faculty member can step back from being the leader of the learning community to being a co-community member.

TABLE 5.4

Phases of Engagement

Phase	Learner Role	Instructor Role	Weeks	Processes
1	Newcomer	Social negotiator	1–2	Instructor provides activities that are interactive and help learners get to know one another. Expresses expectations for engagement in the course. Provides orientation to course and keeps learners on track. Examples: Icebreakers, individual introduction, discussions concerning community issues such as netiquette rules in a virtual lounge.
2	Cooperator	Structural engineer	3–4	Instructor forms dyads of learners and provides activities that require critical thinking, reflection, and sharing of ideas. Examples: Peer reviews, activity critiques.
3	Collaborator	Facilitator	5–6	Instructor provides activities that require small groups to collaborate, problem solve, reflect on experiences. Examples: Content discussions, role plays, debates, jigsaws*.
4	Initiator or partner	Community member or challenger	7–16	Activities are learner designed or learner led. Group presentations and projects. Discussions begin to go not only where the instructor intends but also where the learner directs them. Examples: Group presentations and projects, learner-facilitated discussions.

* In a jigsaw activity, the content is broken into parts with each team member of a group responsible for learning one of the parts and then teaching it to the rest of the team (Sellers et al., 2007).
Source: Conrad and Donaldson (2004).

Recall that one of the goals in faculty communication in any course is to balance the three dialogues of faculty-to-learner, learner-to-learner, and learner-to-resource dialogues. A campus classroom often has a high percentage of faculty-to-learner dialogue, with the faculty at the center of many classroom activities. One of the goals in an online course is to move from a transmission of knowledge mode to a coaching and mentoring mode. Increasingly faculty are shifting to the role of a coach and a mentor and a director of learning to help learners build, reshape, and extend their knowledge structures. When you are talking, learners assume the role of listening, which is a less active role than for them to write and discuss; more learning occurs when learners are processing, writing, analyzing, and questioning.

One of our favorite stories is from an online instructor who was somewhat frustrated with what he perceived as sterile and almost pro forma postings on the discussion boards until he had a family emergency that required him to be away for a few days. He told the students to continue the class discussions while he assumed a less visible, but still affirming and monitoring, role during the week. To his surprise and delight, the learning community that he had been striving to achieve started to happen. The discussion postings took on a new vibrancy of intellectual inquiry and analysis. It is this level of involvement that you want to achieve in your course. And as always, the value of a faculty's presence and confirmation of content accuracy and intellectual vigor cannot be overstated.

Guidelines

Here are a few simple guidelines for refining your decisions as to when to be in the foreground and when to be in the background:

- Provide a virtual forum or space in your course site for learners to talk to and help each other that is totally faculty free. Think in terms of a social gathering place or a residence hall environment for your learners to freely comment, wonder, and ask for help. If students want or need your input, they can post it in the general course area.

- Be specific about your role for each of the discussion board activities. For example, if you have a getting-acquainted discussion posting during the preweek or week 1 of a course, you might want to state that you will be reviewing these postings but not commenting on them until all have responded. You might encourage learners who post later in the week to share or note common interests and experiences. In this way, you are building in some natural grouping or processing of these postings. Later in the course, for a more concept-oriented discussion, it might be appropriate for small groups of two to five learners to review or grade each other's postings according to the prepared rubrics. Your role would be to read the reviews and summarize and comment on the evaluations completed by the learners. This is often a good time to plan to comment on the links, relationships, and applications as noted by the learners.

- At times, your appropriate role may be the active Socratic questioner for a more complex topic requiring analysis and problem solving. This would be a case where you would be more in the forefront, encouraging learners to search within themselves for what they know and think. This means asking questions such as, "What do you think is the main issue here?" and "How does this relate to other core concepts?" With Socratic questioning, an instructor is in the foreground asking questions but not proposing or suggesting the answers.

- Occasionally design activities where you are in the background and students take over the role of questioner, summarizer, and encourager.

Summary—and What's Next?

The first few weeks of a course are busy and time intensive, but by now you, your students, and the course are probably well launched. Everyone is acquainted, engaging in conversations, and interacting with the content resources and core concepts. It is time to stop and breathe deeply and feel satisfied that you have gotten off to a good start.

Chapter 6

Phase Two: What's Happening, Themes, and Tools

Keeping the Ball Rolling in the Early Middle

Chapter Overview

Congratulations! You have likely made a very good start on launching your course and getting to know your students. Now is the time to focus on improving your use of the online communication tools to help you keep the ball rolling. Some tools are excellent support tools for keeping the course moving; others are great coaching and mentoring tools. Your teaching goals during this early middle are twofold: ensuring students are engaged with and using the course content knowledge and nurturing the growth of the course community.

What's Happening in the Early Middle Weeks

By the early middle weeks, learners have generally settled into their weekly rhythm, are feeling comfortable about the course content, and are developing closer relationships with some of the other learners. The learning community is evolving, with all the learners participating at some level.

During this time, it is essential that the faculty member focus on continuing a strong teaching presence emphasizing the core concepts of the content and the nurturing of the learning community. The faculty role in this stage of the course is evolving to include the role of a structural engineer, overseeing how learners are supporting and querying each other in discussion forums (Conrad & Donaldson, 2004). This is also a time for small teams of two or three to be working together if they have not already.

The course content is at center stage as learners are actively exploring and learning new concepts. Learners are also applying core concepts in various scenarios and problem settings.

One of the barriers to community development can be the pressure of needing to cover content. As noted in some of the tips on community building, a feeling of community often arises following a "long, thoughtful, threaded discussion on a subject of importance after which participants felt both personal satisfaction and kinship" (Brown, 2001, p. 18). Pressure to keep moving into new content can short-circuit the time for exploration and for sorting through issues and ideas. Sometimes it makes sense to introduce small changes in content readings in the middle of a course to accommodate the spontaneity of learning.

In summary, in the early middle of a course this is what is happening:

- The learners are engaging with the course concepts and applying the concepts within relatively accessible scenarios and problems. These can be either ill-structured or well-structured problems. Well-structured problems are those that have right or wrong answers; ill-structured problems are more complex and mirror problems in real life, meaning that students need to formulate the question and examine the possibilities and assumptions within the problem.

- Learners are establishing a role within the community and sharing what they are thinking and why. They are working within a small team on various assignments and sharing ideas and comments within the community.

- The faculty member is in high gear, focusing on the core concepts and ensuring that all students are engaged with the content problems. This means that the faculty is exerting a relatively strong teaching presence, but is also encouraging the learners to be clear about what they are understanding and to take the lead on course experiences such as reporting out, sharing, and wrapping up discussions.

Your tasks in this early middle period are to focus on continuing your strong teaching presence: guiding and challenging the student, and implementing the early stages of a learning community. The tasks for learners are to be actively involved with developing their skills, attitudes, and knowledge for the learning outcomes. This early middle period is a very intense time, but less so than the first weeks. This is the time to nurture the learning community and guide and mentor learners as their personal interests and goals begin to emerge.

Early Middle: Themes, Best Practices, and Principles

The themes for the early middle phase of a course expand and deepen some of the themes introduced in the course beginnings. The themes for the early middle include a dependence on the teaching presence, the usefulness of extending your online teaching tool set, and nurturing of a content (learning) community for your students.

Although three types of presence from the community of inquiry model (Garrison, Anderson, & Archer, 2000)—social, teaching and cognitive presence—play a role in each stage of a course, these presences have an ebb and flow (Akyol & Garrison, 2008). In the first phase of a course, almost equal priority is given to establishing social presence and teaching presence. Establishing the social presence launches the community; the teaching presence provides the framework for guiding learning and setting out the goals and expectations for the course learning experience. The third presence, cognitive presence, is launched with the discussion of learning goals but is less prominent.

In the early middle of a course, the teaching presence begins adapting to the individual learners. The community shifts into higher gear as learners depend on the teaching direction to begin serious cultivation of the course content. In the two later phases of a course, the teaching presence can become even more specialized and provide direct guidance to learners on their projects, while also supporting the overall cognitive presence of the community. This shift in emphasis parallels the development of how the faculty role shifts during the stages of a course.

Let's take a look now at the three themes for the early middle.

Teaching Presence

Teaching presence consists of three major categories of teaching direction. The first category of teaching presence is embedded in the course materials prepared before the course begins: the syllabus, discussions, concept introductions or mini-lectures, assessment plans, resources, and policies and procedures. These materials are developed using assumptions of what students probably know and understand and expectations as to how the course fulfills its purpose within a larger certificate or degree offering. In the second category of teaching presence, materials are developed spontaneously during the course delivery and are shaped by the needs, interests, and learning characteristics of the students. This category includes the communication and activities associated with directing, monitoring, and mentoring the particular community of students. As any veteran teacher knows, each group of students develops a unique personality as it moves through the course. The third type of teaching presence that Garrison (2009) calls direct instruction refers to the mentoring and direction of individual students in contrast to the teaching presence of facilitating dialogue within the learning community.

Expanding Your Online Teaching Tool Set

If you have been teaching in the classroom for years or even decades, you have developed a set of comfortable and efficient habits, tools, and practices. Moving to the online environment means developing a new set of habits, tools, and practices, and that takes time, energy, and patience. Recall how you first felt about doing any banking or shopping or social networking online. Over time, it becomes easier until it eventually feels just fine. Developing a comfort level with online teaching tools is similar. The goal is to develop automatic behaviors using the tools, so it doesn't require as much conscious thought. Automatic behavior gets set only when you use a tool on a daily (or almost daily) basis for a month or so. Remember how clumsy you feel every time you return to a tool you use only occasionally and the challenges of remembering passwords and security questions. So part of the learning process is being patient and accepting with yourself, trusting that your skills will improve with use. All experts continue practicing their professions over a lifetime.

The three essential tools that you must use in your course are announcements, discussion board monitoring and feedback, and the basics of grade books and communications tools within whatever course management system you are using. The time and thought needed to develop automaticity with these tools are another reason to give yourself space in the first cycle of any online course and not attempt too much. Once you develop a comfortable level of experience with the basic set of tools, you can quickly move on to some of the more visual and audio tools, such as podcasts, audio feedback, blogs, and wikis.

Nurturing of the Content and Learning Community

Cultivating and nurturing the learning community is a high priority for the teacher during the early middle. In this phase of the course, the learners and the learning community itself might be compared to seedlings, striving to root themselves using an appropriate combination of water (teaching direction), shade (reflection), and wind (dialogue). Part of the teaching task is to provide a shelter and safe place for this rooting. You will have many questions about your teaching presence during this time. How much presence is too little? How much presence is stifling? Will learners feel alone, or will they feel too directed? There are no easy or "this always works" answers here. Just as in the classroom, you will develop a sense of what is right for a particular group of students. Recall these two core concepts about community and cognitive presence:

- Developing community means building a sense of shared understanding, knowledge of one another, and mutual support, even if these values are not shared.

- Cognitive presence is the process of constructing meaning through collaborative inquiry (Garrison, Anderson, & Archer, 2004). Cognitive presence is growing when students express a need to understand ideas more deeply, share insights, connect ideas, and identify patterns and relationships.

Tips for the Early Middle

Fourteen tips are grouped into three sets for the early middle of a course. During your first online course cycle, you may have time to make use of only five or six of these. Plan to come back and use the additional tips for your next course cycles. As before, each of the tips begins with the questions commonly asked by online faculty and addressed by the tip. The tip then suggests practical steps and actions supported by theory, practice, and research and occasional suggestions for further or deeper study.

The first set of tips, Managing Your Course, focuses on your role as a manager of the course directing and supporting learners through the instructional experiences that comprise the course. You want to manage a course efficiently and effortlessly so that you can concentrate your mental energies on supporting and mentoring learners toward achieving their learning goals. In your managing role, keep track of how each learner is doing and monitor his or her progress, providing useful guidance and feedback while establishing a basis for the necessary assessment and grading. This set of tips answers questions about how and when to use basic communications tools such as announcements, discussion forums, and e-mail. It also includes reminders of the tools within most course management systems to make tracking and mentoring students efficient and effective.

One of these tips also provides more detail about establishing a weekly rhythm for the course. Part of this weekly rhythm includes feedback between you and your students. Getting into a weekly rhythm helps learners develop a comfort level with course processes, including the rubrics for discussion posts and other assignments. The weekly rhythm also helps busy professionals with schedules. Another tip focuses on the role of a course assistant if you are fortunate enough to have one. Jointly managing a course with a teaching assistant provides support for the teaching presence but also requires a clear definition of roles.

The second set of tips, Strategies and Tools for Building Community, focuses on the strategies and tools best suited for the initial and early stages of building community. These strategies describe ways to promote peer interaction, including the use of small teaming and peer review. These community-building strategies add another layer to the social and cognitive presences already under way. The first stage of community building, according to Ruth Brown (2001), is "making friends" online with other learners with whom learners are comfortable. This was a significant part of course beginnings on getting acquainted and establishing friendships within the group. In the second stage of community building according to Brown, the communication is broadly expanded to other learners using "long, thoughtful discussions on a subject of importance" (Brown, 2001, p. 24). The long and thoughtful discussions create a shared experience promoting personal satisfaction and kinship that characterizes stage 2 (of 3) of building community. Strategies that encourage such discussions include small teams and peer review. These strategies add team dimensions to the social and cognitive presences launched in the course beginnings.

This set also includes tips on the use of audio and video tools, such as YouTube, podcasts, and other Web 2.0 social networking strategies. Remember that there are two dimensions to these media tools: it is very easy to use those that have been created by others and are ready and available for use; it is another level of skill to create customized ones for your course. Until you are ready, you can easily make a media-rich course by using resources created by others.

The third set of tips, Building the Cognitive Presence, focuses on content. This is the element that has the most direct impact on students' learning outcomes and performance goals for the course. The tips in this set provide strategies for encouraging learners' growth from the types of problems they can handle confidently at the beginning of a course and the problems learners can handle competently later in the course. These tips also encourage student involvement in preparing discussion wraps and summaries and in supporting one another. The final tip in this set discusses processes for launching students' projects. Most online courses use projects for assessment purposes rather than relying on quizzes or proctored tests. The structuring and phasing of key project milestones are integrated into the course and are a critical part of the development of learner outcomes and performance goals.

By the end of the second phase of a course, you will likely be feeling much less panicked about teaching online. If you shared some of your initial trepidation about teaching online with your students, they have probably been accepting and supportive. They may also have provided useful feedback if you used the early feedback tip. You probably have a lot to learn about being efficient and confident, but that will come in time.

Technology Tools

Chapter Four provides an overview of tools mentioned in the course beginnings tips. Many of these same tools are mentioned in the early middle tips. While you've gotten your course off to a good start, you may still not feel that it's the right time for you to learn more tools. You may just be developing a level of comfort with the course management system and don't want to mess around with testing out any new tools.

The pace at which you begin your use of the many available tools is a personal choice. Pick and use the tips that make sense for you. For example, you may choose to use the tips on adding audio and visual media and images in your next online course. There is no need for you to feel compelled to add any of these tools to your online tool repertoire at this time. They are listed as possible additions to your own use in the future. You may hear about other faculty using these tools, or your own students may ask about or use these tools for their own learning and communication purposes. Table 6.1 helps you see where and for what teaching and learning purposes these tools are being used.

Nevertheless, you can encourage students to use graphics and audio and video media in their work as they are so inclined and as it fits the content and their own comfort and skill level. In fact, it is a good way for you to learn about the use of these tools as well.

TABLE 6.1

Tools in Early Middle Tips and Suggested Pedagogical Uses

Tools and Applications in Early Middle Tips	Early Middle Tip Number	Suggested Pedagogical Uses and Purposes
E-mail, announcements, and discussion forums	EM 1	Basic and essential communication tools for guiding learning and building a learning community.
Skype, a free voice-over IP telephone service available using the Internet; a Webcam supports videoconferencing as well	EM 1	A way to hold meetings with people face-to-face. These tools can be good for initial meetings and for sensitive topics that can benefit from actually seeing the whole person.
Text messaging, instant messaging, chat, and Twittering	EM 1, EM 8	Good nearly synchronous tools that learners may use to quickly check facts and ideas, share updates, or arrange for meetings using other tools.
Course management system, such as Blackboard, Desire2Learn, Sakai, Moodle, and WebStudy	EM 2	Systems that provide a virtual place to gather, meet, think out loud, learn, and practice; these systems are like virtual classrooms and campuses.
Performance Dashboard: a subsystem within Blackboard course management system	EM 2	Helps faculty monitor student presence in a course by providing at-a-glance statistics about student presence in a course, grades, and discussion board participation and status of assignments.
Blogs, wikis, and similar collaborative spaces: Flexible tools that support use of audio, video, and images	EM 2	Tools with social networking features that support new collaborative and constructivist pedagogies that encourage peer-to-peer linking, commenting, and messaging.
Polldaddy/Survey Monkey: Survey tools and simple discussion board query	EM 4	Free or almost free tools to solicit informal feedback early in a course to identify the small changes that can make a big difference to learning and satisfaction.
Rubrics	EM 5	Scoring tools that lay out the grading criteria explicitly, often in a matrix using three or four criteria on a scale of 1 to 3 or 4 points.
Quizzes: Testing subsystems within a CMS	EM 5	Timed open-book quizzes that are good for testing and supporting low-level learning objectives such as vocabulary and initial understanding of core concepts.
Peer review: A teaching and learning tool	EM 5	Encourages critical thinking and the building of community by encouraging more dialogue among learners.

TABLE 6.1

(Continued)

Tools and Applications in Early Middle Tips	Early Middle Tip Number	Suggested Pedagogical Uses and Purposes
Synchronous online classroom	EM 9	Can be used to demonstrate steps in solving problems in response to real-time learner questions.
Elluminate, Wimba, and Acrobat Connect: Synchronous collaboration tools and online classrooms	EM 9	Synchronous tools that generally need to be part of the online teaching and learning infrastructure linked to the institution's CMS; can be used for scheduled or spontaneous group meetings.
Google Docs: A suite of free software that includes a word processor, spreadsheet, and presentation application; many others, such as Zoho Office Suite	EM 9	Tools that support instant collaboration and social interaction among learners, either synchronous or asynchronous that can be particularly helpful when working on team or group projects; provide tracking and revision history.
Wimba Voice Board, an asynchronous, audio discussion area	EM 10	One of many tools for incorporating audio into your course communications to add variety, energy, and personality and to save time.
iPods and iPod touch with formats such as WAV and MP3	EM 10	Mobile handheld learning tools that can play back and record podcasts and video files so that students can learn anywhere, anytime and using a choice of media.
Podcasts: Audio files that are as flexible as text files, only using audio	EM 10	Available on almost any topic and can complement text resources; students enjoy creating their own podcasts as well.
Synchronous text chat or audio chat in online classroom	EM 12	A synchronous complement or alternative to a text discussion wrap or summary of module.

When you are ready to dig more deeply into matching learning theories with learning goals and tools, you may want to check out the Distance Education Teaching and Learning Resources Web site at Portland Community College (http://www.distance.pcc.edu/distancehq/lrchq/). One of the resources on the site is a Tools/Theory/Pedagogy Interactive matrix tool that gives suggestions on matching up learning theory approaches with recommended learning pedagogical strategies and the tools to help make it happen.

Chapter 7

Phase Two: Tips for the Early Middle

Chapter Overview

The fourteen tips in this chapter for the early middle phase of a course are grouped into three sets. This is the time to "keep the ball rolling" and build on the momentum from the experiences in the course beginnings. The tips follow the pattern of beginning with the questions commonly asked by online faculty about a topic and addressed by the tip. The tip then suggests practical steps and actions supported by theory, practice, and research.

The first set of tips, Managing Your Course, focuses on your role as a manager of the course teaching and learning experiences and the strategies and tools for establishing your teaching presence. The second set of tips, Strategies and Tools for Building Community, discusses the strategies and tools for the early to middle stages of building community. The third set of tips, Building the Cognitive Presence, focuses on building cognitive presence. Two tools that are particularly effective in engaging students with course content are discussion posts and projects.

Here is a list of the early middle (EM) tips in this chapter.

- EM Tip 1: Tools for Communicating Teaching Presence: E-mails, Announcements, and Discussion Forums

- EM Tip 2: Learning and Course Management Systems: Making Good Use of the Tools

- EM Tip 3: Weekly Rhythm: Challenges to the Plan

- EM Tip 4: Early Feedback Loop from Learners to You

- EM Tip 5: Early Feedback Tools: Rubrics, Quizzes, and Peer Review

- EM Tip 6: The Why and How of Group Projects Within Online Courses: Setting Up and Structuring Groups
- EM Tip 7: Sharing the Teaching and Learning: Working with a Teaching Assistant
- EM Tip 8: Promoting Peer Interaction and Community with Learner-to-Learner Dialogue and Teaming
- EM Tip 9: Online Classrooms and Tools for Synchronous Collaboration
- EM Tip 10: Using Audio and Video Resources to Create a More Engaging and Effective Course
- EM Tip 11: A Good Discussion Post Has Three Parts
- EM Tip 12: Discussion Wraps: A Useful Cognitive Pattern or a Collection of Discrete Thought Threads
- EM Tip 13: Getting an Early Start on Cognitive Presence
- EM Tip 14: Launching Projects That Matter to the Learner

MANAGING YOUR COURSE

This first set of tips focuses on your role as a manager of the course teaching and learning experiences, and the strategies and tools for establishing teaching presence. Developing good practices for the sometimes endless details of managing and administering leaves more time and energy for guiding the knowledge development of your learners and developing satisfying learning relationships. Part of your managing responsibility is paying attention to the engagement and progress of *each* of your students and contacting and encouraging them as needed. It is true that retention of students in an online course is more difficult than retention of students in campus courses.

EM Tip 1: Tools for Communicating Teaching Presence: E-mails, Announcements, and Discussion Forums

This tip answers questions such as these:

- Will teaching an online course require endless hours of communicating by e-mail? How can I allocate my time so that I am a good time manager?
- What course policies help manage effective communications? Will I need to be accessible twenty-four hours a day?
- When and how often should I use the announcement feature?

A common question that comes up with online courses is when to use which communication tools for what. We'll look at the three basic tools: announcements, e-mail, and discussion forums. You may also have questions about instant messaging, chatting, and Twittering (and will have more questions in the future as new tools are introduced). One way to help decide which tools are good for what is to think about the characteristics of these tools, how students use the tools, and what you are hoping to achieve.

Announcements, E-mail, and Discussion Forums

Faculty often err by not using the announcement tool often enough. Keep in mind that students see your announcements as soon as they sign into the course site. New announcements are at the top of the list and immediately visible to the students. Announcements are very useful for your teaching presence. You can use them for reminders about course assignments, insights from your other work, links to current news, and updates or more detail for course events. It's also a good way just to say "Hello" and stay in touch about what's next. In particular, it is sometimes difficult to decide between sending an e-mail to the class or to use the announcement tool.

Here are a few simple rules of thumb. Keep in mind that these rules may evolve as the technologies do:

- *E-mail:* If you absolutely must reach all students quickly and without exception, e-mail is the best choice. E-mail is a push technology meaning that students do not have to actively "go to" anywhere. E-mail lands in the students' mailbox on whatever their favorite tool is: computer, cell phone, iPod, or BlackBerry. If a message is particularly urgent, repeat it in an announcement on the course site. So in this case, it is not either-or but both.

- *Announcements:* The announcement tool is good for general messages and reminders, such as the following:

  - General schedule reminders, such as holidays, assignments, and project deadlines

  - Reminders about the week's activities

  - Announcements about special opportunities and events at the institution and online

  - Reminders about general course processes, such as the importance of making discussion postings early in the week

E-mail is the best tool for private and confidential one-on-one communication. This is the tool of choice when providing individual feedback on assignments and responding to personal events or questions. The telephone is also an effective and convenient tool and the free phone and video applications such as Skype, a free voice-over IP application, can work well also. You may want to schedule a phone meeting with a student when personal life events are impinging on a student's course work or if you need to discuss a particularly sensitive issue, such as exceptionally poor-quality work. Whenever the message might come across harshly or unfeeling without voice inflection, use the phone.

What about using e-mail for general course updates, answering questions, or shaping students' responses to postings? This is where experience comes into play, and it is good to keep general goals in mind, as these are the cases when the right answer is, "It all depends." Here are three considerations to help guide your choice of communication tool.

One primary teaching goal in the online environment is building a learning community. This means creating an environment in which ideas are shared, knowledge is created, and dialogues of one-to-many and many-to-many are encouraged. The course management site is our twenty-first-century classroom, and thus most discussion with small or large groups happens within that environment. With this goal in mind, the discussion board, the announcement tool, or a dedicated faculty discussion forum are probably the first choices for answering questions. These postings become part of the captured course experience and course resources and are thus always available. However, any particular circumstance might argue the other way. Some faculty like to use group e-mail as a way of wrapping up discussions, summarizing ideas, or touching on important current events.

A second goal is that of faculty efficiency. A good general rule is that any question worth answering for one student is probably worth answering for all of them. Thus it's more efficient to do one posting or e-mail to all students than to respond to a single student. Much of the value of a teaching presence concerns the spiraling of content, relating ideas to previous revelations and possible future contributions. As an expert, you can enlighten students with subtleties and nuances that develop over time with many experiences. Sharing these observations within the open space of the discussion forum means the questions and responses are seen, if not read, by everyone.

A third goal is to encourage peer-to-peer communication. This type of networking is one element of a course learning community. Many course templates recommend establishing an open forum space for students to post questions. As appropriate, you can establish a policy that students should first respond to each other. Depending on the class and the students, this approach can work very well, as students learn and confirm what they know and think by responding to others, and it saves you time for responding to more difficult and challenging questions.

Instant Messaging, Twittering, and Whatever Short Messaging System Is Next

Instant messaging has features similar to e-mail or announcements in that it is a push technology that reaches out to learners. Instant messaging as a "cool" tool may already be getting old. The rapidly increasing use by teenagers and young adults of instant messaging for informal conversations is now well documented (Lenhart & Madden, 2007). Teenagers are rejecting e-mail for use among their peer groups while embracing the near-synchronous capabilities of text messaging, instant messaging, chat, and Twittering. While most knowledge exchanges of any significant nature require more time and sophistication than what is usually available with instant tools, such as the 140 character boundary for tweets, these tools can be useful for quick questions and for setting up times and venues for longer discussions.

The use of short messages of all kinds is emerging as a favorite tool of daily life and thus can be a useful tool to support learning communications. A study on the use of instant messaging in teen life included a subject who was an undergraduate teaching assistant who used instant messaging for communicating the times that he would be available for discussing computer programming problems with students (Grinter & Palen, 2002). The authors of the study noted anecdotal evidence that faculty outside the study were using instant messaging to "field questions from students." A Pew Internet study on teens and mobile phones (Lenhart, 2009) suggests that cell phones are now almost omnipresent among older teenagers (71 percent of older teens in early 2008) and adults (88 percent of parents in early 2008). This means that reaching students with important reminders is easier than ever before and that students are in almost constant contact with each other.

Making a Choice

The most important guideline for what tool to use for what depends on you and your students. The goal is to communicate regularly and meaningfully and to cultivate a sense of curiosity and search for truth and wisdom. Tools are just tools. The goal is communicating with and providing guidance to students, while being as accessible as appropriate. The form of the communication is not as important as using the set of tools that work smoothly for the members of the course community. Finally, your student group as a whole may have preferences. So adjust as you go, and consider the benefits of the tools as they become mainstream.

EM Tip 2: Learning and Course Management Systems: Making Good Use of the Tools

This tip answers questions such as these:

- What tracking and managing tools can help me monitor my students efficiently?

- What types of questions should I be asking myself about how my students are doing?

Course management systems (CMSs) provide a sophisticated set of tools that make tracking student engagement in course activities much easier than in the past. Getting a quick look at how your students are progressing online gives you needed information quickly and can help you determine whether any adaptive action might be in order. In classroom environments, we can often see at a glance which students are engaged and which are not. Eye contact in real time can be affirming and reassuring. The tools in many CMSs can also quickly show the state of student activity and even engagement. This tip describes the performance tracking system available in one CMS, Blackboard, and how it can be used to track and evaluate student progress quickly. For other CMS systems and their capabilities, EduTools Course Management System Comparisons—Reborn, (http://www.edutools.info/static.jsp?pj=4&page=HOM) provides a starting point for learning about similar management tools in other CMSs.

Monitoring Student Engagement and Progress: Performance Dashboard

All new tools take time to learn, but the good news is that the Performance Dashboard tool within Blackboard has a great time-to-benefit ratio. The tool contains at-a-glance statistics about student access, grades, and discussion board participation. The customizable Early Warning System tool allows you to set rules for expected performance and then monitor students based on those rules. You can also retrieve reports showing the number of times and the dates on which each student accessed individual course components, course content, discussion forums, and assignments. Other tools offer a student-centric view of one student's postings if you want to focus on one student in more depth. In short, the tool makes it easy to answer questions, such as the following, quickly and with little time or mental effort:

- Have all my students started accessing the course site regularly? This is particularly useful to know in weeks 1 and 2 of a course.

- How can I get a quick bird's-eye view of how one or all of my students are doing on their course assignments?

- Has a particular student, Mehmet, begun accessing the course regularly? How many days has it been since his last course access? Has he been able to address his access and work schedule issues?

- How is Sharmayne doing with the required discussion postings? Do her postings reflect increased sophistication and understanding over time? You can determine this by looking at a collective view of her postings over time.

- Is the class as a whole progressing on schedule for the course assignments and check tests?

- Does the overall data picture for the course suggest the need for any adjustments in the course going forward?

Figure 7.1 shows a view from the Performance Dashboard provided by Barbara Knauff, a senior learning technologist at Dartmouth College.

FIGURE 7.1

Performance Dashboard in Blackboard

Performance Dashboard

Use the links provided to view user progress details for each performance measurement.

Print

Last Name	First Name	Username	Role	Last Course Access	Days Since Last Course Access	Review Status	Adaptive Release	Discussion Board	View Grades
Student	Alexis	alexis.student.bnd	Student	Apr 18, 2007 10:00:36 AM	6	0		0	
Knauff	Barbara	barbara.knauff	Instructor	Apr 24, 2007 4:28:16 PM	0	0		1	
Student	Bernie	bernie.student.bnd	Student	Apr 20, 2007 3:29:55 PM	4	1		2	
Student	Celine	celine.student.bnd	Student	Apr 18, 2007 11:35:40 AM	6	1		0	
Student	David	david.student.bnd	Student	Apr 20, 2007 3:01:23 PM	4	0		1	
Student	Emily	emily.student.bnd	Student	Never	Never	0		0	
Student	Frieda	frieda.student.bnd	Student	Apr 20, 2007 3:08:11 PM	4	0		1	
Student	George	george.student.bnd	Student	Never	Never	0		0	
Student	Helen	helen.student.bnd	Student	Apr 20, 2007 2:59:02 PM	4	1		1	

A demonstration video walking through how to use this tool is available at http://www.dartmouth.edu/~blackboard/bb7/performance dashboard.html.

If you are a Blackboard user, the Performance Dashboard is only two clicks from your course Control Panel. After clicking on Course Panel, the Performance Dashboard link is in the Assessment section under the Gradebook link and the Gradebook Views link. When you click on the Performance Dashboard, a roster of your students appears showing the date of last access, the number of days since last access for each student, and direct links to that student's postings on the discussion boards and the student's grades in your grade book. This feature can save you time in being on top of your whole course.

Thinking Pedagogically: Do CMS Systems Support Learning?

The design of many current course management systems is rooted in the faculty-centric knowledge transmission paradigm that includes the need for grades, faculty lectures, tests, and a focus on access to content. The designs of these systems naturally reflect the technologies and pedagogies of their particular design time or pedagogical era. In fact, many CMSs note with appropriate pride that their systems originated with faculty designing for faculty. Despite the many limitations of CMSs, they have served us well in bringing needed conveniences and efficiencies into online teaching and learning. These systems are in a constant state of change as well, adding technology enhancements such as podcasting, voice tools, blogs, wikis, and synchronous online classroom applications. These enhancements support the new pedagogies promoting collaboration, constructivist strategies, content creation by students, and learning communities, even though they are appended to a system that is basically set in the classroom paradigm. Designing a new CMS with a learner-centered paradigm as the primary design perspective may mean scrapping the old system. A CMS with the learner on center stage will involve moving all the faculty-directed communication into the background, while moving the learner's thinking and communication forward. This redesign will support applications that incorporate what we know about social and cognitive networking, advances in memory and learning, and preferences for hyper and deep attention learning strategies (Hayles, 2007), and current and future technologies.

Nevertheless, effective online courses are possible with the tools available now. Many Web 2.0 tools, including blogs and wikis, have flexible structures and support mixed media, such as audio, video, and graphics. These design features support linking, commenting, and messaging and the new collaborative and constructivist pedagogies. As new CMSs or their equivalents come into use, the features to watch for will be a focus on the learner.

Before moving to any system, try to ensure that learners are front and center, being mentored by the faculty member who is offstage in the director's chair. In addition, a social learning CMS will have a set of tools on hand that support all the media forms of communication we now expect, such as synchronous collaboration tools, quizzes for practice, and discussion forums or conference areas and the necessary administrative tools.

Many CMSs already include features that begin to tap into the power of social networking. WebStudy, for example, houses the beginnings of learner blogs in student home pages. Currently these pages in WebStudy support the building of learning communities while the student forum tools serve as blogs and places for their learning stories. Other CMSs with blog capabilities readily available include the open source course management system Moodle and Blackboard. Because these systems are constantly changing and because new tools are arriving weekly, the best strategy is to ask your institutional contact about whether you have access to a tool or feature that you want to use.

EM Tip 3: Weekly Rhythm: Challenges to the Plan

This tip answers questions such as these:

- What if the weekly rhythm launched in the initial schedule isn't working?
- What about challenges to the weekly schedule due to unexpected changes or demands of faculty or learner schedules?
- What about the potential difficulties of scheduling synchronous sessions with live classroom applications?

In the first tip on the weekly rhythm of a course (see CB Tip 6), the primary reason for establishing a weekly rhythm was predictability and consistency for students and faculty. With this predictability, everyone can create a personal weekly schedule and know the type and amount of work they might be expected to do on any given day. However as Robert Burns, the eighteenth-century poet, said, "The best-laid plans of mice and men often go awry." Here are a few ideas for dealing with the inevitable challenges to a weekly rhythm.

Schedule Surprise Challenges

A common initial problem with a weekly rhythm is the instructor's own schedule. You may have developed the weekly schedule planning that you would have time on Monday for review of the discussion posts and providing feedback to students by 6:00 P.M. Then you discover that you have been assigned an on-campus class on Monday or are chairing a new committee that meets on Monday or you will regularly be traveling that day. What to do? Responding to this challenge can be fairly straightforward:

- Revise the weekly schedule so that students expect your feedback on Tuesday. This is usually the best choice.

- Revise your personal schedule to do it late on Sunday. We do not recommend this one.

- Revise the deadline for the students to be noon on Saturday and do your feedback on Saturday afternoon. Depending on your work/family context, this might work.

Time for Feedback Challenge

A related problem may be the amount of time to complete the planned feedback. What are your choices here? And for planning purposes, how much time is generally needed for feedback and review of discussion posts? Here are some useful data points.

If you have a class of fifteen students, reviewing and providing feedback on the weekly discussion might require three or four hours each week. You will be monitoring the discussions daily, which will take about twenty to thirty minutes to ensure students are staying on track, and then once the discussion closes for the week, you will be reviewing the students' responses more holistically and preparing a discussion wrap for what has happened cognitively during the week. In the first weeks of a course, you may also want to ensure individual contact or touching base with each student. Some strategies for managing feedback include:

- Create feedback templates for student feedback based on the rubrics for the assignments, whether it is a discussion board, short paper, or blog participation. This will allow you to start with basic feedback and then tailor it specifically to a learner, depending on the quality of his or her assignment. Here are some examples:

  "Excellent [or good or fine] participation this week! Your primary postings demonstrated an understanding of this week's topic and were contributed in a timely manner. Your responses to two of your peers were on target, asking them a clarifying question or building on their comment."

"Your primary postings could be improved by substantively responding to the discussion question. Remember that a primary posting is [and then quote from the syllabus]."

"Great job contributing to the community this week, [name]! Your postings met both the quality and quantity requirements. I particularly appreciated your comment on..."

"Your main postings met the requirements, but you needed to reply to at least two peers in question 3."

"Your assignment fulfilled the required elements of [list from rubric]. However, it could have been improved by [tailor to each learner]."

- Create feedback summaries on discussions that address the group as a whole, eliminating the need to provide individual feedback. This is a technique that provides an opportunity to model the type of desirable responses to discussion board postings and is very effective in the first weeks of a course.

- Some faculty are discovering the value of using audio or video tools to reduce the time for writing and composing feedback. Or they are creating a short audio or video podcast for their discussion wrap. This is something to try in cycle 2 or 3 of your course.

- Engage the students more directly in the feedback loop, using peer-to-peer review. This is harder to do in the first weeks of the course, but easier in graduate courses or in the later weeks of any course.

- Be realistic about your expectations for the length and specificity of the feedback you are giving students.

Student Access or Schedule Challenges

Just as schedule surprises can hijack your plans, students may also experience schedule challenges or a related challenge of sufficient and predictable access. Many online students are in the military and occasionally even in combat zones, where predictable access to the network is impossible. Students who are working professionals may experience challenges related to top-priority project work or travel responsibilities, making an occasional adjustment advisable. And then there are always family and life emergencies. If the set schedule works for most students, then the strategy can be to simply adjust the schedule on a case-by-case basis. If the schedule is more problematic, it may need to be revisited and adjusted for your particular group of students. For example, if all of your students are regularly traveling for business, establishing a weekly schedule with fewer and more flexible response times might be appropriate.

Synchronous Meeting Challenges

The new synchronous tools are powerful collaboration and relationship tools. However, scheduling synchronous meetings can be problematic with everyone having so many competing demands. While flexible scheduling is a key reason for learners to take online courses, learners often say synchronous meetings, when available, are the source of greatest satisfaction for them (Abramson, 2007). What to do? If possible, keep synchronous meetings, but be sure to consider doing some of the following:

- Offer sessions twice if possible, each at a different time and day.
- Capture and archive the meetings.
- Make the sessions optional.
- Remind learners to post any questions they have after reviewing the archived meetings in the forum for that meeting.
- Consider shorter sessions, such as twenty to thirty minutes.

While the challenges to a weekly rhythm can seem daunting, a plan and scheduled checkpoint on a weekly basis keep students engaged and in sync with the content and with you.

EM Tip 4: Early Feedback Loop from Learners to You

This tip answers questions such as these:

- How early can I ask for some feedback from students?
- How formal or informal should this feedback be?
- What are some typically effective questions that seem to draw out feedback?
- What should I do with the feedback?

Two or three weeks into a course, you may be wondering about your students' perceptions of how their course experience is going. A student's experience can usually be clustered into three categories: the content of the readings and the overall structure of the course, the course requirements and communications from the faculty member, and their own participation in the discussions and assignments for the course.

Using a Survey

Your institution may have survey tools at the ready for you to use, and in fact a survey tool may be part of your course template. If so, there may be a prepared survey for you to use in the first weeks of a course, so be sure to check. Surveys work best if some of the questions are simple and direct. Providing for open-ended comments is also recommended and often leads to unexpected, and enlightening, comments. Including questions about the content and how useful and relevant the content is to the students is highly encouraged. After all, this is what learning is all about. Here are some questions that you might want to include in an early feedback survey:

- I understand what the course requirements and assignment due dates are.

- The instructor responds promptly to student questions and concerns.

- I have a clear idea how to make a substantive contribution to the weekly discussion through my postings.

- I understand how the rubrics work.

- The weekly discussion questions posted by the instructor are stimulating and cause me to think about the content.

- I feel free to voice an opinion that my instructor may not agree with.

If your institution provides a prepared survey, you may want to modify it and make it shorter or longer or to have it focus on getting feedback on a new activity or process that you are using.

Many survey tools are readily available. One of the best, and free, survey tools is PollDaddy. It is listed as one of the top twenty-five free tools all learning professionals should have in their toolbox from the Centre for Learning and Performance Technologies (http://www.c4lpt.co.uk/index.html). Another popular, easy-to-use survey tool with both free and paid versions is Survey Monkey, also recommended at the site just mentioned previously.

Using a Forum in the Course Management System

Another way of getting early feedback is informal: a special feedback forum that you create and is active for only a week. Ask students to comment on what process or activity has been working particularly well or to provide any recommendations for change that they might have or any questions they would like you to answer. Here are some sample stimulus questions for a feedback forum. You probably want to pick the top two or three that fit you and the course and your students:

- Is there anything you would like to see changed?

- Do you have any "just wondering" questions?

- Are the directions and expectations for the discussion board clear?

- Does the structure of the course—the topics and the requirements—make sense for you?

- Are the course expectations and assignments clear?

- How intellectually stimulating are the selected resources?

- What course communication tools do you check or use every day or almost every day?

Can Students' Responses Be Anonymous?

Students may or may not want to be identified with their responses. Responses to survey items are generally automatically aggregated and anonymous unless students choose to use their name. The forum option in your CMS may or may not support anonymous posting for an individual activity. Sometimes allowing anonymous posting is an option you can select when creating a new forum. Be aware that this option could open the floodgates for the comments to take a rude and harsh turn, so remind learners that constructive feedback is needed.

Obviously the purpose for asking for feedback either early in the course or after the course is to ensure that students are having a quality course experience. An end-of-course questionnaire looks to the future; this early feedback loop focuses on the present, making changes for the current students and faculty combination.

Of course, a key element of feedback is closing the loop back to the students about their comments and making any changes as a result. Sometimes students suggest a different time or a different process for an activity. Small changes that make the course activities complement work, life schedules, and goals can make a huge difference for students. Summarizing the forum results in an e-mail to the learning community and indicating what you will be changing in the course as a result will send the signal that you take their feedback seriously and are listening.

Background Information: Research on Course Evaluations

Research on course evaluations most often focuses on students' evaluating instructors at the end of a course experience. These evaluations are sometimes referred to as postmortems because the faculty member doesn't receive the feedback until it is too late to do anything about it. Also the feedback is anonymous and often comes weeks and even months after a class ends. To be practical about this, end-of-course evaluations are really for the use of the administration. They use the data for faculty portfolios and for overall degree and program evaluation. The feedback recommended in this tip is early in the course so that change can occur within a particular course experience, specific to the configuration of students, instructor, and content. Also, this feedback is informal and direct between the faculty and the students.

One research study (Shapiro, 1990) focused on the relationship between class average evaluations and the characteristics of the instructor and the class in an off-campus setting with nontraditional students. One of the findings was that "evaluations were higher in classes taught with more intensive time formats, in classes taught by instructors teaching more frequently in the program, in classes where term papers were required, and in classes with fewer students." Evaluations also tended to be higher in classes where the "average class grade was higher" (p. 135).

When evaluating those results, one is tempted to theorize that the apparent link between the requirement for term papers and higher evaluations is that writing term papers, or producing projects of various media types, requires students to research a topic and customize some of the content to their own interests. So how an instructor designs and structures the course experiences to stimulate and encourage student customization may be a critical fact. This is just one of many questions for future research. For now, customization is probably a good design feature for your course.

EM Tip 5: Early Feedback Tools: Rubrics, Quizzes, and Peer Review

This tip answers questions such as these:

- What are some good simple rubrics for discussion posts?
- How much individual feedback do I need to provide?
- Should discussion posts be worth any points for grading?

- How visible and prominent should the rubrics be for any particular assignment? Should rubrics be part of the original posting or assignment?

- Should I use the same set of rubrics for all discussions?

- How should I use quizzes? Should quizzes be worth points for grading?

- How can peer review help in the early phases of a course?

All students want to know how they are doing. Yet providing feedback can be time-consuming. These two needs can be balanced by using rubrics, quizzes, and peer review.

The basic rule of thumb as to whether you should assign any points for discussion boards or quizzes or peer review is this: if you want the student to do anything, have points associated with the action or behavior. Remember that online learners, although they are motivated for learning, can be ruthless in only doing what is truly needed to satisfy course requirements. Assigning points to discussion posts and peer reviews is your way of telling the students that engagement and participation are important and make a difference in learning.

Rubrics

One example set of rubrics was included in CB Tip 9. Those rubrics included a measure of time and quantity (when and how often postings are posted), content (resource related, thoughtful, and substantive), and form (adherence to appropriate grammar and communication style) and factor into the points earned. Other rubrics that you might consider using include the following types of measures:

- Engagement and responsiveness to other students

- Demonstrating original thoughts and insights to the field

- Identifying unusual or unique patterns and relationships

- Identifying and establishing links to current happenings

Just which measures you choose can be customized to the overall course goals and students' personal goals as well.

For some discussion boards, using very simple rubrics is a good approach. The primary goal of discussion boards is to get the students engaged. Providing points for assessment in a course is definitely secondary. One example of a simple rubric recommended by an instructional designer at Texas Woman's University follows in Table 7.1. This simple rubric can be part of the discussion posting instructions, and students can

TABLE 7.1

Simple Three-Point Rubric

1 point:	2 points:	3 points:
Minimal response to the module question	Posting responds to the question but does not stimulate further class discussion	Posting fully addresses the question and stimulates at least one substantial follow-up posting

Source: Bartoletti (2007).

TABLE 7.2

Rubric for Participation and Levels of Thinking

Score	Level of Participation During One Week
0 points	Minimum number of postings not met
7 points	Minimums met; all discussion on level I
8 points	Minimums met; at least one example of discussion above level I
9 points	Minimums met; at least one example of discussion above level I with at least one above level II
10 points	Minimums met; at least two examples of discussion above level I with at least one above level III

Source: Palloff & Pratt (2003, p. 91).

even self-grade themselves at the end of the week. Then you can focus on the content in your feedback to the students and simply agree or disagree with their grading. Students often hold themselves to a higher standard than the faculty member does.

Another example of an approach to assessing online discussion board participation and levels of thinking is from Palloff and Pratt (2003) in their book *The Virtual Student*. This rubric uses the quantity of postings combined with a thinking measure (Table 7.2). Palloff and Pratt use five levels of thinking for measuring critical thinking. For example, level I introduces problems or poses questions; level II may identify assumptions; level III may draw conclusions "based on evidence"; level IV might include expressing an opinion on the relevance of an argument; and level V might propose solutions. Palloff and Pratt also provide examples of levels of thinking for how learners are processing information and developing skills.

The power of simple rubrics and self-grading is that an instructor's course energy can be directed toward engaging with the students and focusing on their acquisition of knowledge and skills.

Quizzes

The quiz tools within CMSs are excellent for keeping students on track, increasing learning, and minimizing instructor time on grading. If you have been using quizzes of any sort in your campus classes, it is usually a relatively straightforward task to move those quizzes online. The quiz tools within most CMSs are sophisticated, and once you have quizzes within the system, creating and setting them up is quickly done. Of course, straightforward does not mean that it doesn't take any time.

What about issues of proctoring and ensuring that the students registered in the class are the ones who are actually taking the quizzes? Let's address each of these issues. First, most quizzes should be low stakes. This means that they are worth points, but not many. Students are most likely to cheat and find ways around doing the work if the point value of an assignment is quite high, they are behind in their work, or they are finding the work too difficult. Quiz questions usually focus on facts, discipline-specific knowledge, and core concepts. When online, unproctored quizzes were introduced in a very large lecture campus course, students commented that they could find ways to cheat, but they really did need to know the material, and the point value was not worth the trouble to get someone else to do it.

Other strategies to encourage learning rather than cheating is to be clear about what the purpose and content of the quizzes are, set strict time limits for the quizzes, and provide sufficient but low point value. Also, providing students options to retake the quizzes for a higher point value can encourage the twin goals of competency and self-competition. The goal is for all students to do well. So the bottom-line recommendations on quizzes are to use them for important core concept, factual knowledge, and beginning concept applications; provide a low point value for completion; and let the course management system do its work after you have done your work, which is creating worthwhile and effective quizzes.

Peer Review

One of the challenges in online learning is that we really don't get a chance to be with other learners. Or if we do, we don't know exactly how to interact and have meaningful discussions with one another online. Peer review is one strategy that encourages online learners to work and learn with one another. Early in the course, as students are getting acquainted and establishing trust in one another, setting up learning tasks and experiences that students can share with each other has many positive dimensions. Peer review sets the tone that learning is a social and collaborative experience. (For more on peer review activities, see in EM Tip 8.)

EM Tip 6: The Why and How of Group Projects Within Online Courses: Setting Up and Structuring Groups

This tip answers questions such as these:

- How should I set up and structure online group projects?

- What about criteria for setting up groups? Should learners self-select and form groups on their own?

This tip focuses on guidelines and suggestions for setting up groups, suggested optimal group sizes, and recommendations for collaboration tools during different stages of the projects. These suggestions can be adapted to fit the smaller teams that are often used early in a course.

Setting Up Groups

Setting up group projects in the online environment is similar to the steps in setting up groups in campus-based courses. The primary difference is that group projects in the online environment depend more heavily on the level of maturity and self-direction of teams. Online groups can require more initial direction and less ongoing monitoring, but leave nothing to chance. Here are a few suggestions on setting up group projects.

Group Project Directions and Rubrics

Clear directions about the purpose and task of an assignment or project are essential. It is also recommended that the assignment rubric is included with the project directions. The detail for significant course projects can be quite lengthy; for small assignments, the directions can be brief, and a rubric may not be needed.

Varying the media used to present information on significant course projects can also be helpful for students. For example, the project directions that are part of the syllabus may be text based. For some projects, you may want to have a discussion using an online classroom. Presenting the project requirements in a variety of ways and multiple times provides ample opportunities for students to absorb what the project is about and how to go about it. It also gives students different venues for asking questions.

Include information about the processes, resources, and tools for doing a project with the project directions. For example, discuss and review what technology tools and formats students may find useful for different stages of project communications and presentations. For example, when starting a project, students often find synchronous tools such as phone conferences and chats work well, providing spontaneous brainstorming and problem solving; later stages of a project that can involve drafts and thoughtful analyses can often be best accomplished through discussion boards, e-mail, and online collaboration spaces or even special online breakout rooms.

Criteria and Processes for Setting Up Groups

The way you choose to set up groups can be highly dependent on your course content or program. Some faculty and programs set up groups at the beginning of a course and keep those groups intact for the full course; other faculty prefer to vary the groups for different types of projects and learning experiences. If you have no experience or requirements to dictate otherwise, we suggest the following:

- Don't let students set up their groups themselves because they often do not consider all the factors that make a good team.

- Let the course goals and purposes guide the formation of groups. Ask yourself, "With what learning or skills do I want the students to emerge from the group experience?" For example, learners might be grouped according to their interest in developing skills for working within for-profit or nonprofit organizations or for working in retail or technical organizations.

Factors in Setting Up Groups

Here are factors to consider in setting up groups:

- Amount of content familiarity or expertise of students
- Types of professional contexts in which the students are working
- Types and number of roles the group needs
- Learner goals for the course experience
- Culture, gender, and age (it is often beneficial to mix these)
- Students' online work habits
- Time zones where students are located

EXHIBIT 7.1

Sample Form for Group Availability and Contact Information

Instructions: Enter your available hours for group work or study.

Name:	Sunday	Monday	Tuesday	Wednesday	Thursday	Friday	Saturday
John Doe	Not available	After 6 pm EST	Before 3 pm EST	After 6 pm EST	5:30–7:30 pm EST	5:30–7:30 pm EST	9:00–4:00 pm EST

Study habits: I log on Wed.–Fri. and generally make my group contributions on Wed. Contact info: 555-123-4567 (home), 555-123-4568 (work). Preferences: I prefer e-mail contact over phone contact—really!

It is easy to forget about the impact of time zones and online work habits on team projects. As it turns out, there is nothing more destructive to online teamwork than having a team composed of members who like to work early in the week with those who prefer to work late in the week. As part of the group setup process, you might ask each learner to submit information similar to that in Exhibit 7.1 before you structure the project teams.

Additional Thoughts on Setting Up Groups

Depending on the purpose and context of the groups, you may want to form groups of learners with mixed backgrounds and experiences. In other situations it may be useful to form groups on the basis of similar backgrounds.

Smaller groups of three to five learners generally seem to work better than larger ones. The reasons are many, including working out the roles and responsibilities for the project and arranging times and places to meet to work on the project. A team of two can also be a good choice depending on the project or the assignment. Some of the roles and responsibilities of team members are organizational, such as project manager, note taker, and meeting manager. Other roles and responsibilities are those focused on content, such as researcher, writer, thinker, or reflector. Obviously in smaller groups, learners assume more than one role or task.

The purpose of groups is to increase the time and space available for each learner to express his or her ideas and for you and other students to hear the learner's voice. Groups also by their very nature can produce more content for review and feedback. What is extremely important is for the faculty member to stay involved with each of the groups and monitor and mentor their activities and learning outcomes and products. Without the instructor's active involvement and feedback, learners can discuss topics and possibly reach conclusions without adequate expert overview and guidance. In a classroom, faculty float and walk around, checking on how discussions are proceeding. This same type of overview and guidance is essential to the online group experiences.

EM Tip 7: Sharing the Teaching and Learning: Working with a Teaching Assistant

This tip answers questions such as these:

- When is an online teaching assistant needed?
- What are some of the tasks that an online teaching assistant generally handles?
- What are some of the pros and cons of having a teaching assistant?

As online class sizes grow, administrators often bargain increasing the size of a class with assigning or offering a teaching assistant or offering some type of compensation for additional students. A general rule of thumb is that it is almost essential to have a teaching assistant if an online undergraduate class is more than twenty-five students or a graduate class is more than eighteen to twenty students.

Your first response may be, "I would rather do it myself." Faculty are generally accustomed to doing it all: designing and developing the class, sometimes modifying it along the way, getting to know all the students, and monitoring and guiding the students' learning.

How do you share these complex tasks with someone who might have a different perspective on the content and typically less experience with the teaching process? In fact, sharing the teaching with a teaching assistant is generally a win-win situation and can be a rewarding way of teaching. It is true that sharing the teaching with a teaching assistant can initially require more time and energy than not having one. But the time-to-benefit ratio is usually positive. Moreover, the course community can benefit from hearing and seeing slightly differing perspectives from experts, and this built-in cognitive dissonance can lead to stimulating and lively discussions and debates.

If a teaching assistant is not likely for you, consider whether you can design strategies for students to share some of the tasks.

Teaching Assistant Job Description

One of the most important tasks is establishing roles and responsibilities for the teaching assistant that lay out what you each will do and will not do. Include personal goals and expectations from each party. It also is useful to lay out times that each would like to have (or need) a break from the course responsibilities and how each will adjust the duties during those times.

A good approach is to discuss which elements a teaching assistant might take primary responsibility for and which elements you and the teaching assistant might do together. Many of the tasks involving grading and assessing of students can go smoothly if the rubrics and the scoring are determined collaboratively before the course begins. Here are some of the elements of a course to consider sharing with a teaching assistant:

- Discussion forums—monitoring participation and flow of the dialogue

- Quizzes—monitoring the completion of these and any items that require grading or evaluation

- Support and formation of teams and collaborative work

- Grading and review of course assessments such as discussions and project milestones

- Tutoring and facilitating regular question-and-answer sessions

- Support of course teaching and management tasks, including interacting with and mentoring students who need advice or help

The task that many faculty delegate to the online teaching assistant is the daily monitoring and mentoring of the discussion board and forums, ensuring that all students are participating and interacting and making thoughtful contributions. As the discussion area is the primary site where community develops, daily or almost daily notes and observations by a member of the teaching team give a sense of a vibrant online classroom where interesting things are happening and people care about each other's ideas. At the same time, the students want to regularly hear the voice of the faculty member, so it is important that the senior faculty member make postings and observations, offer encouragement, and answer questions as well. The good news is that these postings need not be a daily task. Also, one of the goals for the teaching assistant will be to increase his or her level of content expertise, and working collaboratively in the discussion forum is a good way of achieving this goal.

By monitoring the discussion areas, a teaching assistant can also be the first to identify individuals who might benefit from outreach and special support at key points in the course. Students may be having technology problems that they feel embarrassed about or life balance issues that they are struggling with. Careful observation combined with outreach as needed sends the message that the teaching team cares about them and their progress. A teaching assistant can also help guide the conversations so that all students' comments can be acknowledged and that rich links, relationships, and connections can be facilitated.

Other tasks that the teaching assistant can assume responsibility for include working with smaller groups for discussions or leading question-and-answer sessions within the live classrooms. Outcomes from these sessions might include innovative problem solutions or alternatives or challenges for the other groups. In fact, the faculty member may choose to participate in these sessions as well but is released from the work of coordinating or leading the sessions. A teaching assistant can also support individual or team assignments. Many online classes routinely rotate the responsibility for preparing weekly summaries and insights from the discussion boards. Teaching assistants can help with these tasks. Another approach that helps teaching assistants develop broad-ranging teaching skills is for the faculty and the teaching assistant to rotate some responsibilities.

The Win-Win of the Teaching Assistant Model

Taking the time to mentor and work with a teaching assistant offers a number of benefits for a faculty member:

- An assistant makes it easier for the faculty member to be away at a conference, meeting, or family event for a few days, when the teaching assistant can be the interim faculty. (In fact, if you do not have a teaching assistant, have a plan in place if you are unexpectedly called away.)

- The teaching assistant can take over the elements or components of a class that a faculty might enjoy the least or for which the faculty might simply not have the inclination. Such tasks can vary dramatically from faculty to faculty.

- The faculty member might develop additional teaching strategies from those of the teaching assistant or develop more comfort and skills with the emerging technologies from a teaching assistant.

There are also benefits for others:

- The learners will likely enjoy the class more, learn more, develop more skills, and recommend the class to others as there is usually more teaching presence and personal attention available to the students.

- Administrators have more flexibility in managing programs, scheduling courses, and enrolling students.

- Students have a teaching team rather than just one faculty person to turn to. They have increased access to expertise when they have questions and benefit from more perspectives on the course content.

Another way to use the information in this tip is when you are coteaching a course. Many online courses use this model as a way of introducing old or new faculty to online teaching and learning. The same principles of collaboration and working out roles and responsibilities, including grading decisions, help make team teaching or coteaching a positive experience.

STRATEGIES AND TOOLS FOR BUILDING COMMUNITY

This set of three tips focuses on the strategies and tools for the initial stages of building community. Building community is launched in the course beginnings with a heavy emphasis on social presence. During the early middle phase of a course the focus shifts to building community focused on course content experiences. The last tip in this set discusses ways of easily adding audio and video to your course.

EM Tip 8: Promoting Peer Interaction and Community with Learner-to-Learner Dialogue and Teaming

This tip answers questions such as these:

- How do I encourage and promote peer interaction and discussion?

- How do I promote meaningful dialogue and questioning within the peer interaction?

- Are students ready for peer-to-peer learning?

- How does peer-to-peer dialogue change the relationship of the faculty to the learners? Is this beneficial?

- How do I adapt to my role of mentoring and coaching rather than telling?

Online learners may or may not eagerly embrace the idea of teaming and working with other learners. Some online learners wish to be left alone to their own learning, welcoming the opportunity to quiet their minds and think for themselves. Yet we know that just as learning happens within an individual, it also happens within a social context. Our own ideas often become clearer when we articulate them in writing or talking or in thinking out loud. Besides being an effective learning strategy, peer interaction reduces the feeling of isolation that often accompanies online learning experiences. Another benefit is that peer interaction often builds a learner's lifelong network of colleagues, one of the primary benefits of lifelong learning.

A benefit of peer interaction for the faculty member is that with well-structured peer interaction and review, learners are more actively engaged in the content, and the faculty member can do more coaching and mentoring. Peer interaction also changes the communication patterns in a course, relieving faculty of the need as well as the possible status of being the center of all communications.

Promoting Peer Interaction and Community

Here are a few strategies for promoting interaction among learners:

- Set a minimum number of required responses that must be made to peers as part of the discussion participation grade. A guideline for responding to two other learners or to 10 percent of the class (a minimum of two students in a class of twenty) seems to work well for many courses.

- Provide a place on the course Web site specifically for students to ask questions of other students. Faculty may choose to monitor that site or not. Sometimes faculty respond to a question if students haven't answered within twenty-four hours, but this needs to be part of the stated policy about the question forum.

- Design pairing or teaming activities in which learners peer-review others' postings, discuss their mutual reviews, and share how their ideas were modified or expanded.

- Design activities for pairs of students. This is a way to begin problem solving and challenges from the learners' respective life or work environments. Working in pairs is particularly valuable in problem-solving courses such as math or biology and in courses where case studies are popular such as business, engineering, and nursing.

- Set up learning experiences with groups of varying sizes. If you have a larger class of twenty-five or so, divide students into groups of three, four, or five; give them their own space for discussion; and have them assume various roles for discussions or case studies. For some activities, the assignment can include students' summarizing what they did in text or audio format and then sharing with other groups. In some cases, you might encourage alternative scenario developments.

- Make some of the grading points based on participation. This is actually a requirement if you want students to do peer-to-peer work and collaboration.

- Provide frequent feedback to each student, perhaps a weekly grade, on discussion contributions, and include comments on the quality of his or her interactions with peers.

The particular value that a faculty expert brings to a course is that of content expertise and coaching and mentoring expertise. Encouraging peer-to-peer interaction is one way the faculty member moves learners into the foreground, or to center stage, while the faculty member supports the dialogue, activities, and conversations of the learners from the background.

Promoting Meaningful Dialogue and Questioning

One way of promoting meaningful dialogue and questioning is to provide a set of rubrics and examples of the kinds of questions students may want to ask each other. Let us assume that you have developed rubrics for assessing discussion posts or a forum dialogue. Let us also assume that learners will be posting and then responding to other learners. A set of rubrics is a good place to include brief examples of effective and superficial postings and a short set of guidelines on Socratic questioning and examples of meaningful responses. Also, as students post effective responses, you can collect them and create a resource of effective postings for future courses.

To get you started, here is a list of four types of responses that students might use as they query the thinking of their fellow students. These types of responses can begin meaningful exchanges of ideas:

"Your point about X is not clear to me. Can you state it another way, or provide an example?" This helps to clarify thinking.

"Do you have any additional evidence to support your thinking about X?"

"You describe how your thinking has changed. What influenced that change?"

"What assumptions are you making about X? How would your statements change with different assumptions?"

Another way of ensuring meaningful dialogue is to do something with the discussion thread so that it doesn't just stop midstream with no resolution. One technique is the discussion wrap that summarizes and captures the essence of the discussion. This is a course task that the faculty member can gradually shift to learners. Discussion wraps are discussed at length in EM Tip 12.

Background

We know that the millennials, those born approximately between 1981 and 2000 and are now in their twenties, enjoy doing, creating, and talking more than listening or reading. They prefer rolling up their sleeves and immersing themselves in projects; they like to find ways to complete learning requirements as quickly as possible without too much of what they refer to as hassle. We also know that members of this same generation are more likely to chat, Twitter, instant message, play games, and create their own profiles, blogs, and wikis (Lenhart, Madden, Macgill, & Smith, 2007). The current and future generations of online learners are generally comfortable with online spaces and social networking tools, but not necessarily for using these tools and spaces for learning. Modeling good learning with these tools is recommended, depending on the age and maturity of your learners.

EM Tip 9: Online Classrooms and Tools for Synchronous Collaboration

This tip answers questions such as these:

- Why should I use synchronous gatherings in my courses? Why do learners and faculty find these types of gatherings desirable?

- What tools should I use for synchronous meetings? Aren't they expensive and difficult to use?

- Are there any synchronous tools that are free and easy to use?

- Do online learners avoid synchronous time commitments?

- Should I use synchronous meeting tools and encourage my students to use them?

"Where are you now? And what are you doing and thinking?" "What is happening where you are now?" This is often the opening line of our social exchanges. We enjoy relationships that are synchronous, social, and interactive. Online learning is no exception. For online learning experiences, we want tools that are flexible, engaging, affordable, and instantly available. Synchronous collaborative environments support open dialogue, study reviews, presentations, and project work. Spontaneous collaboration also supports learning activities such as brainstorming, producing, and revising.

Synchronous gatherings support constructivist and social learning strategies; they support as well the social, teaching, and cognitive presences that combine to make learning effective and satisfying. And they support students' desires to be socially active and related while learning.

Choices in Synchronous Collaborative Environments

The choices for synchronous collaborative environments now range from full-function synchronous environment tools such as Elluminate, Wimba, and Acrobat Connect to sets of mix-and–match instant collaborative environments.

The full function synchronous collaborative environments are invaluable for teacher-led gatherings and smaller group project gatherings, making possible the types of synchronous interchanges between teacher and learners that we value so highly in face-to-face classrooms. Once again, teachers and learners can discuss in real time, bringing real-time spontaneity back into teacher-learner interactions.

Sara Cordell, a writing professor at the University of Illinois-Springfield who also teaches British Victorian literature, commented that she values her online classroom for the real-time give-and-take with her students (J. Boettcher, personal communication, January 3, 2008). She added that the synchronous environment provides a way of "pulling things together for her students." She noted that the synchronous online classroom saves her time because she can talk through an essay, for example, discussing how the argument and flow of a student's essay work or not and weighing the thoughts of other students in real time. She commented that her students have shared with her that they feel as if there is more of a "real person teaching the class." (More about how Cordell uses synchronous tools for teaching is in an NPR interview in Abramson, 2007.)

Faculty often ask how students respond to the expectation of participating in synchronous events, particularly because one reason they are taking an online course is for the flexibility. Anecdotal data give us some insight. Sara Cordell, for example, requires her literature and writing students to participate in ten of thirteen live classes and to watch the archives of the classes they miss, setting up a separate forum discussion for those students. These classes also extend her day: she meets with her students for between two and three hours, starting at 6:00 P.M. After using the live classroom for five terms, Cordell has concluded that although students find it difficult to participate in the synchronous events, they enjoy the real-time spontaneity. Other faculty provide flexibility by offering a choice of synchronous sessions or by making the synchronous sessions optional.

Access to Full-Functioned Open Live Classrooms

Depending on the infrastructure for your online course, creating online classrooms can be very easy or a little more difficult. As powerful as the full-functioned environments are for teacher-learner collaboration, they need to be part of your institution's IT infrastructure. If your institution has one of the online classrooms mentioned (Elluminate, Wimba, or Adobe Connect), all you have to do to access this tool is to contact the IT department and request that the service be added to your course site. Other CMSs such as WebStudy provide this service as part of their suite of applications.

Among the questions that you may want to ask of your contact at your institution are these:

- "How do I create and set up online classrooms for my course?" In some CMSs, the online classroom appears as an option under a Communications tab. If so, you click on it and create a classroom just as you might create a forum or discussion board.

- "How do I record and archive the online classroom sessions?" Press the archive button at the beginning of the session and again at the close of it. Once the session is archived, you can post the link to the recording anywhere it is convenient in your course.

- "How do I prepare technically for an online session?" Most online classroom systems have prerecorded or live tutorials available on their Web sites, or you can prepare by attending sessions offered by your institution.

- "How do I prepare the content for an online session?" Preparing well for the content of online sessions is extremely important. The goals for everyone need to be clear, and everyone who is a leader for the session needs to be ready with questions, demonstrations, or polls to make it useful and engaging.

Some institutions offer and even require that you be certified in the use of the tool, but this generally takes only an hour or two and is fairly straightforward. Also many quick-start reference documents for both learners and faculty are available at the vendors' sites.

Informal and Free Options for Instant Collaboration

While live classrooms work well for planned interaction and events, we have also needed easy ways for online students to set up collaborative environments with little demand or effort on the part of the faculty member or the IT staff and infrastructure. New tools supporting instant collaboration and social interaction among learners are now free and readily available. Two of these tools are Google Apps for Education (www.google.com/a/edu) and the Zoho Office Suite (http://www.zoho.com/). More may be available as you are reading this.

The suite of Google tools includes communication, collaboration, and publishing tools such as e-mail, calendaring, document sharing, and chat and talk tools. A particularly useful feature of the document applications for student projects is a tracking and revision feature. A group of students working on a report, problem, presentation, production, or some other project can quickly review the revision history and the content of the revisions and access earlier versions. The tracking feature also records who made the changes. Many of these features may be integrated into a new application called *Google Wave* (EDUCAUSE, 2009).

Mixing and Matching for Spontaneous and Customizable Instant Collaboration

Learners can mix and match the tools to create whatever type of collaboration environment is needed for their purposes at the time. In other words, they can create their own customized synchronous environment—in a sense, their own mobile ecosystem that fits their particular needs at the time. Learners can set up collaborative environments such as these:

- Use their cell phone text messaging and Google calendaring for setting up meetings

- Use their phones and Web sites for initial brainstorming of projects, determining roles and responsibilities, and setting up time lines with calendaring applications

- Use group text chat and Google documents combined with phones for creating, planning, editing, and revising reports and other learning content

The only major constraint in setting up these mix-and-match environments is the need for relatively good and predictable network access and relative quiet in physical spaces. Quiet is often hard to come by in popular "offices" such as bookstores, cafés, and other public meeting places.

What is also promising about these tools is that they are currently either free or free for education and are readily available on the Internet, resulting in fewer demands on IT infrastructures. Learners can be more in control and be able to reach out and be productive with other learners without much preplanning, as schedules are often so unpredictable.

In 2001 Elliott Maisie, an e-learning futurist and analyst, suggested that we might want to use a metric called "Steps to Instant Collaboration" that would be the number of steps needed for "2 individuals or 2 groups of people ... to start collaborating via technology." The desired goal was that setting up a synchronous collaborative meeting would be as natural as going to a meeting room. Are we at this point yet? If not, we are getting very close.

EM Tip 10: Using Audio and Video Resources to Create a More Engaging and Effective Course

This tip answers questions such as these:

- How can I build audio and video into my online course? Why is the use of audio and video important?

- What are some easy ways to identify and integrate audio and video resources if I don't have much time to learn new tools?

- Can I use audio and video podcasts and learning objects created by someone else?

- How do I get started with finding quality podcasts?

- How long should podcasts or other media resources be?

You may wonder about the emphasis on adding video and audio to your course. Investing time getting familiar with and using audio and video tools creates a richer, more interesting, and more satisfying course experience for you and your students. More specifically, consider the following:

- Using audio is natural.

- Using audio can save you time. It takes less time to provide feedback on papers or on e-mail. This reason alone makes it worthwhile.

- Audio adds personality, feeling, and tone to discussions and comments.

- Audio makes doing presentations and project reports much easier and again, simply more natural. This means that students can practice the skills of real-time discussions, reporting, and presenting.

That we can easily incorporate audio into a course should not be viewed as a good reason to recreate a campus classroom environment. In other words, using audio online is not an opportunity for you to think, "At last I can lecture online." For great teaching and learning, long, rambling lectures are definitely out; quality mini-lectures, concept introductions, dialogue, and interaction are in. Podcasts and audio introductions are tending to be shorter rather than longer. Many published podcasts range from one minute to about twenty at the longest. When you are ready to make your own, you may want to start with a podcast that is three to five minutes long.

Strategies for Getting Started

There are two primary ways of adding audio and video to your course. You can use what someone else has created or published or you can create your own. Here are some strategies for getting started. If you are a novice at using audio or video, you may want to skip ahead to the section on using someone else's audio and video resources.

Add Audio to Your Biography and Introductory Posting

A good place to start is to add audio to your picture and bio and your getting-acquainted posting. Our voices are another dimension of our personality and part of getting to know someone. Think about how CNN uses audio. When correspondents are in far-flung and sometimes dangerous places such as war zones, where it is difficult to send video, they use the correspondent's picture in an inset with the audio, frequently accompanied by a Google Earth shot of the terrain where the correspondent is. So we hear the voice, and our mind almost fills in the missing video.

Adding good audio requires getting familiar with the volume controls on your computer and buying and using an external microphone if you want quality audio, but this is easier than it has ever been. In a pinch, you can even use the built-in microphone on some laptops. Capturing your voice is almost as easy as talking on a cell phone. Usually you press a red button in the application to start recording. As you are recording, a volume meter helps you gauge whether your voice volume is appropriate. One of the major suites of audio tools is the Wimba Collaboration Suite that includes the Wimba Voice Board, an asynchronous audio discussion area. Detailed instructions are available on many sites, including this site at Palomar College in California: http://www.palomar.edu/atrc/Training/How-to/Wimba/VoiceBoard.pdf. Once audio files are created, they can be exported to other places and devices, such as the iPod and iPod touch with formats such as WAV and MP3. The same processes work for creating your own podcasts and course announcements.

As with learning any other new tool or application, use audio in non-critical course elements as you develop confidence in it and introduce your students to this way of bringing voice energy into your course.

Use Audio in Course Announcements or for Discussion Feedback

Two other places for using audio as you are getting started are course announcements or discussion board postings. Think of announcements as ways of talking naturally with your students and giving them reminders of what's next, what might be happening in the world that is particularly relevant to their course content, and schedule changes.

Incorporate Published Audio or Video Resources

An even easier way to start with audio is to use published audio and video resources. In addition to text content resources, select a course learning activity that requires students to do some research. For example, you may have a discussion board posting that requires your students to identify a reputable reference that supports their position on a business strategy. In addition or instead of the text reference, expand the choices that students have to include finding an audio or video podcast or interview on that topic. Your instructions to the student might go as follows:

> *One of the topics that we will be studying over the next week is X. This might mean a topic such as consumer markets in China, the characteristics of leaders, the ethics of open software, or the pros and cons of intellectual property. To support the ideas in your posting, find an audio/video resource from a reputable reference discussing these issues. Include the URL and a short description of the resource in your posting. Then other students can review these resources as part of their response to the postings.*

This is a good initial audio experience, as it means that you and your students need to ensure that your personal computer or learning resource works well with audio and video.

Enrich and Expand the Course Resources

Select one of the learning activities in your course for which you believe that current events or reports are particularly relevant. Information is being updated so quickly that the textbook and other resources for your course may have already been eclipsed by new developments. Once you have identified a topic, search the Internet for relevant resources. Once you have found a good source, you may want to download the file to your computer or MP3 player for off-Net listening. Then think through how that resource supports one of your core concepts and add that podcast to assignments. Podcasts can be a good source for discussion questions.

Podcast Starting Points with Specific Publishers

Although there are portals dedicated to podcasts such as the iTunes store (www.apple.com/itunes/store/podcasts.html), podcasts are now so ubiquitous that a simple search using *podcast* usually works well. You will soon develop a favorite set of content providers. The *Wall Street Journal, Harvard Business Review,* American Public Radio, CNN, *Scientific American*, and *Chronicle of Higher Education* are some popular sources of podcasts. The iTunes University site (http://www.apple.com/support/itunes_u/) offers free audio and video podcasts from many universities in the United States and around the world, including Stanford, Yale, MIT, Duke, and Penn State.

If you teach in areas such as business, management, or society, the *Harvard Business Review* offers a weekly series, called *Ideacasts,* that features "breakthrough ideas and commentary from leading thinkers in business and management." The podcast from May 25, 2007, for example, features an interview with Bill George, professor of management practice at Harvard and author of *True North: Discover Your Authentic Leadership*, about "how leaders who are true to themselves add significant value to their organizations." This fifteen-minute podcast can be streamed to your computer, or you can download it and put it on a mobile player for use in your car or while exercising. This series currently has an active archive of about fifty podcasts.

Subscribing to Podcasts

Once you start exploring the world of podcasts, one of the decisions a podcast provider always presents is whether you want to subscribe to a podcast series.

Podcast subscribing means that you can choose to store a series of podcast links on your computer. A convenient way to subscribe to a series of podcasts is by using a free downloadable application, iTunes (http://www.apple.com/itunes/download/), that works on both Macs and PCs. This application is also a portal, making it easy to search and find podcasts from universities, museums, and public radio and news sources.

Once you download the iTunes application and respond, "Yes, I want to subscribe," to a podcast series, the names, dates, and descriptions of all the podcasts in the series are downloaded to your computer, essentially creating a catalogue index of available podcasts from that provider. If you want to download a specific podcast, you can do that from within the iTunes application that is now on your computer by simply clicking on a Get button next to each podcast description.

Sharing Podcasts

Sharing podcasts is simple. With a URL in your syllabus, assignment, announcement, or discussion board, you can direct your students to a podcast that they can use on their computer or a handheld device. Students can share podcasts in this same way. Best of all, most of these podcasts are free.

Exciting Discoveries

Online book sites also offer a wealth of media, although it seems to be more ephemeral. For example, Borders bookstore often features audio/ video podcasts with authors of books that are favorites of book clubs. One podcast that was temporarily available was with Khaled Hosseini, author of *The Kite Runner* and *A Thousand Splendid Suns*. Authors such as John Grisham and Stephen King have also been featured. Podcast research, however, can be dangerous. You may well be snagged and diverted in a thousand unanticipated directions, but you will likely be rewarded with new exciting discoveries.

Tools Within Course Management Systems

Asynchronous audio can enhance the existing asynchronous tools in your course management. Students can add audio data and information to their postings as well. Audio can make the process of sending out announcements easy and natural.

Background

Following are some of the reasons that you may want to take your time about using audio and video in your course:

- Using audio takes some learning and setup time.
- Your computer needs to be equipped for audio input and output. Almost all recent computers have these capabilities built in. Many new computers even have cameras embedded for doing video (which means that you may have to give up working in pajamas or your exercise togs if you are working from home).

- Hearing audio from published resources or from collaborative meetings requires that you have speakers either built in or attached to your computer for audio output.

- Creating audio messages or resources requires a good microphone built in or attached to your computer. This is for audio input.

- Good synchronous audio, talking real time live with your students, is better with a comfortable headset.

- Using audio requires that you find where the volume controls are on your computer and on your microphone and how to adjust the volume to a comfortable setting. By experimenting with playing a podcast, you learn at least two of these three items.

- Your students will need to learn how to use and control audio on their computers, including use of the mute button, so ambient noise does not distract live meetings.

This list is not intended to discourage but to clarify the steps and the requirements for incorporating audio and video. This list can help mentally prepare you and help you be realistic about getting started. Taking it one step at a time will build your confidence and make learning how to do this a pleasant experience. You may also find personal advantages. Those of us with grandchildren many states and time zones away can now feel closer by seeing them in real time and sharing the treasures they have to show us. Other faculty are using these audio and video tools to visit with their elderly parents.

BUILDING THE COGNITIVE PRESENCE

This last set of early middle tips describes strategies for building cognitive presence and includes tips on discussion wraps, characteristics of good discussion posts, and designing projects.

EM Tip 11: A Good Discussion Post Has Three Parts

This tip answers questions such as these:

- What are the three parts of a good discussion posting?

- How can I encourage student interaction in discussion postings?

- What posting directions encourage learner-to-learner responses and interlocking conversations?

The question of what makes a good discussion post is particularly important because the discussion board in an online course is the functional equivalent of the discussion part of a face-to-face class. The discussion board is the tool of choice in an online course for connecting socially and cognitively. The discussion board is where we express what we know and why, what we don't know, and occasionally what we wish we knew. The discussion board is where the community happens.

Building cognitive presence requires sustained communication over time on important content. Here are two specific ways to encourage discussion posts that create community and sustained conversation.

Three-Part Post: What, Why, and What I Wish I Knew

One simple way of encouraging peer dialogue is the three-part post. These guidelines work well on discussion posts that present problems or queries about opinions. This three-part post works whether a learner is doing an initial posting response or a response to another learner's posting:

Part 1: State what your considered thought or recommendation might be. In other words, answer the question, "What do you think or recommend doing in this situation?"

Part 2: State why you think what you do. This is a good place for learners to probe their thoughts, experiences, and beliefs. It is also a good place for learners to provide references, links, and resources to experts, events, and beliefs that share and support that thinking.

Part 3: State what you wish you knew or what problem or challenge will follow or accompany the original question.

Characteristics of Quality Online Discussion Posting or Message

We often are ambivalent about how strict we ought to be about guiding learners in their posting behaviors. At the same time, discussion posts are a reflection of minds and thoughts. Here is a set of recommended characteristics of discussion posts derived from multiple sources on the Web. See whether you agree with these and how many of these you generally require for the postings in your class:

- *Substantial:* Messages should relate to the subject matter and provide information, opinions, or questions about that subject matter.

- *Concise:* Studies have shown that messages that are several screens long do not get many replies. The message should be clear.

- *Provocative:* A good message is one that prompts others to reply or object.

- *Explanatory:* A good message explores, explains, or expands on a concept or connection.

- *Timely:* A good member of the learning community gets on regularly and replies to messages in a timely fashion.

- *Logical:* A good message should contain a clearly stated conclusion or thesis supported by premises, reason, evidence, or grounds of belief.

- *Grammatical:* A good, clear, and concise message should be well written and free of typos and sentence fragments.

This set of characteristics was adapted from the Quality Online Messages at St. John's University (www.stjohns.edu/faculty/portable_old/portable1/tools/messages.sju) and derived from a rubric at Mercy College.

Background: Observations on Learner and Community

One shift that is occurring in online learning is from a focus on the individual learner to a focus on the learner within a community of learners. This shift is supported by the observation of Heckman and Annabi (2005) that a key advantage of online learning is that the interaction pattern of online courses tends to be group centered rather than authority centered. This shift moves the instructor to the role of a group mentor or group coach in addition to mentoring individual students. In other words, the teaching goal will include how the group as a whole is moving toward understandings.

To ensure that the group moves forward, each learner must fulfill his or her own individual responsibilities. The individual learners contribute to the whole by embracing the content that is brought to the course, integrating course content with their existing knowledge, and creating and contributing ideas in a process of knowledge creation and discovery (Garrison, 2006).

Shift from Turn-Taking to Reflective and Developed Conversation

Another observation made by Heckman and Annabi (2005) is that online discussions, operating asynchronously and thus often more reflectively, can shift groups away from the turn-taking atmosphere that often characterizes classroom discussions. One of their findings was that virtually all student utterances in face-to-face were responses to the teacher, while in asynchronous discussions nearly two-thirds of student utterances were responses to other students. This shift in communication patterns is highly desirable. Thoughtful posts and responses to them build on the thoughts and knowledge that the learners bring to the conversation and in return elicit responses by other individuals. The totality of these posts creates a sustained conversation or a "stream of meaning flowing among and through and between us" (Bohm, 1996, p. 6) about important ideas.

Sustained conversation on important topics needs to be nurtured as it does not usually happen naturally. As with many other new types of communication, effective use of online contexts requires practice. Also, sustained conversation that includes responding and building on others' thoughts is rare in this time of Twittering, instant messaging, and constant interruptions. So it is worth finding ways to encourage students not just to post what they believe, but to read and understand what a fellow student is saying and integrate those thoughts with their existing thoughts and mental models. Students may have to learn this process, so an instructor should take time to observe and comment on the process of how the content is being taken in, absorbed, and integrated. As Bohm (1996) noted in his many reflections on dialogue, listening openly and suspending our own beliefs for a time is the only path to what he calls "shared meanings" and "collective thought." This may be an elusive goal for many of us. Nevertheless, the results in learning and community make it a worthwhile goal.

EM Tip 12: Discussion Wraps: A Useful Cognitive Pattern or a Collection of Discrete Thought Threads

This tip answers questions such as these:

- Why is a discussion wrap beneficial?

- My students have done a great job at discussing our current weekly discussion. How do we wrap it up and move on to the next?

- How can I involve my students in the wrapping-up process? Can they sort through and identify the essential core ideas of the discussion?

Weekly discussions are the basic online tool for getting to know what students know and what they think they know. Weekly discussions are also the best tool for creating a learning community. Think of weekly discussions as the formal equivalent of late-night dorm conversations or extended student union discussions. How to close out online discussions is not a topic discussed regularly. Part of the learning cycle is pruning our investigations down to the essential principles, patterns, and relationships. What is the essence of the knowledge that we want students to take away from a discussion? Can you remember a discussion that was intense, thoughtful, and stimulating? It can be hard to move on. The goal is to summarize briefly what you believe your students are going to remember, think about, and question from that discussion.

Using the Discussion Wrap

The purpose of the discussion wrap is to bring closure, if only temporary closure, to a topic. This does not mean having answers, but rather identifying the core messages and pruning to the essentials. We know from memory research that we remember very little of what we encounter and, with good reason, given the amount of information we encounter (Damasio, 1999). Summarizing the discussion is an opportunity to help students focus and reflect on key concepts. Summaries can help students develop useful knowledge rather than having only vague recollections. Here are two practices that you may want to try.

Summarize the Discussion

Keep in mind that when we are learning, we are changing and growing links in our brains. We are identifying patterns, finding hidden relationships, delighting in new insights, and pondering challenges and questions for the future. As students are exploring and discussing ideas, the questions, perspectives, and ideas that they are bringing to the conversation tend to be broad-ranging and dispersed. Often just as the conversation gets to the point of identifying key challenges and interesting relationships, the week comes to an end and a new topic begins. The students are left with wondering questions such as these:

- Where has this discussion taken my understandings? Our group's understandings?

- What have I learned? What do I know now that I did not know before?

- What is next? Are there actions that we should pursue at some point?

- Have I changed how I think about these ideas or this problem?

- What do the experts think?

- What does our faculty leader think? (It is important for students to know our opinion, because we are a guide to the experts, if not one of the experts.)

The discussion summary can take one of many forms. Here are four common formats:

- Create a closing discussion thread labeled "Summary," "Wrap-Up," "Key Ideas," or "Key Concept." Good labeling will help students with course reviews. Faculty who teach a particular course each semester can create a template for reinforcing some of the key concepts. Then the insights and contributions of the current group of students can be woven into this summary.

- Create a text or audio/video wrap-up summary or podcast that encapsulates the key postings of the week and integrates these statements with the key concepts. For example, if you are using YouTube or an instructor blog or weekly preview announcements for your students, you can book-end your week with a summary closing.

- Create a group summary by asking each student to identify the key concept for him or her from the discussion. The concept might be a key insight, challenge, action, change, relationship, or pattern.

- Hold a live synchronous text chat or audio chat with your online classroom and review key ideas from a two- or three-week unit. Then create a summary from that activity.

Involve Students

The creative process of preparing a summary from a week's discussion requires critical thinking skills such as analysis, synthesis, questioning, linking ideas, and identifying patterns—the types of skills that we desire for our students. As faculty, we want to share this type of creative experience and involve students. You may want to ask students to volunteer to take on one or more roles for some of your weekly discussions, or if you have a small class of mature students, you might assign the weekly summarizing task as one of the elements of your assessment plan. If you have a larger class whose students have less experience with complex analysis tasks, a team of two students might work on the summary together. If you have quite a large class that you have separated into groups, you can create separate discussion groups for the weekly discussions. Then each group can summarize the discussion, and the summaries can be posted in a separate forum or blog for summaries. If you actively involve your students in these discussion wraps, remember how important your voice is in taking the next step of providing confirmation, affirmation, or disagreement with the student's summary. Your opinion, next challenges from an expert, and links forward are key components of the community summary from that week's discussion work.

Background and Other Resources

Diane Schallert of the Department of Educational Psychology at the University of Texas has created a one-minute video clip explaining why she uses the technique of creating a separate word document for weekly summaries (www.utexas.edu/academic/blackboard/examples/videos/schallert_02.html). Other research at this same site affirms why "the process of compiling discussion threads and posting them again might increase learning"). Reder and Anderson (1980) showed that college students remember more important material from reading chapter summaries than from reading entire textbook chapters. In addition, Mayer et al. (1996) showed not only that students remember more of the important material when it is presented as a summary but that they also better understand the material.

Whatever strategy you use for discussion wraps, keep a focus on the core concepts of the course and identify the essential relationships and ongoing issues of your discipline.

EM Tip 13: Getting an Early Start on Cognitive Presence

This tip answers questions such as these:

- What is cognitive presence?

- What are some of the behaviors that help to create the stages of cognitive presence?

Presence—social, teaching, and cognitive—is a characteristic of online courses that makes a difference in learner and faculty satisfaction and learning benefits. For learning goals, the greatest of these presences is cognitive presence, that is, "the extent to which the participants in any particular configuration of a community of inquiry are able to construct meaning through sustained communication" (Garrison, Anderson, & Archer, 2000, p. 89).

As work on this model has progressed, the processes involved in creating cognitive presence and the stages of the process have been further defined. Garrison and Vaughan (2008) now offer this definition of cognitive presence that includes four stages of a knowledge-building process: cognitive presence is "a recursive process that encompasses states of puzzlement, information exchange, connection of ideas, creation of concepts and the testing of the viability of solutions" (p. 22). This definition describes a knowledge-building process that might require the full term of a course to achieve. What does it mean we ought to be doing in the early middle? One way to approach this is to map the four stages of the cognitive presence to the four stages of a course. In the course beginnings, the focus may be on the initial set of questions students have about the core concepts of the course. This is the puzzlement stage. In the early middle, the focus is on gathering information and exchange of ideas, or the exploration stage. In the late middle, the work of cognitive presence might be connecting and relating the ideas within the course framework, which includes theory-building. The closing weeks might be the testing and problem solving and scenario building. The practical inquiry model that graphically shows these four stages is in Figure 7.2 (also see http://communitiesofinquiry.com/files/practicalinquiry.pdf).

Another way of applying this knowledge-building process is to plan out the four stages. Use the puzzlement, exploration, theory-building, and problem-testing cycle with simpler problems, and complete a cycle in one or two weeks.

FIGURE 7.2

Practical Inquiry Model

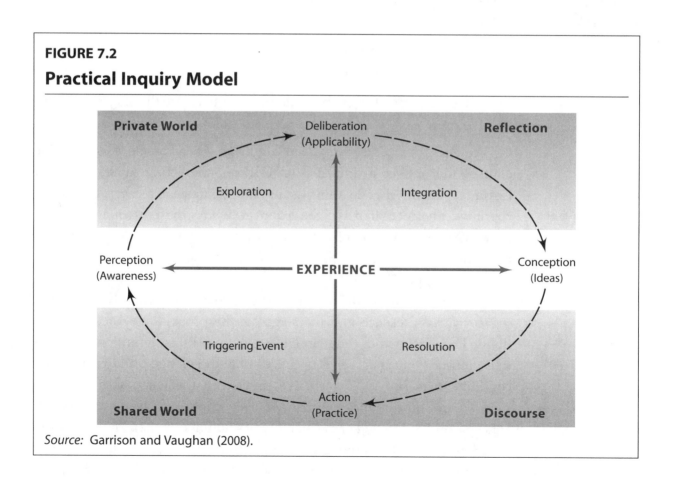

Source: Garrison and Vaughan (2008).

Tools and Behaviors by Faculty and Students

Establishing cognitive presence and moving through the stages of the inquiry model requires attention and commitment from the faculty and learners in a course community. Cognitive presence seeks an understanding on an intellectual and affective level of how the learning activities are engaging an individual's meaning structures. This requires knowledge and time for the processes of reflection, discussion, and confirmation of meaning. Cognitive presence requires a focus on meaning, so occasionally this may mean that depth and problem solving of topics is favored over concept awareness. Tending to cognitive presence requires time, listening, reflecting, and careful responding to encourage sustained conversation.

Here are some of the behaviors that help to create and sustain cognitive presence and what is real learning growth by the learners:

- Faculty set high expectations for student inquiry.

- Faculty examine student responses and probes, challenges, and questions, encouraging analysis of ideas and content.

- Learners participate thoughtfully in the discussions, responding to content and thoughts and questions from other learners so that a sustained communication occurs.

- Faculty and students strive to ensure that project outcomes are long-lasting and meaningful.

Striving for Cognitive Presence

Achieving cognitive presence requires significant and ongoing emphasis on core concepts and how learners are progressing with their understanding of those concepts. In evaluating student responses, be aware of the states they may be experiencing: puzzlement, information exchange, connection of ideas, creation of concepts, and the testing of the viability of solutions.

EM Tip 14: Launching Learner Projects That Matter to the Learner

This tip answers questions such as these:

- When should course projects get started?

- Should course projects be individual or group projects?

- What are some guidelines for designing projects and tasks that really matter to the learner?

The second half of a course is the time that students are often doing more intensive individual and collaborative projects. However, it is important for project work to begin early in the course, and the early middle is definitely the time to start, if not sooner. By this point, the requirements of the course project should be clearly defined and communicated. However, it is not too late to tweak the project if you would like to do so now that you know your students better.

The focus of assessment in online learning often shifts from a set of two or three proctored tests or quizzes to multiple assessment activities. The most important of these activities are the creative projects, or what might be called learner performance tasks. Some online courses are now totally structured around the project that the students design and complete during a course. These courses demonstrate an important shift toward an apprenticeship model of learning. Just as developing cognitive presence in a course has four stages, the task of designing and creating assessment tasks and projects course generally has three to four or more major milestones.

The Assessment Plan

The assessment plan, generally set out in your course syllabus, summarizes the points of assessment and how the learning outcomes of each learner will be assessed. Assessment plans generally have at least four types of experiences important to evaluation—for example:

- Participation in discussion posts—the class conversation
- Automated low-stakes quizzes
- Individual projects that include analysis such as critical thinking and communication of that work to others in a final product of some type, such as a paper, interview, report, podcast, or presentation
- Team projects of various sizes and purposes

The Importance of the Assessment Project

This tip describes a shift from the common practice of overdesigning a course project to designing open-ended course projects that focus on difficult and complex problems for which a ready answer is probably not available.

Effective course design practices place a high priority on designing assessment experiences that matter to the student. This usually means designing enough choices so that learners can develop projects that provide for personalized and customized knowledge and require some innovative thinking.

One excellent example of the importance of such an assessment is from David Gibson, who directs the Global Challenge, an ongoing project funded by the National Science Foundation. This project, actually for high school students, is designed around a fundamentally subtle but profound shift in assessment. The common approach to assessment plans is similar to the three-step process later in this tip: developing guidelines and directions for the projects and experiences that learners will use to demonstrate the discipline performance goals for competency. By contrast, the Global Challenge describes for learners the required features and characteristics of the response, the task model or project, and leaves the processes and tools unspecified. This difference cycles us back closer to the model of apprenticeship. It is likely that current practices encourage an "overdesign" of course projects, consistent with directing learning. We often design projects that match our knowledge structure and our favorite tools and concepts.

In contrast, the Global Challenge project focuses the work of teacher-mentors on designing a task model for students that enables, indeed encourages, wide-ranging discovery, teamwork, analysis, and global awareness. It is a project in which learners are not assigned to solve a problem for which we have known answers and ready responses, but a project that is of social, economic, and global significance for which we need innovative, creative thinking. In other words, students are given the tools (such as Web sites, electronic portfolios, and in-house global simulation frameworks) for the project and the task model. Then they work in a team of three—two students and an advisor—and collaborate with international counterparts from October to May to address global climate change. The task model is to propose a global business solution for mitigating climate change (http://www.globalchallengeaward.org/display/public/Home).

This model can be readily implemented in online courses by building sufficient flexibility into course projects so that students can follow their own interests. Effective designing for learning recognizes the power of the passions and interests of the individual. For example, a course on framing global policy issues can integrate a project in which an individual or a small team identifies a global policy issue and then applies the core principles and strategies of the course content to that policy issue.

So, in summary, three key features recommend themselves to our assessment practices:

- Do not overdesign a project; leave ample room for learner exploration.

- Focus on problems that need innovative ideas and solutions.

- Encourage work on projects that students like and want to do rather than projects that might be important to faculty.

Background: A Three-Step Process for Planning Assessment

Here is a three-step process for planning your assessment (McTighe & Wiggins, 1999):

1. Identify results that you want for your learners. These results will probably include enduring understanding (similar to concepts), knowing the vocabulary and syntax of a discipline domain, and being familiar with the exemplars of a discipline, for example, the most famous representatives and case studies.

2. Determine the acceptance evidence by which the learners can demonstrate their knowledge, understanding, and integration of ideas.

3. Design the learning experiences to ensure learner accomplishment of these understandings and the processes for demonstrating their learning.

This process can guide the development of an assessment plan focusing on knowledge and effective use of core course concepts.

Summary—and What's Next

This is the end of the tips for the early middle. By now, your learning community is growing and projects are planned, if not already well under way. Your teaching presence has likely already started a subtle downward shift into more coaching, mentoring, and deeper questioning.

Chapter 8

Phase Three: What's Happening, Themes, and Tools

Letting Go of Power in the Late Middle

Chapter Overview

You are now at the halfway point of your course. By this time, you and your students are likely well acquainted with each other from both a social and cognitive perspective. And your teaching presence is actively guiding both group and individual learning goals.

In this chapter, we reflect on what is happening in the late middle part of the course and summarize the teaching and learning themes of questioning, assessing, project coaching, and empowerment. The tools section provides a quick guide as to which collaborative tools, such as blogging and wiki tools, might be best suited for achieving certain types of desirable learning outcomes, such as critical thinking and effective problem solving.

What's Happening in the Late Middle Weeks

By the time an instructor and learners arrive at the late middle of a course, processes are well established, and a certain equilibrium has often been reached. The course learning community has a history of trust, and a feeling of comfortable camaraderie has been established from the work learners have been doing in supporting, challenging, and helping each other. With these processes operating smoothly, you can relax a little and continue your shift from directing the learners to more facilitating. Rather than a focus on actively directing learning experiences as you did earlier in the course, you will be devoting more of your time and energy to responding to questions and supporting learners thinking about the content and acquiring knowledge. Time on project work is intensifying, and this is the time to individualize some of the mentoring and coaching for personalizing and customizing learning. Learners need to be progressing well on their course projects and interacting with the other learners on those projects.

The growing maturity of the learners makes it easier for faculty to begin letting go of power and sharing it with learners. While an instructor continues to make key course decisions, such as the timing of certain events in a course, appropriateness and fit of projects, and major grading, learners can share other responsibilities, such as peer review, expanding learning outcomes, helping others to develop knowledge, and leading in the development of activities in the course.

During the late middle, a key teaching responsibility is to encourage students' movement from exploring and researching ideas to integrating knowledge and producing knowledge products. Recall the stages of the practical inquiry model: triggering events, exploration, integration, and resolution (Garrison, Anderson, & Archer, 2000). This is the time to support students as they complete the exploration stage and begin integrating that explored knowledge. Some course activities will also begin moving beyond integrating core concepts to defining problems and searching for resolutions.

Other important teaching responsibilities during this stage are to identify, review, and highlight patterns and relationships in the content and cycle back as appropriate to earlier course content. New group content is often concentrated in the first three-quarters of a course, and the last part of the course focuses more on the integration and application of content in solving problems. The late middle can be the best and last time to identify and correct misconceptions.

In summary, this is what is usually happening in the late middle:

- Learners are moving from the rapid and expansive knowledge exploration stage to working with more challenging problems and scenarios that require the integration of some of the core course concepts. They are responding to others and providing comments and suggestions on other students' proposed projects. Learners are generally working in small groups during this stage.

- The faculty is focusing on feedback to learners on the shaping and fit of the projects and how the projects are progressing. The role of the faculty is shifting to being primarily a facilitator of learning experiences and supporting the learners as they lead, summarize, and integrate content experiences. Faculty are striving to encourage the building of relationships, patterns, and connections and spiraling and layering the core content concepts. The faculty member continues in high gear, focusing on the core concepts, but also shifts to challenging the learners even more, sometimes with complex discipline problems for which there are no known answers.

In brief, your task in this late middle phase of the course is to subtly shift the responsibility for directing learning more and more to the learners, their projects, and their learning outcomes, while at the same time ensuring that the course core concepts are well integrated into their knowledge frameworks. The tasks for students in this phase of the course are to move aggressively to complete the exploration stage of their learning, refine their course project plans, and complete sections of their projects while assisting and supporting the projects of their fellow learners.

The late middle is our favorite part of the course: the learners are actively engaged, the community is functioning well, we are developing insights spontaneously with our learners, and the stress of the final weeks is still in the future.

Late Middle: Themes, Best Practices, and Principles

The themes for the late middle—questioning, assessing, project coaching, and empowerment—capture the work of the third stage of the course. This is where the learners come into their own as to what they are thinking and knowing about the course content. This is also the place in the course where they use their questioning and thinking skills to integrate the course knowledge into their own personal and customized knowledge base. This means that guidance in developing good questioning skills best accompanies guidance in developing critical thinking skills. Almost all curricula goals include critical thinking as a desired learning outcome. Critical thinking is also one of the cross-functional skills recommended by the well-known report, *Building a Nation of Learners: The Need for Changes in Teaching and Learning to Meet Global Challenges* (Business-Higher Education Forum, 2003). Planning and doing course projects and being an active member of the course community encourage student learners' individual content integration, resolution, and critical thinking processes.

We haven't discussed much about the resolution process, which is postulated as the fourth stage in the practical inquiry model. As noted in the literature, resolution happens less often than we would like in higher education. That is something to work toward. It may be our course structures and other administrative constraints limit these possibilities. Capstone courses that focus on projects and complex scenario building are the courses that probably come closest to that goal.

Let's take a closer look now at the late middle themes.

Questioning

Questioning is at the core of teaching and learning. It is through questioning that we learn what students know, why they think, what they do, and what they want or need to know next. Questioning is one of the tools that enables us to learn each learner's zone of proximal development, that is, what he or she is ready to learn. Effective questioning also reveals misconceptions and sources of possible confusion. By hearing students' thoughts, voices, and questions through text, audio, and video postings, we come to know their minds and their current knowledge structures. Some of the topics in the tips for this stage include how questioning makes students' knowledge visible to us. The techniques include turning questioning upside down and inside out by having students pose the questions to try to stump the instructor. The tips offer references for classic resources such as Bloom's taxonomy and the updated Bloom's taxonomy by Krathwohl (2002) and examples of the categories of Socratic questioning.

Assessing

Assessing is a major management and administrative task that we may avoid because of the potential conflicts and disappointments that can occur. One of the major differences between campus and online courses is that an online course design plans for continuous and multiple points of assessment (Moallem, 2005): individual, small group, and larger group team assignments; feedback cycles and self-review; and peer and expert review. Continuous feedback and assessment means that assessment grading usually brings few surprises. Students should have a fairly clear idea of how they are doing throughout the course.

Project Coaching

For us, projects are where the rubber meets the road. In much of the first half of a course, students are encountering and experiencing resources in a domain of knowledge that may be quite unfamiliar to them. They are being exposed to content at a rate that can seem as if it is coming at them through a fire hose. There is usually insufficient time for pausing, reflecting, and thinking. We hope that the course design recommendations that we have made in the first chapters encourage a more realistic and practical, while still challenging, approach to acquiring course knowledge and achieving the performance goals of a course. It is one thing to have the goal of covering a certain amount of content, but it is even more important for students to engage with and process course content.

Projects are excellent knowledge integration tools; projects are also excellent tools for supporting personalization and customization goals. Projects should be designed with multiple assessment points so learners start their projects earlier, staging this work throughout the course. With multiple assessment points, such as an initial proposal and concept review, an initial draft and a final paper and presentation, you, other students, and potentially invited experts get to know the students and the problem that they may be grappling with or focusing on. With multiple assessment points, students can review, discuss, and provide feedback on other learners' ideas and projects. Projects can be individualized so that students have an opportunity to focus their learning on topics of interest to themselves while still learning the core content. An additional value is that every course expands your own expert knowledge as you coach students through the design, selection, and execution of projects that the learners really care about.

Empowerment

The subtitle of this chapter, "Letting Go of the Power," captures much of what should be happening within a course at all times, but in particular as the learners progress through core content. The ideal mentor coaches his or her apprentices so that they outgrow their master. A learner's performance goals should challenge the learner toward solving real-life complex problems. We know that simulating real-life disaster scenarios prepares people for automatic responses when met with real disaster. And we know that pilots practice in flight simulators so they are prepared for complex real-life challenges. The same is true for the learning environment. We want to simulate as much as possible the types of scenarios that learners will encounter in life and prepare them for those situations and problems. So the theme of empowerment means encouraging students to think and analyze each other's work and support each other in the community and, as a whole, challenging learners to go beyond the course content. One of the future learning shifts will likely be to enhance learner-centered teaching to include the learner within the community teaching, developing the socially responsible learner.

Tips for the Late Middle

There are four sets of tips for the late middle and letting go of the power. The first set, Leveraging the Power of Questions, explores how questions and students' responses provide insights into what learners know and what they think they know. These tips provide examples of probing questions that you and your students can use for querying learners as to what they think and why they think what they do. These questioning techniques encourage peer-to-peer dialogue that supports the goals of creating community. In fact, of all the skills drawn on in online teaching and learning, developing effective questioning skills is one of the most important.

The second set of tips, Assessing Learning as You Go, offers help in providing feedback to learners. These tips provide guidelines and hints on strategies for ensuring timely and efficient feedback to learners on an ongoing basis. Recall that one of the differences between campus-based and online courses is the need for ongoing assessment. Ongoing assessment ensures that you get to know your students as individuals and thus minimizes the potential for cheating or other types of fraud. As you become familiar with the manner of a student's expression and perspectives, you can detect any abnormalities in his or her work. Other tips in this set suggest ways of personalizing and customizing learning experiences to better fit a learner's interests and readiness.

The third set of tips, Project Work Practices, focuses on the tasks of managing and assessing an individual learner's projects as well as group projects. These tips complement the earlier ones on projects and include a rubric for analyzing critical thinking and a set of best practices during project time. The last set of tips for the late middle, Community Empowerment and Social Networking, brings together hints on using social networking tools such as blogs and wikis for putting conversations into high gear. The final tip in this set describes strategies for personalizing and customizing learning and the power that these strategies bring to learning.

Just when particular tips are going to be useful will vary with the course, your students, and where you are in developing expertise as an online instructor. Be sure to use the tips as you are ready for them.

Technology Tools

Your key teaching responsibility regarding tools in the late middle is to continue developing good habits in your own use of the communication tools. At this point in the course, you want to encourage learners in using the tools that are most useful for supporting collaboration, teaming, and project coaching. Some tools that are particularly well suited for these tasks of collaboration and knowledge building are the basic discussion forums and the newer blog and wiki tools. In addition, your students may want to be adventurous in using the many communication tools that reduce the distance separating them from each other—among them the audio tools such as Audacity and Skype and the Google free work project and collaboration tools. Keep in mind that not all students have to use all the same tools for their communications and process work. Some learners may come to your course using Skype on a daily basis and want to use it with their team of two or three other students. That is similar to letting them choose whether to use a landline or cell phone. However, you determine the tools and the environment for the submission, community discussion, and presentation of work.

Table 8.1 lists the tools mentioned in the late middle tips and the suggested pedagogical uses and purposes of these tools.

TABLE 8.1

Tools in Late Middle Tips and Suggested Pedagogical Uses

Tools and Applications in Late Middle Tips	Late Middle Tip Number	Suggested Pedagogical Uses and Purposes
Online classroom: a place for synchronous real-time presentations and discussions	LM 1	Particularly well suited for question-and-answer sessions such as those that might involve invited experts.
Discussion boards and blogs	LM 1	The classroom spaces for an online course; used for discussion, questioning, and thinking out loud about concepts and issues.
Audio tools	LM 5	Individual or group feedback. One's voice carries more personality and energy than text alone. Voice feedback can be more spontaneous and energetic.
Open forum: an open discussion board for learners	LM 6	A place where learners can ask general questions of the instructor or other students.

TABLE 8.1

(Continued)

Tools and Applications in Late Middle Tips	Late Middle Tip Number	Suggested Pedagogical Uses and Purposes
Team blog or wiki	LM 7	Provides an open collaborative thinking and working space for project work, including collaborative work on phased milestones such as proposals, ideas, and resources.
Google Docs: a suite of free software that includes a word processor, spreadsheet, and presentation application	LM 8, with additional information in EM 9	Tools that support instant synchronous or asynchronous collaboration and social interaction among learners; can be particularly helpful when working on team or group projects; provides tracking and revision history.
Skype and Google Gmail (voice and video chat)	LM 8	Tools that stream audio and video for getting to know people and what they look and sound like and for synchronous discussions for collaboration and community building.
Audacity: free open source software for recording and editing sounds	LM 8	Can be used for group project presentations in low-bandwidth situations.
Flickr: photo-sharing application	LM 12	A place for collecting or storing photos that learners might use in a project, simulation, or problem-solving scenario.
VoiceThread: a place for having an asynchronous or almost synchronous discussion about an image, video, or document	LM 12	A place to go for a conversation about an important image, graphic, document, or video and to post comments that are saved and archived.
Facebook and LinkedIn: social networking sites	LM 13	Places for more extended social networking and community that can supplement course places and carry networking beyond courses and programs.
YouTube: a Web site for posting short videos	LM 13	A place for posting videos and demos so students can see you and see process demonstrations.

Chapter 9

Phase Three: Tips for the Late Middle

Chapter Overview

Be sure to take time to enjoy the late middle of a course—the time for deep thought, exploration, sorting out confusions, and getting to the real questions of your discipline. Students bring a host of new perspectives, relationships, and patterns from other disciplines. These varying perspectives can often illuminate tough problems for all of us.

The tips in this chapter for the late middle phase of a course are grouped into four sets. There is a lot going on during this phase of a course. As a faculty member, you are facilitating, coaching, and supporting; learners are integrating their new knowledge into their knowledge structures. This is a significant shift as the learners take responsibility for directing more of their learning and sharing in the learning direction of their fellow learners. Students are moving into their own in terms of developing content knowledge and pursuing creative projects. This can be a stimulating time for discipline insights and for novel approaches to traditional perspectives.

The tips follow the pattern of beginning with the questions commonly asked by online faculty about a topic and addressed by the tip. The tip then suggests practical steps and actions supported by theory, practice, and research.

Here is a list of the tips for the late middle (LM) of the course:

- LM Tip 1: Questions and Answers: Upside Down and Inside Out
- LM Tip 2: Three Techniques for Making Your Students' Knowledge Visible

- LM Tip 3: Moving Beyond Knowledge Integration to Defining Problems and Finding Solutions

- LM Tip 4: "Are You Reading My Postings? Do You Know Who I Am?" Simple Rules About Feedback in Online Learning

- LM Tip 5: Feedback on Assignments: Being Timely and Efficient

- LM Tip 6: Reshaping Learning Habits of Online Students

- LM Tip 7: Customizing and Personalizing Learning

- LM Tip 8: Managing and Facilitating Group Projects

- LM Tip 9: Assessing Group Projects

- LM Tip 10: A Rubric for Analyzing Critical Thinking

- LM Tip 11: Four Effective Practices During Project Times

- LM Tip 12: Course Middles and Muddles: Souped-Up Conversations That Help Build Community

- LM Tip 13: Using Social Networking Techniques to Build a Learning Community

- LM Tip 14: Experts: A Touch of Spice

LEVERAGING THE POWER OF QUESTIONS

The first three tips delve into techniques and strategies for making the best use of questions. They suggest empowering students with questioning skills as a way of furthering their own critical thinking and offer specific questions that can clarify what your learners are thinking. The third tip extends these questioning techniques into uses in problem formulation and resolutions.

LM Tip 1: Questions and Answers: Upside Down and Inside Out

This tip answers questions such as these:

- What are some alternatives to the questioning model in which instructors ask questions that students answer?

- Why are students hesitant about asking questions?

- How can we make questioning more natural and more open?

Faculty ask questions and students answer questions. Then we know what students know. Right? Well, maybe not. We may want to turn this traditional model upside down and inside out and try some variations on the traditional model of faculty questioning and learner answering. We are now at the point in a course where students have been working with the course content for some time, and you want to know what they know now about the concepts and ideas presented thus far. Remember the principle that concept development is not a one-time event. Research into concepts confirms that students build knowledge over time as a result of a series of experiences. The likelihood that students will be familiar with and conversant with key concepts from the first part of a course is generally low (Hake, 1998, in Wieman, 2008). We know it is important to revisit, discuss, review, and reference the concepts from the first part of the course as students are grappling with the course concepts in the latter part of the course.

One technique to probe the state of each learner's knowledge and skills is to turn the tables and design activities in which students ask questions. These questions then reveal the structure of how and what they know; the downside is that they may ask questions that show they have acquired very little of what we had planned. They may also ask difficult or complex questions that may lead the course conversation in unplanned but needed directions. If that happens, it may mean shifting gears and revising the course to meet where students are.

Student Questioning: Inquiry as a Reflection of Knowledge

We often can't move forward on a problem or learn something new until we can specify what we don't know. By stating what we don't know, we are creating a holding space within the structure of our knowledge base for that new knowledge or concept.

Consider what is required of learners when they are asked to generate questions. They generally need to think, review what they know, and identify what they don't know. Learners are often afraid of asking questions, and with good reason. A question reveals the structure or lack of structure of existing knowledge, links, and relationships. Answering factual questions, for example, is often a simple stimulus-response action, requiring little deep thought or analysis. More complex questions, such as clarifying questions, require tapping into a learner's state of conceptual development and examining the links and relationships that are either formed or beginning to form.

Discussion Boards for Student Questioning

The discussion board in online classes is often used for questions to the students—for example, "What do you know? What do you think you know? How do you know what you know?" And, "What is the basis for your knowledge, and what are the relationships and other links to that knowledge?" We ask students to analyze articles, news reports, Web sites, or podcasts. We ask them to respond to statements and support what they know with references and research. We ask them to research topics specific to their own interest area or region. The students' task is to answer, analyze, and suggest possibilities and strategies for addressing the problem or scenario.

These types of discussion postings are excellent and generally can stimulate sustained conversation and inquiry. But teachers and students like a variety of experiences, so asking students to do the challenging and questioning is a way to provide variety.

Here are a few specific ideas for challenging students to come up with tough questions. Any of these activities could also be used as team activities. The simpler activities could be dyad activities and the more complex activities involving scenarios might be done with a team of three or more students:

- Play a variation of "Stump the Faculty Member" in which the learners generate scenarios or questions for the faculty member. Another strategy is to arrange for an external expert to participate in a discussion and be available for answering questions over a few days to a week. This variation could culminate with a "Stump the Expert" in an interview. Either of these experiences could have a wrap-up activity in a synchronous event using an online classroom.

- Post a statement, article, scenario, or video news clip on the discussion board, and ask students to generate a set of data-gathering questions that they would like to have answered to help address that problem.

- Set up a discussion board that students use to describe problems that they have learned to address and problems that would still stump them. Students can do research over the Web for examples of such problems.

- Establish an open forum for a week. Have the students generate questions and problems related to the readings and challenge others to find the answers.

- Encourage students to question the information they gain from a Web search. Questions that should be encouraged include: "Who asserted this? What are this person's credentials? Who had the opportunity to critique this idea? Who supports and who disagrees with it?" (Bruckman, 2005, p. 36).

So turn the tables, and have students generate questions for themselves. Questioning by students in an online class can become a form of testing and evaluation; it can also build useful critical thinking skills, inquiry skills, and cognitive inquisitiveness about what it is we really do know and even how we came to know something.

LM Tip 2: Three Techniques for Making Your Students' Knowledge Visible

This tip answers questions such as these:

- What are some examples of questions that shine a light on a student's state of knowledge?

- What types of questions show how students are linking new information and core concepts to what they already know?

- How can I develop a questioning mind-set in my students?

- What is concept mapping, and how might this technique make students' knowledge visible?

Getting to know your students' state of knowledge and zones of proximal development is an ongoing part of the teaching experience. Here are three techniques that help stimulate the students to spend reflection time in integrating their listening, watching, and thinking experiences. These techniques also help to balance the input experiences of reading, listening, and exploring with output experiences such as reflecting, questioning, and producing learning products for you to observe and evaluate.

Technique 1: Interviewer-Expert Modeling

As part of a reading, research, or listening assignment, ask your students to develop their own set of two or three questions as if they were interviewing an expert, leader, fellow learners, or you. For example, use a question like this: "What three questions would you ask this expert or leader?"

Developing questions requires the student to pause, reflect, and assimilate knowledge or content. One strategy for using interview questioning is to assign the role of interviewer to some of your students and the role of expert to another group of students. The interviewers' task is to develop the questions and post them to the discussion board, and the "expert" students then have the task of responding to the questions as best they can. If it makes sense, students can switch roles for a follow-up activity.

The questions that students ask and the student responses to questions help you to observe how students are putting things together in their heads and whether they are creating a useful and accessible body of knowledge.

Technique 2: Identifying Patterns, Relationships, and Linkages

Making new knowledge one's own requires linking ideas and new incoming knowledge to existing items and nodes in our physical brain and knowledge structure. These knowledge-integration processes include identification of patterns and relationships, and differentiating the characteristics of one item from another. Here are some questions that might elicit this type of knowledge work in your students:

- What do the ideas in [a chapter, reading, discussion, podcast, or news article] remind you of?

- What relationships are fundamental or inherent in these ideas?

- What patterns, if any, are you observing?

- Are these patterns or relationships present in recent or significant past events or experiences?

Technique 3: Identifying Insights

Part of being a lifelong learner is an awareness of how our minds work, that is, an awareness of when insights happen and when we are aware of discrete and separate data elements and information pieces coming together. Here are a couple of questions that can lead students to think about their own minds and how learning happens.

- What insights or "aha" experiences have you had in the past two weeks?

- What do you know or understand now that you did not have at your intellectual readiness just a couple of weeks ago?

Students' responses to these questions and your affirmation of what they observe can help students develop their metacognitive skills, one of the goals recommended by the How People Learn research analysis. (Bransford, Brown, & Cocking, 2000).

LM Tip 3: Moving Beyond Knowledge Integration to Defining Problems and Finding Solutions

This tip answers questions such as these:

- Getting students to formulate the problem space is itself a difficult task. Are there any models that help in defining problems?

- What are examples of good problem definitions?

- What are examples of effective problem resolution?

- Can the course learning community arrive at any problem resolution over a course duration?

The early stages of inquiry and learning deal with clarifying the issues and challenges of a domain, and researching and exploring ideas. By the time the course has reached the late middle phase, it is time to encourage more complex use of the knowledge, including active and creative use of the content to propose solutions and strategies.

A learner's awareness of and exposure to the content knowledge may be expanding, but the ability to use the knowledge in any meaningful way may not be developing. New knowledge will be lasting only if it is used. Defining problems—getting to what is the question—and then deciding on a way to approach them are steps in the practical inquiry model of Garrison and Vaughan (2008), mentioned in EM Tip 13 on cognitive presence. The steps in practical inquiry help develop students' critical thinking and problem-solving skills. They also provide rich opportunities for mentoring by the faculty member. As a reminder, the four steps in the model are (1) the triggering event where the issue or problem is identified; (2) exploring the problem and gathering relevant information; (3) making sense of the data and defining some possible solutions; and (4) testing the possible solutions.

Defining Problems and Deciding on Resolution Strategies

It is helpful to remind ourselves occasionally that the underlying process of all learning is growth (Dewey, 1916). Part of that learning process requires identifying areas of dissonance and inconsistency in course content, as well as dissonance and inconsistency in other resources and learners' own beliefs.

To translate this process into specific behaviors, it is helpful to look at a recent study that defines cognitive actions and behaviors. Murphy and Manzanares (2006) identified a set of nineteen behaviors that are often used in defining and formulating problems and then working on finding a resolution to a problem. The study identified eleven behaviors common in formulating problems and eight behaviors common to resolving or testing solutions to problems.

Problem Formulation Behaviors

In the analysis of the transcripts of online discussions, Murphy and Manzanares identified eleven behaviors that might be part of formulating or defining a problem. These behaviors can be helpful in providing suggestions and guidance for students as they might proceed in problem formulation. These behaviors are also useful for developing rubrics for assessment or simply as guidelines:

- Agreeing with the problem as presented
- Specifying ways in which the problem may manifest itself
- Redefining a problem within a modified problem space
- Minimizing or denying the problem
- Identifying the extent of the problem
- Identifying the causes of the problem
- Articulating the problem outside the problem space
- Identifying unknowns in knowledge
- Accessing and reporting on sources of information
- Identifying the value of information

Problem Solution Behaviors

Murphy and Manzanares associate three types of high-level cognitive behaviors with problem resolution: identifying solutions, evaluating solutions, and acting on solutions. Here is the list of behaviors they identified used in problem resolution:

- Proposing solutions
- Hypothesizing solutions
- Agreeing with solutions that others propose
- Weighing and comparing alternative solutions
- Critiquing solutions
- Rejecting or eliminating solutions judged unworkable
- Planning to act
- Reaching conclusions or arriving at an understanding of the problem

Developing Problem Solvers and Critical Thinkers

Many reports and books on the state of higher education stress the need for graduates who are good problem solvers and effective team players (Bransford et al., 2000; Business-Higher Education Forum, 2003; Bok, 2007). Becoming familiar with and using these behaviors help students develop an understanding of the processes and the knowledge needed for problem formulation and problem solving. In many cases, the work that is done in formulating and clarifying a problem often takes us halfway to a solution, and this is a valuable lesson as well. Working with others on sustained and thoughtful interaction to clarify and solve problems results in the shared knowledge discovery and co-creation that are also characteristics of a successful learning community.

ASSESSING LEARNING AS YOU GO

Tips LM 4 and 5 offer guidelines and suggestions on providing feedback to learners and the importance of developing good habits of staying in touch with them about how they are doing in the course on discussion posts, assignments, and general participation. Tip LM 6 speaks to some strategies that you can suggest to students to help them develop good online learning habits, and Tip LM 7 suggests ways for personalizing and customizing learning experiences.

LM Tip 4: "Are You Reading My Postings? Do You Know Who I Am?" Simple Rules About Feedback in Online Learning

This tip answers questions such as these:

- How important is feedback?

- How many types of feedback are there?

- When is feedback important?

- Does feedback always have to address an individual's work, or can it address and summarize the work of groups?

Research is showing that mastering the art of giving students feedback in an online course makes a substantive difference in student satisfaction and retention (Kim and Moore, 2005). This study affirms that "students' interaction with classmates and their instructor have an impact on their satisfaction with Web-based courses." In other words, getting feedback right often results in good feelings about a course and, by extension, about an institution.

Here are quick answers to the initial questions:

- How important is feedback? (Vital!)

- How many types of feedback are there? (Lots!)

- When is feedback important? (Almost always!)

- Does feedback always have to address individual's work or can feedback address the work of groups? (Both types can be useful!)

This tip focuses primarily on feedback channels from instructor to learner. Other types of feedback are peer feedback, feedback from students to faculty, automated feedback, and rich feedback. Research on feedback embraces interaction and dialogue between faculty and students as well, including the use of audio.

Feedback is an element of any communication or dialogue. In fact, there is no real communication or dialogue without feedback. Feedback continues or closes a train of thought. The image of a train of thought is very useful because you don't want to interrupt a train that is moving along, and you want to allow flexibility in learning experiences so that learners can occasionally diverge and follow a train of thought or inquiry important to their own knowledge integration.

In online learning, the type of feedback that first comes to mind is that from faculty to student. This is the most important feedback from a student's point of view. Learners want to know what you think about the work they are doing. The most important rules about feedback from faculty to student are simple.

Provide Feedback Early and Often

Providing feedback early in a course can mean providing it even prior to the formal launching of a course when students have just introduced themselves. One technique that works for some faculty is to take the time to mine the information about learners' expected learning goals and purposes for the course and create a reminder that profiles key information about each student, such as the name of the company that he or she is working for and his or her particular area of interest.

That information can help you make connections and suggest relationships to help students connect their goals and purposes to the content and goals of the course. The simple act of taking a personal data element and incorporating it into feedback to the student sends the message that postings are not going into a black hole. Other connections that you might comment on can include shared working environments and similar life experiences, such as a love of baking or biking or having roots in Minneapolis. These observations create connections that build a foundation of community.

Other connections can be made between course content and goals and a student's background experiences and goals. You might observe, "Your background in the XYZ industry may be especially relevant to the rest of the class when we discuss ABC topic in weeks 5 and 6." This observation signals to the student that you have connected with him or her in a unique way. Making these kinds of observations requires first noting the connections between what learners reveal about themselves and what we know of the content and also students' work context. This personalizing and individualizing helps keep students engaged and motivated. Fortunately, everything that a student posts online, such as the getting-acquainted posts, is captured and can be returned to at any time.

Provide Feedback on Assignments When Expected

If you do not tell students when to expect feedback on their assignments, they will expect it within minutes of hitting the send or upload button. So state your general rules for feedback turnaround times clearly and provide regular reminders. For example, you might state that your general rule of thumb for providing feedback on questions is twenty-four hours during the workweek. You might also restate that guideline in the assignment information. For large projects, the turnaround time may be longer; other times you may want to adjust deadlines given your own schedule. This does mean planning assignment deadlines around your own teaching and life patterns and special events. For example, if a week's postings close on Saturday, you will likely need to schedule time on Monday for review and feedback on them. Also, if you know your final course grades are due three days after the end of the final week, you may want to move the submission deadline for a final assignment up a few days or a week to give you adequate time to provide feedback to students. The average turnaround time for larger projects is around seven days, dependent, of course, on other variables, such as the length of a course.

Online learners are particularly concerned about the first cycle of assignments and feedback because it is a benchmark for what will likely follow. They will use the feedback from the first assignment as a marker for what you think about their ideas and how they express themselves. It often determines how much time and effort they put into subsequent assignments. Some of the questions learners often have include: "How closely do you follow the assignment rubrics?" "Do you count timeliness?" "How much do you recognize or expect analysis, innovation, or creativity?" "How much research do you expect?" "Do you notice grammar and spelling?"

Provide Rapid Response to Questions

For general discussion questions, it is important to answer questions promptly or have a system for ensuring that questions are answered in a timely manner. An efficient use of the course site is to encourage an online forum where students can answer questions from other students and that you can monitor for questions that you may need to respond to or supplement a learner's answer. A cautionary note here is to avoid providing expansive feedback in e-mails except for the personal feedback on assignments or lack of progress as might be needed. The course site is the place for discussion and feedback on assignments in general. A good rule of thumb is that if a student asks a question, three to five others are probably also wondering about the same issue but didn't have the courage or take the trouble to ask. Thanking students for their questions is feedback that says, "I value your questions. There's no such thing as a dumb question, so keep the questions coming."

Provide Feedback That Is Personal and Formative for Learning

Providing feedback to learners can be very time-consuming. In an effort to save time, systems with automated or embedded feedback are available, and some of these are proving to be excellent and effective, as in the example of using rich feedback in quizzes in large introductory biology classes (Cooper, Tyser, & Sandheinrich, 2007). Nevertheless, these systems do not provide personal feedback or a relationship with a live faculty member.

The best feedback is personal and formative for learning. Effective feedback assumes that the faculty is reading or listening to a learner and then analyzing and reflecting on his or her work and ideas. Personal feedback means that you are getting to know the student as a person and as a mind, and that you are helping to shape and challenge the learning of the student. This type of feedback creates long-lasting and satisfying links and connections. No wonder that feedback is an element of student satisfaction and loyalty! Many of us have stories where feedback to a student has made all the difference in someone's life or learning. Quality feedback means that you have taken time to know an individual and to care about him or her as a person and a learner.

LM Tip 5: Feedback on Assignments: Being Timely and Efficient

This tip answers questions such as these:

- How do you give feedback in a timely and efficient way to many students?

- Does feedback to students always have to be private? Can I use the open community forum or a faculty blog for summarizing feedback?

- Can I use rubrics to guide learners' self-feedback and peer feedback?

- What is the usual turnaround time for feedback on small assignments? Larger course projects?

An ongoing concern for online faculty is how to give good feedback in a timely and efficient way to many students. The ideas offered in this tip are a good fit for the late middle phase of your course. Note that they focus on feedback on assignments and not the feedback on the weekly discussion postings, which can be more public, open, and part of the course community dialogue. With the use of blogs, wikis, and the shift to a learning community, more and more feedback is shifting to the open community, where it contributes more to the entire community and advances sustained conversation and inquiry. Feedback on assignments is often more private. It is typically part of the faculty-to-learner dialogue and is more personalized and customized to shaping an individual's growth.

Timely Feedback

Always let students know when they will receive feedback on their assignments. You can do this by posting a note in an announcement or however you regularly communicate with the students. The weekly discussion post area or an instructor blog is a good alternative to the announcement tool. The standard time for providing feedback for larger or major assignments is one week. If assignments are stacked, one building on a prior one, as happens in phased project assignments, you may want to provide feedback more quickly. In general, however, one week is a good guideline. Be explicit and reaffirm the feedback time frame with your students. Posting a note about the expected feedback schedule is also an opportunity to change this time frame if your schedule requires such an adjustment.

Also tell students the process by which you will provide feedback. Will you be making embedded comments with detailed observations based on a rubric? Or will you be providing more of a holistic grade and comments? The "how" will likely change with the phases of a project. Will you also be providing summary feedback for the entire group? The new audio tools might be a good way of providing feedback as well.

Using a grading rubric for assignments guides student projects and saves you time. A rubric lays out the criteria for grading and becomes useful as a checklist. You can counsel students to work on the assignment with one eye on the rubric as a way of self-assessment. (Examples of rubrics are provided later in this tip.) A grading and assessment rubric also helps to avoid unwelcome surprises because students generally can predict their own grade from the rubrics.

Part of the assignment direction might include a discussion of the rubric, or you can encourage discussion of the rubric. If the highest points are reserved for papers or presentations that show evidence of research or deep thinking about the issues evidenced by noting patterns, relationships, and insights, are there any examples or models from earlier courses that students might examine? Will the grade include assessment of communication elements, such as writing, grammar, clarity, and citation accuracy?

Conceptual Feedback Reminders

Here are other reminders for feedback to individual students that particularly address content issues:

• • •

- Keep an awareness of a student's particular zone of proximal development front and center. Learners are not ready to learn everything at one time. Our brains process information chunk-by-chunk and piece-by-piece, depending on the knowledge structures already in our heads. As you review the student's assignment and prepare the feedback, structure your comments so that you tap into where the student's ideas are coming from based on what they likely know, and then mold or shape their thinking by reinforcing the strengths of their ideas and guiding them to the next steps of integrating those ideas. Viewing an archive of the student's postings, including a personal archive, so that you refresh your view of the student's state of thought can help in providing effective feedback.

- If you prefer a more holistic approach that combines simple criteria with personal comments, create a simple template for the feedback to use for a short thought paper. This template can consist of two sections: the first part lists the criteria you are using for the assessment, and the second part sets out examples of how you might encourage, challenge, and reinforce the core concepts. Providing thoughtful conceptual feedback can take time. Building a template that includes reinforcing concepts and principles can make this process more efficient.

- This technique can be used with assignments or a long and rich discussion forum. Review the postings or the assignment, and respond with one summative cohesive discussion and analysis, weaving in and making reference to contributions by students by name. This feedback technique has the advantage of taking less time than individual responses to students while creating a useful summary.

- Audio feedback tools offer new strategies for providing substantive feedback to individuals or to the class as a whole. For summary feedback to the class, you can comment back to the public forum or discussion board and highlight the strengths of the work of the learning community. This is an opportunity to reinforce, praise, coach, and direct. You can also do this same type of community feedback in the public discussion board.

Examples of Feedback

Here are two examples: a rubric for a written assignment and a checklist for a short written assignment.

A Rubric for a Written Assignment

In this example, the final paper or project is an individual project and is worth 20 percent of the final grade:

- *The paper/media project is well organized, easy to understand, and well written or produced. The project is presented well, with no major grammatical or spelling errors and citations are in accordance with APA guidelines, as appropriate. The project is the right length for the assignment. It includes a descriptive title, an introduction, a conclusion, and appropriate section headings. 5 points.*

- *The paper/media project is responsive to the content of the assignment. It includes a summary statement of your thoughts, the research, and the rationale supporting your recommendations. 12 points.*

- *All tables and figures presented are thoroughly discussed in the paper/media project. Additional resources are included as appropriate. 3 points.*

A Checklist for a Short Written Assignment

This example of a checklist (adapted from Briskin, 2005) guides students through an evaluation of their own writing:

Directions to the student: Before submitting your assignment, use this checklist to ensure that your assignment is complete. If you find problem areas, revise. This checklist is used in grading your assignment, so you can even self-grade your work.

1. *Do you have a clear introduction? Does it identify the thematic and organizational structure of the essay? Does it indicate the point of view you will argue?*

2. *Have you organized the material effectively, that is, is the sequence of presentation appropriate for the content?*

3. *Is the content presentation user-friendly? Do you "talk to the reader" and indicate clearly the transitions from one section/ argument/theme to the next? Do you use headings and subheadings appropriately?*

4. *Do you make a persuasive argument to support your point of view? Have you considered other points of view?*

5. *Have you used relevant source material? Have you referenced all your sources, including those you have quoted directly and those that you have paraphrased?*

6. *Do you provide a conclusion and summary?*

7. *Have you included a bibliography?*

8. *Have you spell-checked your work and checked it for punctuation and grammar errors?*

9. *Is your assignment the required length?*

LM Tip 6: Reshaping Learning Habits of Online Students

This tip answers questions such as these:

- Are learners natural online learners? How much guidance do they need?

- What types of habits should online learners develop?

- How are online learning strategies different from learning strategies for face-to-face courses?

This tip focuses on strategies to help students adapt their learning habits to an online environment rather than hanging on to the habits they may have used for face-to-face environments.

Some learners enjoy more guidance and introductions to the online environment. Some online programs have tutorials and practice exercises that help students learn the basics of navigating and using the learner-to-learner spaces and applications within a course management system. For example, learners might not be familiar with the norms of discussion postings, such as posting their own responses, and then reading, responding to, and questioning the postings of the other students. Also, students might want to communicate with faculty the same way they communicate with their friends by texting and instant messaging rather than the more formal expression and evidence writing.

Teaching Strategies for Managing Learner Expectations

In an online class, there may well be a small group of students or even a single student who is insistent on a one-on-one dialogue with you. While this dialogue is occasionally necessary, an online community is one in which students open up and talk with other students. Consider these strategies:

- When a student sends you an e-mail with a good question, don't answer the e-mail. Rather, praise the student for the good question, and ask him or her to post it in the student open forum. Leave the question there for twelve to twenty-four hours, and encourage the others to address the question. The value of this strategy is that it involves the entire community.

- If a group of students is not using the open forum area for student questions and conversations, you might want to post a question or observation to get them started.

- Have the group of students name the student question space for themselves. For example, in some courses, this space is called The Cyber Café, The Water Cooler, or simply The Question Place. Use a name that suggests an informal gathering space where students can think aloud, exchange process ideas, and bond and network with each other.

A general set of tips from Roper (2007) that you might share with your students was developed from a survey of graduate students who had completed degrees by taking 80 percent or more of their courses online. Here is the list of those seven tips, some of them with student comments from the survey:

1. Develop a time-management strategy.

   - *"Setting and staying to specific study days was one factor that worked for me. For example, in the evenings, throughout the week, I read my lessons. Saturdays were generally reserved for writing assignments. Saturdays were also devoted to responding to other online postings and building on what I had already submitted."* (p. 63)

2. Make the most of online discussions.

- *"Weekly discussions were best when the teacher encouraged it, especially by having pro versus con discussion, or asking 'why' or 'how' questions." (p. 63)*

3. Use it or lose it. Interpret and restate key concepts while in an active dialogue with other students or apply the concepts in work environment.

4. Make questions useful to your learning.

- *"Going deeper [by asking questions] makes the subject matter more understandable." (p. 64)*

5. Stay motivated. Online courses require additional discipline, so each student needs to identify personal or life goals that keep him or her motivated.

6. Communicate the instruction techniques that work for you.

- *"I liked instructors who logged in often and asked a lot of questions. Not only did this help to increase understanding of the subject, but it gave people the opportunity for class participation." (p. 64)*

7. Make connections with fellow students.

- *"The experience was enriched greatly by the relationships and interaction with my fellow students." (p. 64)*

Background

Keep in mind the "designing by threes" principle (Boettcher, 2009) for guiding the design of an online course that encourages variety in the size of groups, the types of interactions, and the types of content resources. Designing for a balanced dialogue (Pelikan, 1992; Moore, 1997) is one of those principles. Strive to achieve a balance somewhere roughly approaching the following: one-third of the course dialogue is between faculty and learner, one-third is between students, and one-third is between the student and course resources (readings, writings, and other resources). The faculty-to-student dialogue somewhat depends on how much the faculty member is writing, summarizing, and providing feedback to students. Remember that the teaching presence combines the prepared design course materials that direct learning experiences and the teaching presence for both the community and learners that occur as the course progresses.

As we develop more experience and even better online tools and as we adjust to learners' goals, the percentage of dialogue from faculty to learner may decrease even more as faculty assume more habits of facilitation and mentoring. One well-known adult learning educator, Elizabeth Burge (2008), follows the 80/20 rule: students are responsible for 80 percent of the dialogue, and the instructor owns only 20 percent of the dialogue. The particular percentage is not as important as working to achieve a balance of dialogue, so that the faculty member is not the one on center stage and doing the talking. If what the faculty member is saying is going to have any impact on the students' knowledge structures, learners must be actively processing the ideas. Otherwise the faculty member may be talking, but no one is listening.

The literature review and discussion in Kim and Moore's research study (2005) grounds the effectiveness of a balanced dialogue in Vygotsky's philosophy and the theory that "learning is a social activity that involves interaction with the instructor and among students." In their conclusion, the authors encourage the move to "self-regulated and social learning activities" and for "innovative instructional activities that encourage student engagement and ownership of the learning process."

So while we as faculty need to encourage learner-to-learner interaction, we need to continue to improve our instructional strategies to make that interaction constructive and dynamic.

PROJECT WORK PRACTICES

Projects are learners' opportunity to integrate and consolidate their knowledge and make it their own. Earlier tips focused on setting up groups for projects and also on designing the project so that it was a good fit for learners. One of the tips in this set provides hints on what an instructor can do to assist learners with their projects and provides ideas for helping learners get "unstuck" as we often do. Projects are by their very nature somewhat messy, often requiring iterations and revisions and involving false starts. Acknowledging the messiness of projects from the start helps everyone. One of the tips includes another rubric; another gathers together four best practices during course project time. Many of these ideas work for all types of course projects, individual and group.

LM Tip 7: Customizing and Personalizing Learning

This tip answers questions such as these:

- How much flexibility for student choice and personalization should I include in course project requirements?

- What are the three components of a task model for a course project?

While one of us was teaching a faculty workshop celebrating ten years of a faculty support center, a faculty in charge of an online master's degree program in nursing administration had a question regarding teams. His program had been online for almost five years and was doing very well, but he was looking for ideas on the design of team projects. One of the courses had a significant team project with the students working in groups of five. The feedback from the students was that the team project didn't work well. Some of the problems centered on communication challenges and how difficult it was to coordinate the team across distance, work, and family responsibilities; other problems centered on appropriate sharing of roles and responsibilities; still others focused on the choice of topics that didn't quite fit. And then of course there is the ever-present challenge of team evaluations.

Guidelines for Developing Project Requirements

Have you faced similar quandaries? How might you change project requirements to accommodate learners' interests and learning conditions while still respecting the performance goals of a course? Here are some guidelines and hints for developing project requirements with built-in flexibility.

Reduce the Number of Team Members or Vary the Size of the Teams

Striving for consistency and fairness is important, but there is no reason that all groups need to be the same size. Projects can usually be adapted quite easily to varying sizes, and the learners can be responsible for proposing how they will do that. So the default project team size might be three or four learners, but those who want to do projects in groups of two or five, or even alone, can propose a revised project for approval.

One good place to communicate flexibility regarding team sizes is in the project overview: your document that provides an overview of the course project, including your purpose and learning goals for the project, dates, and reporting processes. As part of this project overview, you can indicate flexibility in the team size, giving students the responsibility of preparing a revised project team for approval by a specified date—probably no later than the early one-third of the course. Recall that your directions to the students are a key component of your teaching presence and that it is hard to be overly explicit about processes and requirements.

Broaden the List of Possible Topics for the Project

Most online learners are working adults and have preferences and interests that influence their choice of project and commitment to course requirements. Just as providing flexibility in team size is important, so is flexibility in the choice of a topic. Early in the course, even in the first two weeks, focus the students on choosing a topic and developing a proposal for their course project. Another option is to set up a team blog or wiki and have the students post their project proposals there. Having students post in a public forum also makes it possible to invite comments and recommendations from the other students.

For faculty, the most important reason for having a course project is that a project is a focused and complex type of learning experience that engages students in the course content, helping them to consolidate concepts and make meaningful connections, aiding in their achieving course performance goals. A course project is also a primary tool for assessing online learning because high-stakes proctored tests are not generally part of an assessment plan for online courses.

For students, the most important part of a project (other than meeting course requirements) is doing something that will be meaningful to them in their current position or future ones. A student who is working on a project that is meaningful and relevant usually willingly and enthusiastically expands the time and energy invested in it. For employers who are providing tuition aid, project choices that have positive and visible ripple effects into the workplace also provide a win-win scenario, creating a closer relationship with a program or institution.

Be Explicit About the Task Model for a Course Project

Task model is a term that describes three variables of any assessment task: (1) the key features of the task, such as the content area and the level of difficulty or complexity, (2) the directions provided to the learner, and (3) the expected work product that "allows one to observe the students' performance" (Gibson, 2003). Effective task models describe the expected work product in general terms, leaving room for learners to customize and personalize learning by selecting how and by what means they will complete the work product. Part of the task model requires that directions be clear and explicit about the need for an effective and professional end product but still providing flexibility.

Complement the Task Model Guidelines with Process Guidelines

Course projects have many purposes relating to content acquisition and integration, but another important goal is developing the cross-functional skills of project planning, teamwork, and project management. Thus, providing guidelines and coaching for the process of completing projects is as important as the directions and explicit guidance on the task model for the project. It is the process model that is often repeatable long after the class has concluded.

Encourage Course Projects That Combine Challenge, Confidence, and Interest

Vygotsky's zone of proximal development is a good principle to guide us in how flexible we might want to be in the design of course projects. Recall that Vygotsky's zone of proximal development defines the space that the learner is ready to develop into useful and independent knowledge and skill. Ideally, if the project task model is sufficiently flexible, learners can define and select a project that fits their personal zone of proximal development. Because this zone of learning readiness combines a confidence level as well as a challenge level, learners naturally gravitate to a project that more or less fits their learning needs. A key role of the faculty mentor is to ensure a good choice and guide learners to a project fit that combines challenge and know-how. Time spent ensuring this fit is well worth it.

Guiding Questions for Project Work in Courses

To determine whether a project is a good fit, ask if the learners are doing more for the teacher or for themselves and whether the student cares enough about the work to make a significant investment in it. These questions help to balance the trade-off between making the work a product that demonstrates what students have learned and a product that will be of lasting value to them (Gibson, 2006).

The process of fitting the project to the learners and to the course goals and content simultaneously takes time and energy, but the result is committed, enthusiastic, and customized learning that can also be shared with the other students.

Designing for Discovery and Discernment

In closing, here is a quote that we would like to share: "The skills required by knowledge-based economies are not absorption and recall, but discovery and discernment" (Weigel, 2005). Designing projects that fit the learners can help build these skills.

LM Tip 8: Managing and Facilitating Group Projects

This tip answers questions such as these:

- What are some simple guidelines for facilitating group projects to ensure that all students contribute to the project?

- How many project checkpoints are recommended?

- What communication and presentation tools work well for students when working on projects? Project wikis, blogs, forums, discussion areas, Google Docs, or something else?

- What should I do if teams aren't working well together?

This tip provides suggestions for matching the appropriate tools for different stages of group projects and techniques for helping to ensure that students stay on schedule. If students will work in groups on a project, set up a group space online within the CMS as a place for students to share ideas, resources, and drafts of their projects. This group space might be a blog, a wiki, or a simple discussion forum. If you have offered the flexibility of learners to do a project on their own, it is still recommended that the learner have a personal space such as a blog or discussion space for capturing and tracking project progress. Learners can then invite classmates to this project space for comments, suggestions, and brainstorming.

Monitoring and Guiding Group Projects

Once work on a project has begun, check regularly with each project team to see that everyone is participating and that the project is moving along. Here are a few things you can do to support the team process, and they work as well for individual projects:

- Establish a minimum of three checkpoints on all projects. The first checkpoint is a project proposal that describes its goals and purposes; the second is a project design or definition that serves as a blueprint for the project plus a set of initial or probable resources for the project; and the final is the project paper or presentation. Other useful checkpoint products might be a team task schedule, an ongoing summary of discussions and decisions, and an outline of final project components.

- Monitor the team project space, and make comments or suggestions as appropriate, such as indicating that the group seems to be proceeding appropriately. If little progress is evident, you can ask for a progress report on what questions they might have or hold a conference call or live classroom meeting. The team can then discuss how the work is proceeding and if they are encountering any barriers or have any questions. Also, there are useful team tools within most course management systems that enable you to monitor and track team participation and activity, such as those that track discussion participation in group areas.

- Provide reminders of the schedule using a milestones approach—for example: "We are now halfway through the time allotted for the project, so you should have completed the following …" Or, "The project proposal or design is due by Friday of next week, so you should have met with your team and have a draft of your sections under way." Or, "If you would like feedback at this time, let's meet in the open forum space."

One of the principles for facilitating online projects is to provide enough instructor presence to remind team members that their activities and progress are not invisible to you and yet not provide so much presence that the project shifts from being team led to instructor led. You want to provide sufficient help so that the students are successful, but not more help and presence than their level of maturity and experience suggests is needed.

It is easy for students to get lost in the process of group work, especially in larger groups. One team member could be the project or group manager; this person directs the project and monitors that each student is working on his or her particular role or responsibility and doesn't get lost. This is a good leadership role.

Communication and Presentation Tools

Online asynchronous teamwork can bog a group down because everyone tends to wait for everyone else to do something. Synchronous tools are particularly useful in the early stages of a project when groups need to reach consensus as quickly as possible about project content and tasks. Low-tech conference calls sometimes can be the best tool for group formation and task negotiations. The faster the communication mode, the better for initial team communication. Synchronous communication tools such as the telephone, online conferencing tools such as Skype (www.skype.com), and Google Gmail voice and video chat (www.google.com/talk/) are free, easy to use, and work on both Macs and PCs.

Once the team has organized itself, asynchronous tools such as the discussion board forums, wikis, and blogs are useful for sharing progress and resources, collaborative writing, and critical reviews by team members and other teams. Students can also use Google Docs as preliminary work sharing spaces for Word, spreadsheets, and presentations (www.google.com/educators/p_apps.html).

Many of these tools are free and readily accessible. Students may have their favorite tools to use as well: they may want to chat, Twitter, or instant message. Basically students should be given the task and then left to determine which communication tools work best for them. Provide help and suggestions as needed or requested.

When learners are ready for reviews of their proposals for final projects before presenting projects to the larger group, asynchronous tools work well so that everyone in the course has an opportunity to review the projects. Group project presentations can be synchronous with the use of live classrooms or a combination of tools such as Audacity and Skype or other conferencing tools.

Managing Groups: Additional Thoughts

When problems arise with one of the project groups, and the law of averages pretty much ensures this will happen, a set of guidelines for students as to how to proceed will be useful. The usual rule of thumb is that the problems are best resolved within the group itself. The faculty member should be reserved for the very difficult problems that the group cannot resolve itself. Faculty, of course, can be asked general questions to help guide the students as they work through difficulties, but the best outcome is for the group to resolve its problems. A good resource for both faculty and students working within teams is *Building Blocks for Teams* from the Teaching and Learning with Technology Group at Penn State (2001–2005). You can post this resource in the same folder or space as the group project directions and rubrics. Each of the topics in the frequently asked questions on this resource is a link to extended discussions. Here is a sampling of some of the questions and answers:

- How can we work together without wasting time? *Place reasonable limits on planning and brainstorming activities, define tasks and maintain a central archive and checklist.*

- How can we deal with group conflict? *Try to make collective decisions professionally and democratically.*

- What do we do if a group member is not contributing? *Deliberately take turns presenting ideas or updates.*

- What happens if we don't get along? *The response is that disagreement is common, but you don't want it to escalate.* This question then links to a Web page with conflict resolution tips.

Another good resource on collaborative group work is at the University of Guelph Learning Services site. This resource, *Fast Facts: Group Work*, has a useful Getting Started section that provides a list of questions ensuring that the group understands the assignment. Here are a few of those questions:

- *Are you familiar with the requirements of the format(s) or will you need support, resources, or instruction?*
- *What avenues of support are available to you?*
- *Are the necessary resources readily available or should you secure them as soon as possible?*
- *What criteria will be used to assess your work?*
- *What are the main components of the project?*

The resources for remotely collaborating continue to improve in both functionality and ease of use. The best advice for selecting technology tools today is to pick a tool that is available and works, and simply go with it. Much time can be wasted making decisions concerning virtually identical tools. The discipline and study of group processes also is changing rapidly. Keep in mind that the option of allowing students to work in teams of different sizes or as individuals sometimes is the best way of handling difficult situations while keeping an eye on the required learning outcomes and course performance goals.

LM Tip 9: Assessing Group Projects

This tip answers questions such as these:

- How do I assess group projects?
- Is there a way to have students participate in the review and grading of projects?

This tip focuses on strategies for assessing group projects. A common thread among all projects, whether individual or group, is that projects are powerful and satisfying teaching and learning experiences. They provide an opportunity for students to customize course performance goals to their particular life and work goals, making the learning experience meaningful and satisfying. Papers, presentations, interviews, podcasts, talk shows, and other projects also make students' thinking and learning visible. They require students to link the new content to their existing knowledge, creating a larger networked knowledge structure.

Techniques for Assessing Group Projects

Online group projects can be assessed in much the same way that they are in the classroom-based learning environment. However, two recommendations can make a huge difference. One is to assess both the process and the final product. The process includes the interim milestones such as a project proposal milestone and the project design. Assessment of these interim stages mirrors professional processes more closely and provides an opportunity for peer review (Moallem, 2005). Interim reviews thus become part of the dialogue of the learning community as a whole, and comments tap into the collective thinking and expertise of the group. The processes in the planning and the execution of the project then become part of the course content and goals.

The most useful tool in assessing group projects is the project grading rubric that you develop at the same time that you create and design the task model for the project. By referring to the rubric in your reviews and comments to the students, you help to ensure students' awareness and understanding and reduce unpleasant surprises. The rubrics used for discussion postings are a good place to start when developing rubrics for projects. Simple scales of four to five points or one to four levels are often most workable. Here are some of the criteria areas that you may want to consider; they include metrics for both the processes of teamwork and the project, as well as the completed product:

- The process of how the team worked. For example, how effective were the team members in participating in group formation, task definition and progress, and finished product? This is the classic process assessment.

- The end product. How well did the team execute the design for the project, and how well did the project achieve the intended goals and objectives? Criteria such as innovativeness, thoroughness, readiness for action, and professionalism might be considered.

- The presentation of the product to the larger group. Encourage the students to branch into a varied set of presentation techniques that might feature interviews, multimedia news releases as well as Web sites.

- Participation in the peer reviews and evaluations of the product and responsiveness to comments.

A useful resource for more detail about assessing group projects is the Assessing Group Work Web site at the Center for the Study of Higher Education at the University of Melbourne, Australia (http://www.ucd.ie/teaching/goodPracticeAssessment_sub/groupWork.html).

More About Peer Reviews by Students

An effective tool for encouraging effective and appropriate participation in teams is a peer review process. Ideally, this is designed as an integral step in the project. It can be most useful while the project is still in the proposal or design phase. Peer review of the final project also helps with the final assessment and grading of the students from both the process and the product perspectives. Involving students in the process of review increases networking and collaboration among them and deepens the peer-to-peer dialogue that contributes to a vibrant learning community. Students often need coaching in the process of doing peer reviews, but the skills of evaluation and honest and fair review of work are valuable cross-functional skills.

Exhibit 9.1 provides a sample peer assessment form that you may wish to adapt to the nature of the particular project in your course.

EXHIBIT 9.1

Team Member Evaluation Form

Team member name:

Using your best, objective, and fair professional analysis, complete the following evaluation form concerning your team member's performance on your team project.

1. The LEVEL of effort this team member gave
   toward the project was …

   Below Expectation   Met Expectation   Above Expectation

2. The QUALITY of that effort was …

   Below Expectation   Met Expectation   Above Expectation

3. The INPUT this team member contributed to
   the team discussions was …

   Below Expectation   Met Expectation   Above Expectation

4. How would you rate this team member's level
   of participation?

   Below Expectation   Met Expectation   Above Expectation

5. How would you rate this team member's level
   of time on the project?

   Below Expectation   Met Expectation   Above Expectation

6. This team member participated in team
   meetings and work:

   Below Expectations   As Expected

7. This team member met team deadlines:

   Below Expectations   As Expected

8. How would you rate this team member's
   OVERALL work and contribution to this
   project?

   Below Group Grade   Same as Group Grade   Above Group Grade

9. Additional comments regarding this team
   member's work on this presentation:

Each member should submit a form for every team member as well as themselves. Question 8 is really the crucial question. Sometimes a team member may be disgruntled about a particular behavior of a teammate but overall still rates the team member as having done a good job. It's only in those cases that the team feels that the grade should be lowered that it is good to consider doing so.

Another good starting point is the Web site at University College/Dublin Centre for Teaching and Learning, particularly the section providing different ways of assessing group work (http://www.ucd.ie/teaching/goodPracticeAssessment_sub/other_forms.html). Here is a sampling of strategies.

- *All students get the same mark for the product of the group and then peers assess contributions to process out of an additional ten marks, e.g. $a = 23 + 9, b = 23 + 4, c = 23 + 7$.*

- *All students get the same mark for original task and then get different marks for an additional or separate task or responsibility, or for their individual contribution to a presentation event.*

The major challenge in searching out good resources in the assessment area is to avoid being overwhelmed. So the best strategy is to start with one or two good sites and go from there. For example, you may want to bookmark the University College/Dublin Centre for Teaching and Learning site and explore the related areas on teaching and learning. One other good starting point for assessing group work is *Assessing Group Tasks* (Isaacs, 2002) at the University of Queensland. This document addresses topics such as

- When should group tasks be assessed?

- Best practices in the assessment of group tasks

- Examples and theory

- Assigning marks to individuals versus the group as a whole

- Self and peer assessment

- Freeloading and plagiarism

- The logistics of forming groups

The most comprehensive of all sites on assessment is the *Internet Resources for Higher Education Outcomes Assessment* Web site, at North Carolina State University (http://www2.acs.ncsu.edu/UPA/assmt/resource.htm). It currently contains about a thousand links, including about 375 college and university assessment sites.

LM Tip 10: A Rubric for Analyzing Critical Thinking

This tip answers questions such as these:

- What are the stages of critical thinking skills?

- Is there a rubric for critical thinking skills?

- How can I create instructions for assignments that encourage critical thinking skills?

Earlier tips focused on discussion questions that invite reflection and responses from students. Every success is often followed by another challenge. If you have developed a wonderfully effective post and the students start responding thoughtfully and expansively, your existing rubric for analyzing the discussions might not be as robust as you would like it to be.

The rubric set out here has been custom-designed for analyzing critical thinking responses. You may find it valuable if you are ready to refine an existing rubric or would like a more robust rubric for some course assignments.

The Critical Thinking Rubric

This critical thinking rubric, Guide to Rating Critical and Integrative Thinking, is the result of a multiyear research project at Washington State University. (Many of the background and application materials are available at wsuctproject.wsu.edu/.) This rubric defines these seven criteria for evaluating a learner's progress in developing critical thinking skills:

1. Identifies, summarizes (and appropriately reformulates) the problem, question, or issue

2. Identifies and considers the influence of context and assumptions

3. Develops, presents, and communicates his or her own perspective, hypothesis, or position

4. Presents, assesses, and analyzes appropriate supporting data/ evidence

5. Integrates issue using other (disciplinary) perspectives and positions

6. Identifies and assesses conclusions, implications, and consequences

7. Communicates effectively

These are the desired critical thinking skills for learners and are independent of any particular discipline or course of study. With little adaptation, you can use some or all of these criteria to develop rubrics and instructions for assignments. You can include examples from the rubric in

TABLE 9.1

Examples of Critical Thinking Criterion 5: Integrates Issue Using Other Perspectives and Positions

Stage 1: *Emerging* critical thinking
- Deals with a single perspective and fails to discuss others' perspectives.
- Adopts a single idea or limited ideas with little question. If more than one idea is presented, alternatives are not integrated.

Stage 2: *Developing* critical thinking
- Begins to relate alternative views to qualify analysis.

Stage 3: *Mastering* critical thinking
- Addresses others' perspectives and additional diverse perspectives drawn from outside information to qualify analysis.
- Integrates own and others' ideas in a complex process of judgment and justification. Clearly justifies own view while respecting views of others.

Source: Washington State University (2006).

your teaching instructions and grading rubrics to make your expectations to the students clear and explicit.

Emerging, Developing, and Mastering of Critical Thinking

This rubric goes beyond listing criteria: it expands each criterion and lists examples of the types of evidence pointing to three stages of critical thinking skills: emerging, developing, and mastering. These example statements can be used to measure the maturity of a student's critical thinking skills. Table 9.1 shows examples of these three stages for critical thinking criterion 5.

You may also want to review CB Tip 8, which discusses the characteristics of Socratic questioning. The web site of the Center for Critical Thinking and Moral Critique (www.criticalthinking.org) is another excellent resource. This site is supported by a cross-disciplinary group that promotes excellence in thinking and provides resources to help educators improve their instruction in critical thinking.

LM Tip 11: Four Effective Practices During Project Time

This tip answers questions such as these:

- What types of support do students most value during project time?

- How flexible should the projects be in customizing and personalizing them to learners' interests?

- How closely should an instructor monitor project progress?

As a course reaches the halfway point and beyond, work on projects, papers, and presentations picks up steam. Project time for students can be a bit stressful as course work shifts a balance from receptive or exploring work to creative, productive work. And of course learners are always balancing work, life, and learning responsibilities. This is a time to be sure to stay in close touch with your students. A few learners always need additional support and encouragement at this time.

This is a good time to stop and check yourself on four best practices to guide you and your students through these creative project and team-work experiences.

Help Learners Get Unstuck on Projects

The most difficult part of many learning tasks is getting started. Large projects require skill at planning, segmenting, and organizing. Finding planning and collaborative time with other busy people can also present barriers. For working adults and professionals who often turn to their course work in fifteen- to thirty-minute segments (listening to podcasts while jogging, reading while waiting for children or between appointments), finding time to do project work that requires a dedicated effort can be a challenge. One of us used to enjoy flying because it offered the best uninterrupted thinking time.

One best practice during project time focuses on techniques for supporting and encouraging students during this time. A technique recently popularized in the business arena (Allen, 2002) is being explicit about answering the question: "What is your next step? And then what is the next step after that?" Often students find that their next step is something they can do while doing other things and that one of their next steps is planning for learning time, getting access to a resource, or arranging a meeting.

Another technique for getting unstuck on getting started is described in the title of a book by Brian Tracy (2007): *Eat That Frog! 21 Great Ways to Stop Procrastinating and Get More Done in Less Time!* The message behind this book is, "If you eat a live frog first thing each morning you'll have the satisfaction of knowing it's probably the worst thing you'll do all day." We're not certain we agree with that, but certainly finding a way to get started on a complex task is good to do first thing in the morning if you can. A good alternative is putting it on the top of your "learning time" list. In fact, when starting a project, Tracy recommends building a plan of all the steps in the projects and then organizing them by priority and sequence. Sometimes doing this plan is the worst "frog" of all, but it can make the difference in getting started well.

Here are a few more ideas to help students get started on projects or get unstuck if they have made a good start:

- Ask students to share their questions, difficulties, and successes with their ongoing papers and projects. Sometimes they answer their own questions once they formulate them.

- Ask your students what their next one, two, or three steps on their project are.

- Ask how their teams are working, what they are working on now, and what they plan on doing next. This is a good time to reinforce the feeling of a learning community. Encourage the teams to share templates, process tools, and good ideas. The goal is for everyone in the learning community to succeed.

- Remind students about the resources, tools, processes, and rubrics that you developed to guide them through the tasks. As they share what helps them, you can expand that set of resources for future students.

- Encourage learners to customize and personalize their projects.

We have discussed the three types of content in a course: prepackaged authoritative content (books, resources, tools), director-mentor faculty teaching presence content that guides and supports learners through the course, and performance content that is generated by the learners during the process of learning.

An ideal time to personalize and customize the performance content so that it is maximally useful and of most interest to learners is when they are working on projects. Encouraging them to select and do learning tasks that are of most interest and use to them is also healthy because it reduces their level of anxiety about how much time they are spending on their course work.

Coach Learners on Personalizing Their Projects

If you have used a multiphase approach of proposal and design steps in the project, you have a built-in opportunity to coach students to be wise about their selection of their project.

Defining projects and papers so they can be most useful to an individual and to a larger, potentially external group can be an excellent community brainstorming activity. Peer review of proposals also means open and public discussion about how best to personalize and customize a project. Once students have identified a project that meets these characteristics, they may find it useful to post or otherwise share in a discussion forum why they have made the selection and how they feel it will be useful to them. This can have the ripple effect of reminding the other learners in the community about potential applications that they may not have thought about.

Ask Learners to Post Progress Reports or Updates

This best practice is closely linked to the technique of having the learners identify their next step. As they move on to planning out a project, creating a task list, finding a needed or seminal resource, or completing one of the steps in an assignment, openly sharing that success is a way to build community. As they share their completed steps and identify their next steps, other students often praise, encourage, and suggest, building a stronger network of learners. One habit that I (Judith) have developed over the years is to always pause before putting a project away, whether it is an article, chapter, or teaching or quilting project, and make some notes about my next steps. When I return to the project, sometimes after a significant delay, my next step is right there for me. This is not foolproof, but it works more often than not and always saves time. In fact, sometimes my subconscious has been working on it in my absence.

Communicate Your Availability and Schedule

Be sure to continue your use of the announcement tool and other communication channels to let students know your schedule. Another good strategy is to schedule open question-and-answer times by phone, e-mail, chat, or live classroom. Students then can feel comfortable about contacting you during those times, knowing that they are not intruding on your personal time.

Students may be so overwhelmed that they may not even be able to frame questions with ease, but setting a time and a place to talk some ideas through might work for them. Setting times and places where you will be more or less available is comforting even if learners do not make use of them. Also, be sure to be present on the discussion board. Students do want to hear your expert perspective while exploring the perspectives of the other students.

COMMUNITY EMPOWERMENT AND SOCIAL NETWORKING

These next two tips on community empowerment and social networking highlight some of the networking and social learning power that is possible with discussion boards, blogs, and wikis. The last tip for the late middle describes the value that experts can bring to a course experience and hints on making it happen.

LM Tip 12: Course Middles and Muddles: Souped-Up Conversations That Help Build Community

This tip answers questions such as these:

- How can you energize your learners in the late middle?
- What are some other strategies for encouraging challenging questions and substantive knowledge building?

It is easy to get bogged down in the middle of courses. Lots of things might be going on, but you may not feel as if it represents real learning, or the amount of interaction and discussion can be underwhelming and you may feel that everyone is just going through the motions. How can you energize your learners at this time? Here are three ideas for stirring up your course middles.

Team Up for Course Discussions for a Week

Team your students into groups of two for one discussion week. Working in a pair means that the students will collaborate and discuss a topic in more depth. To do this, create a set of three or four open-ended questions for the week, and have each team select a topic to explore for three to five days. Then have the students post the results of their collaboration by Friday of that week. This technique results in a set of more elaborate postings than usual. For the next week, select one or more of those threads for the entire class to respond to and extend. These conversations typically result in a more sustained conversation and an in-depth focus on a topic of interest in the course.

Why do this? One of the more difficult behaviors to cultivate in students is effectively responding to their peers' comments. From a student's perspective, it is more efficient and takes less time to just prepare his or her own post and then exit the online classroom. This exercise structures a learning task that requires students to respond, comment on, and analyze the comments and responses of their peers.

In the three-stage model of building community (Brown, 2001), stage 2 requires a feeling of "sharedness." Brown found that that feeling of having shared an experience in online classes often follows a "long, thoughtful, threaded discussion on a subject of importance after which participants felt both personal satisfaction and kinship." It is this type of discussion that we want to be striving to have students participate in. And this often does take time. Being patient and providing time for exploration and even confusion is sometimes needed.

Make Time for Learners to Develop the Tough Questions

Sometimes the most difficult cognitive work is figuring out what the question is, and this frequently happens as we approach the middle and muddled part of a course. By this point, students' heads are "getting filled up to overflowing," but they don't know what they know or don't know. There's a lot of stuff in their minds, but no accessible framework or set of relationships that helps it all come together to make sense. All students may know that they have covered a lot of material and the multiple-choice questions weren't too hard. But what can they do with this knowledge they have been busily acquiring?

This is a good time to challenge the students to propose tough questions for the faculty member. Think of this as a variation of the "Stump the Chump" challenge from NPR's radio program *Car Talk*. Set up a time for a synchronous, or almost synchronous, class discussion thread or perhaps a session in the interactive classroom and have students submit questions to see if they can either stump each other or stump the faculty member or teaching assistant. This can be a lively experience, highlighting what they know, what they don't know, and what they might like to know or be able to do.

Here are a few additional variations on this theme of having students generate difficult questions:

- Post a statement, article, scenario, or video news clip on the discussion board and ask students to generate a set of data-gathering questions that they would like to have answered to help address that problem.

- Set up a discussion board for students to describe problems that now seem easy and problems that still stump them.

- Establish an open forum, blog, or wiki for a week, and have the students generate questions and problems related to the readings. Or set up a space at Flickr or VoiceThread for students to submit photos that might help in solving a problem or answering a question.

- Encourage students to question the information from a Web search. They might ask, "Who asserted this?" "What are this person's credentials?" "Who had the opportunity to critique this idea?" "Who supports and who disagrees with it?" (Bruckman, 2005, p. 36).

Construct a Round-Robin of Knowledge Construction Tasks

Another way of encouraging substantive knowledge building is to design a learning experience using the five phases of knowledge construction from the interaction analysis model by Gunawardena, Lowe, and Anderson (1997). The five phases that follow combine a description of both the task and the skills needed in that model to do the task:

- Sharing/comparing of information (researcher, data gatherer)

- Discovering/exploring of dissonance or inconsistency among ideas, concepts, or statements (analyst)

- Negotiation of meaning and co-constructing of knowledge (interpreter)

- Testing and modifying of proposed synthesis or co-construction (proposer)

- Agreeing on final statement and applications of newly constructed meaning or insights (consensus builder)

This can be a good team project. A team of two or three learners can choose a particular problem, scenario, or case to examine and then assume roles as suggested by the knowledge construction model. The end goal includes both the end product of a set of recommendations as well as the metacognitive awareness of the process of knowledge builder.

LM Tip 13: Using Social Networking Techniques to Build a Learning Community

This tip answers questions such as these:

- What are social networking tools?

- How can social networking tools help build community in my course?

- What performance goals can blogs, wikis, and other social networking tools help learners to achieve?

Social networking tools are Web applications that make it easy to share and interact with others online. Some of the most popular sites are Facebook and LinkedIn, photo and video sites like Flickr and YouTube, and commercial sites like Amazon.com and eBay.com.

These sites use applications that characterize what is often called Web 2.0 because they go beyond the first wave of Web applications that mostly just displayed and organized data. These tools are creating a new communications milieu that you and your learners are most likely already using with family, colleagues, and friends.

This means that learners of almost every age are already accustomed to the Web 2.0 environment, which makes it easy to create, share, and stay in touch with hundreds of others. The online learning environment will seem foreign and strange if we do not integrate some of these same social networking techniques into our courses.

Social Networking Pedagogical Strategy with Individual Course Projects

This pedagogical strategy incorporates a social networking sense and works well with course projects, personal or course blogs, or other medium to complex assignments. This strategy can use either the discussion board or a blog tool as its base:

1. Create a personal project blog or discussion board area for each student.

2. Each student posts a project topic or abstract as the first proposed phase of a course project. This is another good pedagogical strategy of phasing course projects to ensure timely progress and personal responsibility.

3. Other students, from a designated small group or the class as a whole, review the project abstract and add comments, ideas, and suggestions and offer additional resources, adaptations, or cautions. This is similar to the comment and tagging features of the photo-sharing sites such as Flickr or blogs of all types. All comments become part of an individual project as it evolves.

4. Each student responds and makes changes and tweaks to the project as appropriate.

5. The faculty member blogs and comments on the project progress and the learners' input. This can be private or public or a combination of both.

6. Each student integrates the ideas and suggestions as appropriate into his or her project. Each also posts regular notes that update the project status similar to the "what I am doing now status" feature on Facebook. This status can be something as simple as, "I am researching some of

the suggestions this week," or "I am not making much progress right now."

7. Each student posts the completed project as required by the course assignment.

8. Each student's group or class members then review or see the final product and again make comments or evaluations.

This strategy can work for individuals or small groups. The cycle of posting and commenting is repeated depending on the number of project phases or complexity of the project. Cycles of posting and commenting shift the project from being the sole production by one student to a collaborative group project.

Tweaks and Comments on Encouraging a Social Networking Environment

Here are a few observations about using blogs, wikis, journals, and discussion boards for building community:

- Using a blog for project planning and progress is almost like a student's private journal in that it is individually "owned" and created by one student. It is the student's own place, similar to one's own space in Facebook. But it is social because it can be open for review, comment, and adaptation. The student can invite and respond to comments and suggestions. With this type of blog project, there is an end product—a project report, paper, or presentation of some ilk—just as with a wiki.

- This strategy shares characteristics of a journal in that it is authored over time and serves to track and record activities and progress.

- It is also like a blog or a discussion board in that it is organized chronologically from first posting to most recent.

- It shares with blogs, wikis, and discussion boards the ability to include media of all types, such as pictures, video, text, and Web links.

Incorporating social networking into your course encourages interaction and the building of community. It is likely that learners are comfortable with this type of interaction and pleased that it is part of their learning environment as well. Social networking sites encourage regular, daily, and even hourly checking in and commenting and seeing where everyone is and what they are doing and thinking. This can be helpful with project work. Sharing where they are in a project and what they are thinking of doing next encourages awareness of their own thinking and working strategies.

The cycles of comments and responses also promote community because students no longer focus solely on their projects. Through their review and support of their fellow learners, they develop ownership and critical thinking about many of the other projects.

No doubt there are more adjustments to a social networking strategy, but the best part of this approach is the social aspect of learning and creativity that it promotes. It provides a way to sense an individual and his or her particular knowledge and skill development for grading and assessment purposes.

Essential Features of Web 2.0 Tools: Interconnectivity and Interactivity

One of the most fundamental truths about learning is that it is active, specific, and internal to the learner. Web 2.0 tools empower learners to comment on and develop their own work and build on the work of peers and experts. These tools enable real-time and asynchronous collaboration and encourage, stimulate, and motivate learners to create new content and support and challenge each other in the process.

Most CMSs now have blog and wiki and voice tools as part of their systems. Be sure to select and try one tool to see how it can used for your course performance goals. The basic principle of these tools is that learners add value to the community learning experience. This means that you learn more too.

The next wave of Web applications, now on the horizon, is part of what is being called the "semantic Web," or Web 3.0. The critical feature of this next wave of tools is that applications will not only have the power to display information, they will have the power to extract embedded meaning and actively select pages that are likely of greater interest and use to you. This means we will be able to search and find faster, better, and more coherently. The tools in Web 2.0 helped build community; the tools in Web 3.0 wave will help build knowledge (Ohler, 2008).

LM Tip 14: Experts: A Touch of Spice

This tip answers questions such as these:

- What are some good times for inviting experts to a course?
- Where can I find experts?
- What types of learning events are good for experts?

Invited experts can add a bit of spice to your course for you and your students. Most courses by necessity are planned well in advance and often use a textbook or a set of published readings and content in a field or discipline. These resources, together with the designed learning outcome goals, provide the framework for a set of course experiences. Yet many of our most exciting experiences occur when we see the application of course content to current and innovative events. This is what guest experts can bring to a course: customized and authentic application of course content as embodied in a real personality within an authentic career experience.

Expert guests also provide a change of pace with a large group community experience. Most faculty bring expertise from a particular field of knowledge; other authoritative voices come from the textbook and other resources, such as readings or podcasts. Bringing in an expert provides another perspective that helps round out some of the core concept knowledge as used within a particular context.

Another benefit of bringing an expert into your course community is that the experience creates learning opportunities prior to, during, and after the experts' participation. Prior to the expert's visit, learners can research the person, organization, and subject of that person's expertise; during the event, students have a chance to inquire and dialogue; and after the expert interaction, the knowledge can be integrated with the other course content. Experts often have wisdom that clarifies why and how the content matters.

Expert events often help in the community-building process of a course as well. We are often an event-driven world and enjoy the feeling of anticipation and novelty prior to an event, getting ready to be good hosts and preparing challenging intellectual inquiry, sharing the event experience, and then following up with the specific application of that intellectual inquiry. Many disciplines, including the world of information technology for higher education, host regular podcasts featuring experts on various topics. For example, the virtual world of Second Life, an online international world, regularly uses events to create community.

Note: The Second Life Grid site is a good place to start to see how higher education is using Second Life (http://secondlifegrid.net/slfe/education-use-virtual-world). A general list of Second Life events can be found at http://secondlife.com/community/events. Another good starting point is a newsletter, *The NMC Campus Observer*, which publishes the latest news related to New Media Consortium activities in higher education and can be found at http://sl.nmc.org/calendar/.

By now you may be saying, "Yes, sounds like a good idea! Just how do I go about incorporating experts into my course?" Here are a few questions that you might have about how to incorporate experts into your course and some starting points for answers.

Is There a Preferred Time in the Course to Have an Expert Event?

Usually sometime in the second half of a course is a good time. By the second half of a course, students have developed sufficient understanding and curiosity about a topic to prepare good interview questions for the expert and to place the expert's comments in context for a useful conversation. However, there are few hard-and-fast rules about inviting experts. Sometimes inviting an expert to pose significant challenges at the first part of a course can work well for advanced learners.

How Do I Go About Finding an Expert?

Experts are plentiful and often willing to participate as long as it doesn't take too much time. Serving as an invited expert is usually a pleasant and rewarding experience.

Friends and colleagues are always a good place to start. As you become more experienced with using experts, search out national and even international experts. With online classroom technology, plain old telephone conferences, and asynchronous discussion tools, experts can come from anywhere. Program graduates are an excellent source of experts. Alumni often have warm feelings for their institution and a natural affiliation with future graduates. Such invitations build ties back to the institution that are beneficial to all.

What Type of Content Is Good for an Expert?

You can set your own criteria, of course, but a good place to start is by focusing on one of the following areas:

- A core concept application. If you are working on scenarios with difficult leadership challenges, you may want to invite an expert who has personally experienced a difficult leadership challenge and can share some lessons learned and the need for flexibility and confidence.

- A current trend or development in a particular discipline. If a significant development in your field has occurred in the past six to twelve months, possibly in the area of impending legislation, managing response to economic conditions, significant natural events such as Hurricane Katrina and the subsequent support leadership, or new technology developments, invite an expert to share his or her perspective or analysis of that trend, event, or development.

- An area in which you have a particular strength or weakness. If you have a colleague you have worked with over time and with whom you share expertise, hold an event where you and your students can probe areas in greater depth with dialogue and debate. And if you have an area of relative weakness, try to identify an expert in that area to provide greater depth.

- Or you can invite an expert in to listen to, judge, or evaluate one or two key team projects.

How Do I Set Up the Expert Event?

The best type of event is one that feels comfortable to and challenges both experts and learners. Some of the possible structures are a mix of one or more of the following:

- A simple question-and answer-format. If the expert is sufficiently well known, the preparation can consist of a set of questions prepared by students and sent to the expert in advance. Years ago, Steve Jobs of Apple accepted a keynote invitation from a higher education technology group on the condition that he didn't have to prepare a talk. The format would be a question-and-answer session.

- A magazine, journal, or other content or media resource that has been authored by the expert or features the expert combined with the question-and-answer format.

- A short PowerPoint presentation (about ten minutes) that forms the basis for the conversation and dialogue.

- A podcast by an expert used as a base resource and then a conversation and discussion with the expert after all the students have listened to it and prepared questions.

- Experts can also be invited to serve as discussion board or seminar leaders for a week. In this scenario you serve as host or moderator and support the dialogue of the expert with the students.

Generally it is important to prepare for the unexpected that can occur for an event. Something can always go wrong, so having a backup plan is highly recommended. This plan might be as simple as moving to a later day or time or substituting an article authored by the invited expert or a related resource, such as an equally relevant article, podcast, or archived presentation.

Are There Other Resources on Using Experts in Online Courses?

Here are the links to a two-part resource, "Guest Lecturers in the Online Environment," by Virgil Varvel of the Illinois Online Network:

- July/August 2001: Guest Lecturers in the Online Environment. Learn the benefits of bringing in the outside lecture into your online courses. http://www.ion.uillinois.edu/resources/pointersclickers/2001_07/index.asp.

- September/October 2001: Guest Lecturers in the Online Environment. Where can you find a good guest lecturer? What do students think about guest lecturers? http://www.ion.uillinois.edu/resources/pointersclickers/2001_09/index.asp.

Summary—and What's Next?

With the late middle of the course behind you, you probably have a set of mixed feelings. You may be feeling elated that some of your students obviously are doing very well and progressing on innovative projects; you may be feeling a little disappointed that some students are still on the edge and that their projects may be only minimally successful. If this is your first online course, you are also probably feeling pleased at how the course has progressed but also anxious about the final weeks. This is all normal. Enjoy the range of experiences. It probably brings back memories of your first face-to-face course.

Chapter 10

Phase Four: What's Happening, Themes, and Tools

Pruning, Reflecting, and Wrapping Up in the Closing Weeks

Chapter Overview

The closing weeks of a course bring a mixture of feelings, often ranging from concerns and worry about getting everything done to feelings of relief, satisfaction, joy, and camaraderie. As an instructor, you want your students to be feeling confident about the new skills and knowledge they have acquired. And you want to be fair and efficient in your assessment of their learning.

During this part of the course, your role as a coach should be front and center as the students direct more of their own learning and contribute to the learning of others. Your teaching goal now is to help your students know what it is that they are learning and how they will likely use the skills and knowledge they are acquiring in their lives and careers. In these closing weeks, support your learners as they integrate their knowledge and reach some level of resolution with what they know now and want to know in the future.

Some of the tips in these closing weeks could be put to good use earlier in your course, but just as the content for a course needs to be sequenced in some way, so too it is not wise to try to do too many new things at any one time. When we started planning this book, we decided that it would be great for a new online teaching faculty to move from a novice to an expert online teacher state in a twinkling. Without that as an option, we had to make some choices as to which tools might best be introduced or used in each phase of the course. Also some tips may well favor certain disciplines. For example, problem-solving strategies are essential for more hands-on courses such as mathematics, statistics, and practicum types of courses. We decided to trust your judgment and your book-scanning skills.

What's Happening in the Closing Weeks

In this phase, the course is pretty much in the hands and minds of the learners, and the key tasks of the faculty member are to direct, mentor, and support learners as they integrate and frame their new knowledge and finish projects and other course requirements. The major cognitive push is to ensure that the learners receive feedback on their knowledge work and hear, see, and benefit from the results of the creative work of the other learners. The students want to bring their learning together in a form that leaves them with a sense of satisfaction and fulfillment at what they have gained. They should be clear about what concepts, skills, perspectives, and goals they have developed. In addition to bringing the current session to an end, it is also desirable for faculty and students to reflect on the course collaboratively, determine what elements worked best in this course, and consider what changes might be good for the next set of learners.

In summary, this is what is usually happening in the closing weeks:

- Learners are finishing up the course projects and requirements. They are taking the lead in community discussions and integrating their knowledge by grappling with difficult problems and working on challenging tasks such as concept mapping, scenarios, and integrating feedback from learners and possibly experts beyond the course. They may be feeling stressed and a bit overwhelmed with what they need to do.

- The instructor is directing learning at the community level and at the individual or small team level. The instructor is also coaching and encouraging the learners through the final weeks and what needs to be done. A high priority is to provide customized and personalized feedback on projects and other assessment tasks in a timely and efficient manner to ensure that students have time to reflect and act on the feedback. The faculty member also supports the learners in establishing appropriate follow-up and future networking with learners, particularly important in online courses and programs.

- To-do lists are important for both learners and faculty to ensure that the work of teaching and learning is well coordinated.

Closing Weeks: Themes, Best Practices, and Principles

The principal themes for learners in the closing weeks are learner independence, pruning and reflecting on course knowledge, and course project completion. The major theme for the instructor is coaching the learners in these tasks. By this time, work on course projects is well under way, and discussions in the project forum should reflect learners' growing sophistication and understanding of course knowledge and concepts. Course projects and complex scenarios should reflect learners' progress toward identifying possible strategies for addressing difficult course or discipline issues.

Learner Independence

By the closing weeks of the course, learners should be familiar with the core concepts of the course knowledge and be able to say how these concepts relate to one another and to core concepts outside the boundaries of the course knowledge. They should be able to apply these core concepts in their course project and in the ideas they are contributing to other learners' projects. They should also know how to make their contributions to their peers in a constructive and helpful manner. The learning community should be operating smoothly with the goal of everyone helping others in achieving the course goals. Learners should be independent, but strong links within the course community should encourage them to help each other as appropriate as well. While there are a lot of "shoulds" in learner independence, they may need to be adjusted to fit individuals' readiness and skill levels.

Pruning and Reflecting

Memory research confirms that we retain only a small percentage of our experiences. Rather than railing against this natural memory process, it is best to work with it, identifying the specific and explicit core concepts that we want learners to take forward into their lives and careers. As each learner begins the course with his or her own particular area of interest and readiness, so too the particular set of core concepts that the learner will identify as his or her own from the course will be specific to each learner. The probability is high, and in fact desirous, that there will be a great deal of overlap among the learners for the core concepts, but the likelihood of a fair amount of divergence is also high. The divergence is natural and rooted in the desires and recommendations for encouraging learners to customize and personalize course knowledge. In brief, including an assignment or exercise specifically asking students what they have learned in the course and how they plan on using the course knowledge is beneficial. This is similar to the technique of a one-minute summary (Cross & Angelo, 1993) popularized in lecture classes. A one-minute summary asks students to respond to a question, such as, "What was the most important thing that you learned in this [class, paper, reading, podcast]?" or, "What important question do you have that has not been answered?" This can be the focus of one of the closing forums.

Course Project Completion

Ideally, course projects and other creative assignments are the expression of the integration of the course content and the newly acquired knowledge skills of the learner. The project is where it can all come together. Course projects enable the creative expression of course knowledge. The steps in creating a course project require the full range of learning experiences: reading, writing, research, listening, and revising and restructuring ideas. Rather than just covering content, this is where students use and apply content in their projects and help other learners do so. Thus, time dedicated to projects, such as proposals, design, draft, review, revision, and presentation, is a period of active learning.

Coaching

In the view of some teachers, the closing weeks of a course are easier for instructors. The students are actively engaged in projects and, ideally, supporting and helping each other. The role of the instructor during these closing weeks is similar to the work of a coach. To coach well, instructors need to balance providing their voice and encouragement with the need to ensure that the amount of help is neither too much nor too little. That means staying in close touch with what each of the learners is doing and providing the help and challenges as appropriate. It also means keeping the learning community moving forward and assisting unobtrusively, with individuals or teams helping each other. This is also a good time to review the literature on cognitive apprenticeship (Collins, Brown, & Holum, 1991) and the steps in helping learners develop expertise: modeling and observation, scaffolding, and increasingly independent practice. So while this time may be easier for some instructors, it is probably more appropriate to say that the focus of teaching practices is different. Faculty work now is directed to coaching to ensure learner independence and assessing to provide feedback and closure.

Tips for the Closing Weeks

The closing weeks have two sets of tips: Meaningful Projects and Presentations and Preparing for the Course Wrap.

The Meaningful Projects and Presentations tips focus on strategies for managing and directing meaningful projects and presentations, including suggestions for learners to assume some leadership roles in the learning community and to tailor and customize their learning. These tips also address topics such as authentic problem solving, working with what-if scenarios, and strategies for achieving a stimulating and comfortable camaraderie within the course community. One of the tips describes concept mapping, also known as mind mapping, which asks learners to create a graphical representation or map of what they know, identifying the nodes, relationships, and dimensions of the course content.

The Preparing for the Course Wrap tips describe some of the actions for planning and celebrating the closing experiences. Just as it is helpful to wrap up discussions and other assignments during the course, it is helpful to explicitly design closing wrap-up experiences for the course. One tip focuses on the pruning and reflecting processes of learning. These processes are natural to integrating knowledge and contributing to the cognitive growth of the course learning community. This tip provides a number of strategies for identifying what students take with them from a course. We know that no one can possibly remember everything from a course, so being explicit about what is known and not known helps learners put their knowledge into perspective. Two tips in this set discuss celebrating the closing of a particular community and making plans for future gatherings and networking. The closing tip in this set focuses on the learner experience, encouraging learners to think critically about their course experience and in doing so, providing useful feedback for enhancing the course.

Technology Tools

Table 10.1 lists the tools that are mentioned in the closing tools tips and the suggested pedagogical uses and purposes of these tools. Do not be intimated by this list of tools. Although these tools are becoming a

TABLE 10.1

Tools in Closing Weeks Tips and Suggested Pedagogical Uses

Tools and Applications in Closing Weeks Tips	Closing Week Tip Number	Suggested Pedagogical Uses and Purposes
Simulations and virtual worlds	CW 1	Applications and resources that support the use of authentic learning scenarios and complex problem solving.
Prerecorded tutorials	CW 1	Static resources useful for demonstrating the thought processes that experts use in solving math, engineering, or any type of problem. They might be open source resources, freely available on the Web; published resources available as part of a purchased set of course resources; or part of the teaching direction of a faculty. Many tutorials are posted and discoverable in YouTube.
Synchronous online classroom	CW 1	Used to demonstrate steps in solving problems in response to real-time, spontaneous questions from learners.
Discussion boards, blogs, wikis, and collaborative spaces	CW 1	Places for recording problem definitions, requirements, and potential strategies for approaching a problem by individuals or groups.
Second Life	CW 2	A virtual three-dimensional world that could be used as a site for what-if scenarios. Assumptions and variables could be changed.
CmapTools and iMindmap: Tools for concept mapping and mind mapping	CW 4	Graphic representation tools that promote integration of new with existing knowledge; can be used for problem solving using focus questions; support organization and framing of knowledge.
iPhone and iPod Touch	CW 4	Mobile handheld learning tools for audio, video, and Web access; thousands of free or almost free applications.
YouTube: Web site for posting short videos	CW 4	A place for posting videos and demos so students can see you and see process demonstrations; students can also post videos of practice and presentation here.
Synchronous online classroom	CW 5	A space and time for question-and-answer sessions supporting knowledge integration and review sessions summarizing core concepts.
Synchronous online classroom	CW 8	Can be used for student presentations and closing celebrations.

standard part of online courses, they are not essential, and you can have a successful first online course without using most of them. As discussed in the course beginnings, the essential tools for a successful course are the basic course management system and the key communication features of that system: the discussion forum, course site and e-mail, and the phone, which remains an excellent choice for spontaneous, synchronous communication.

Many of the tools listed in the table were also referenced in previous tips. In the closing weeks their use may change somewhat. For example, the online synchronous classroom tool is mentioned in CW tips 1, 5, and 8, but the primary purpose for the tool may change. Also, while the online classroom is a good choice for mini-concept lectures, question-and-answer sessions, problem-solving demonstrations, presentations, and celebrations, you can use basic asynchronous tools such as text, discussion forums, blogs, and wikis for some of these interactions.

The first offering of a course is just that: the first offering. As you continue to teach in the online environment, you will have many opportunities to test, explore, and refine your use of these tools and the plethora of tools that will be available.

Chapter 11

Phase Four: Tips for the Closing Weeks

THE TIPS IN this chapter focus on complex cognitive growth, managing a vibrant and dynamic community, and wrapping up assessment and course projects. The tips also include strategies for getting feedback from your students as to what resources and activities worked for them and that they would recommend to future students.

Here is the set of closing weeks (CW) tips:

- CW Tip 1: Reaching the Heights of Learning: Authentic Problem Solving
- CW Tip 2: Using What-If Scenarios: Flexing Our Minds with Possibilities
- CW Tip 3: Stage 3 of a Learning Community: Stimulating and Comfortable Camaraderie
- CW Tip 4: Learners as Leaders
- CW Tip 5: Course Wrapping with Concept Mapping: A Strategy for Capturing Course Content Meaningfully
- CW Tip 6: Pausing, Reflecting, and Pruning Strategies
- CW Tip 7: Creating a Closing Experience: Wrapping Up a Course with Style
- CW Tip 8: Real-Time Gatherings: Stories and Suggestions for Closing Experiences
- CW Tip 9: Debriefing Techniques with Students: What One Change Would They Recommend?

MEANINGFUL PROJECTS AND PRESENTATIONS

This set of tips suggests teaching strategies for managing and directing meaningful project and presentations.

CW Tip 1: Reaching the Heights of Learning: Authentic Problem Solving

This tip answers questions such as these:

- What is authentic learning or authentic problem solving?
- What makes authentic learning effective?
- Why is authentic learning important?
- What are some ways to incorporate authentic problem solving into a course?

This tip focuses on activities and strategies for creating and directing problem-solving experiences. The general rule of thumb for problem learning is to incorporate problems that are as authentic as possible. What is meant by authentic? One definition is that authentic learning uses "real-world problems and projects that allow students to explore and discuss these problems in ways that are relevant to them" (Carlson, 2001). The future of problem solving may look quite different within the next few years as games, simulations, virtual worlds (such as Second Life), and Holodeck-type (*Star Trek*) environments continue to proliferate. Designing more learning experiences using actual and complex scenarios increases engagement with the content and in all probability increases learning.

Types of Course Content

The content model described earlier (Figure 2.2) categorizes course resources into four content types: (1) core concept content, (2) simple application content, (3) more complex applications and problem solving for which solutions are available, and (4) authentic, real, and complex problems for which solutions may not be known.

In the face-to-face classroom, a faculty often leads a group in a simple problem-solving experience in a synchronous class meeting. In this traditional teaching experience, particularly in math and science, the instructor takes the learners step-by-step through a problem and its solution, explaining the reasoning and the process.

Modeling problem solving in the online environment is often done with prerecorded tutorials, text resources, or the synchronous online classroom.

More complex problem-solving activities usually combine individual and small group work, followed by sustained synchronous conversation or projects. In other words, complex problem solving is not one activity but a sequence of actions and experiences. The experiences might include individuals doing some initial thinking and searching on their own, then sharing some of this thought or exploration with others, and then perhaps generating possible solutions and alternatives in a group setting.

Steps in Problem Solving

Learners can often benefit from guidance in using a structured approach to problem solving. You may want to adopt one or more problem-solving "step" approaches that are recommended for general real world problem solving. Here is a seven-step process derived from the work of Chang and Kelly (1999) that you might consider adopting (a Web site with descriptions of each of the seven steps is available at www.pitt.edu/~groups/ probsolv.html):

1. Define and identify the problem.

2. Analyze the problem.

3. Identify possible solutions.

4. Select the best solutions.

5. Evaluating solutions.

6. Develop an action plan.

7. Implement.

For math problems and other engineering types of problems, a four-step process developed by G. Polya, a mathematician from Stanford University, and considered the prototypical problem-solving approach in these disciplines might be preferred. Polya's four-step process is similar to the seven-step process but is a bit more compressed. (More detail on the process is at http://www.physics.ohio-state.edu/~kilcup/261/pdf/ polya.pdf.)

Polya's process is an inductive reasoning process that can be used for any problem-solving need. Here are the steps:

1. Understand the problem, which includes an analysis of it and identifying what is known and what is not known.

2. Devise a solution plan. This includes many questions to guide the plan's development, such as, "Have you seen the same problem in a slightly different form?"

3. Carry out the plan.

4. Look back, which is a review-and-check step that the solution fits the problem at each step in the plan.

Ways to Approach Problem Solving

Following are some examples of how to approach problem-solving strategies in your course—for example, focus on two or three parts of the more complex and authentic problem solving in any one course, particularly if you have a short six- or eight-week term. We examine three major phases of an authentic problem-solving assignment.

Problem-Solving Phase One: Individual Starting Points

Let's assume that the end goal of this authentic problem-solving assignment is to do one of the following:

- Create a vision for the next stage of growth for a company.

- Develop a report on possible alternatives for solving a leadership succession problem.

- Critique and provide alternatives to the statistical methods used in a research study.

- Develop recommendations for a problem—tied to the course content, of course—in the workplace that one or more of the learners is experiencing.

- Identify and analyze environmentally safe or friendly products for cleaning in a learner's county, region, or state.

The first step to solving any problem is to analyze the problem and envision a successful outcome. As this is a skill that we want all learners to develop, students should spend some time analyzing just what the problem is, what the knowns and unknowns are, what the constraints might be, and what that end result might look like.

Therefore, this first phase might be structured with all learners approaching the problem individually and recording their initial thoughts about what the problem is and how to approach it. This step can be done as an assignment that is then posted on a blog, wiki, or discussion board. This assignment is not intended to be long or complex, but a starting point that shows thought, likely questions that need to be answered, and avenues for possible initial research. Another option is to have the students work in small groups or teams in this phase as well, depending on their maturity and the complexity of the problem.

Problem-Solving Phase Two: Small Group or Team Collaboration

In this phase, the learners work in small groups or teams and bring their initial thoughts, questions, and observations to a brainstorming meeting. This is sometimes difficult to do in the online environment. The best brainstorming is synchronous or almost synchronous, so the best online tools might be the online classroom or a chatroom. Another possible gathering strategy is to use a combination of wireless networking, cell phones, and free online collaborative spaces.

It is usually wise to record and report the results of this brainstorming session, because the next step will be for the small teams to collectively agree on the definition of the problem and then work on generating possible solutions or approaches to it. The results of the brainstorming session, including work on possible solutions, can then be shared with the larger course community in the next phase.

Problem-Solving Phase Three: Course Community Sharing and "Consulting"

Now the learners share the results of their work with the rest of the course community. If all of the learners are working on similar problems, they can compare and evaluate the approaches. If the learners have problems that are quite different, they can serve as advisors and consultants to each other. Tools that support this phase include general discussion forums, live classrooms, and team blogs.

Segmenting the Authentic Problems

Designing complex authentic problems into your course might be too ambitious or unwieldy. In addition, learners may be intimidated or overwhelmed by difficult and real problems in their course—on top of the very real problems that they may have at work and in their personal lives.

So if your students are undergraduates or less experienced graduate students, segmenting the problem-solving process and focusing on fewer parts of a problem can be a way to incorporate authentic problems into your courses. For example, segmenting would mean to focus on the first steps in any problem-solving scenario, such as analyzing and clarifying the question and determining some potential approaches to the problem. As John Dewey observed, "A problem well stated is half-solved." In the same course the next time around, an approach would be to focus on one of the next steps in the problem-solving process, building on what previous students have done. Other options might be generating some possible approaches and then having the students evaluate some of the solutions and develop an action plan.

Other Resources for Authentic Problem Solving

Many disciplines, including health, business, and leadership courses, use case studies for problems. Case studies are often readily available, for example, at the Harvard Business Online site for educators. For example, a Web-based simulation, Leadership and Team Simulation: Everest (Roberto & Edmondson, 2007), uses the dramatic context of a Mount Everest expedition to explore processes of group dynamics and leadership.

An alternative to using prepared case studies that can become dated quickly in our age of constantly breaking news is to complement prepared case studies with updates from Internet research or to have a class develop its own real-time case study. A 2007 article by Theroux, a UMassOnline professor of business, describes the challenges and possibilities of creating real and immediate cases by using the Internet to develop communications between the faculty, students, and a company. A tool that can support this type of development is a collaborative wiki or course blog.

Closing Thoughts

A common, and valid, concern about problem-based learning is that it is difficult to cover all the content in a course. The best way to deal with it is to analyze your course in terms of the learning outcomes and performance goals. Finding enough content is no longer the biggest challenge; interpreting and using content well in incorporating authentic problem solving is.

CW Tip 2: Using What-If Scenarios: Flexing Our Minds with Possibilities

This tip answers questions such as these:

- What are what-if scenarios?

- What are some examples of what-if scenarios?

- Will I have time to do these types of intense, collaborative activities?

Picture this. You are the manager of a large grocery store, but the number of new food products and variants, such as yogurt Cheerios, apple cinnamon Cheerios, milk, soymilks, and varieties of organic products seems endless. If only you had infinite shelf space. How would you manage it, and how would your customers navigate it? Or picture a variant of our current political and philosophical worlds. In alternate history studies, historians ponder and explore scenarios that might have been if our familiar history was not so familiar. Some alternate history scenarios explore questions such as these: "What if Socrates had died before his philosophy was written down by Plato?" (Hanson, 2002) or "What if FDR's life or circumstances had been different in the 20th century?" with seven different possible scenarios (Ward, 2002) or "What would have happened if Martin Luther King Jr. had not been assassinated and become president?"

In the case of the store manager wistfully desiring a world with infinite shelf space, this wish has virtually been granted and a new world of niche culture is one of the ripple effects. This new world is persuasively described by Chris Anderson, an editor at *Wired* magazine, in *The Long Tail: Why the Future of Business Is Selling Less of More* (2006). Anderson states that examples of infinite shelf space abound today. We have infinite shelf space for books, music, and other media, enabling businesses to profit from low-volume items desired by the specialized interests of consumers. One ripple effect of this phenomenon, Anderson argues, is that common culture will reshape itself into an array of infinite overlapping niche cultures. How the effects of this reshaping of mass culture will play out is unknown, but even a partial reshaping of mass culture will have significant effects.

Do you think that a scenario of infinite shelf space might have been the focus of a business course fifteen or twenty years ago? What types of scenarios might you want to use in your course today, looking out fifteen years or so to encourage thinking in new ways and of new possibilities?

This tip examines some possible uses of what-if scenarios in your course and when you might want to use them.

What Are What-If Scenarios?

What-if scenarios generally pose a question inquiring about some of the possible scenarios or ripple effects of something that happened in the past differently, in the alternate history example, or what might happen in the future, such as scenarios of the future of health care in the United States. What-if scenarios are a specific type of problem-solving experience that includes role-playing activities, simulations, and case studies. These types of activities enable students to be involved and engaged on an intellectual level, and often an emotional level as well. When working on these learning activities, students research, evaluate and analyze, make decisions, observe results, and then make additional decisions dealing with the consequences of earlier decisions.

Why Use What-If Scenarios?

Here are four reasons for using what-if scenarios in your course:

- Using what-if scenarios encourages spontaneity and flexibility in thinking. When a group explores these scenarios, they are basically dealing with fictionalized events. One requirement for this fiction, however, is that once a context has been established for a scenario, the happenings within the event must have internal consistency.

- What-if scenarios typically have possibilities rather than right or wrong answers. Devising scenarios is relatively straightforward because all scenarios, real or imagined, depend on a set of assumptions. Change the assumptions, and you have a new scenario. Have Socrates die earlier, and his philosophy is not written down. Assume that you have fixed shelf space, or assume that you have infinite shelf space. Assume that gas will cost six dollars a gallon or, alternatively, two dollars a gallon. Change the assumptions, and then examine the possible consequences.

- Using what-if scenarios in your course often helps students develop confidence in what they know or don't know or might need to know of the course content and related areas. Exploring the assumptions behind the scenarios requires that students examine their own assumptions and knowledge structures, and clearly communicate what they think and why.

- Using what-if scenarios is often an excellent device for keeping the course content fresh for both faculty and students. It also offers ways of personalizing and customizing content.

Getting Started with What-If Scenarios

To get started with scenarios, search out case studies in your field, and then change some of the variables and some of the assumptions. In fact, taking a case study and then having the students identify the core assumptions and suggest a different set of assumptions can itself be an excellent collaborative group activity. If you want to control the design of a scenario, build your question for a group activity around a change in an influential figure in your discipline. In a leadership course, explore a scenario in which Al Gore was elected president in 2004 or John McCain was elected president in 2008. In biology, examine a scenario in which significant plant life is found on Mars.

Background

What-if scenarios are engaging and effective interactive teaching and learning tools, but they can present challenges. It can take time on your part to design an appropriate scenario, and then scenarios can be time-consuming to set up and complete. They can also present challenges in assessing just what students have learned. However, if scenarios are derived from the desired learning outcomes, assessment can be straightforward, if not easy. Overall, what-if scenarios are powerful learning tools and worth pursuing.

CW Tip 3: Stage 3 of a Learning Community: Stimulating and Comfortable Camaraderie

This tip answers questions such as these:

- How do I know if the learning community has reached stage 2 or stage 3?

- Is it possible to reach the stage of stimulating and comfortable camaraderie in a single course term?

When a course is in its closing phases, it is good to return to one of the most fundamental themes of teaching and learning online: community and collaboration. In particular, be sure to revisit the development stages of a course community and the characteristics of stage 3: reaching a state of stimulating and comfortable camaraderie.

Three Stages of Building Community

One of the earlier tips (LM 12) referred to the three stages of building a course community (Brown, 2001). Here they are again, this time in greater detail.

Stage 1: Making friends online with students with whom we feel comfortable communicating. This stage is part of the early social presence in the course beginnings.

Stage 2: Community conferment (acceptance). Community conferment often occurs following a "long, thoughtful, threaded discussion on a subject of importance" (p. 18). The discussion may have included feelings of a shared experience and generated feelings of satisfaction and kinship with the other participants. This stage usually occurs during the early middle to the late middle of a course.

Stage 3: This is characterized by camaraderie generally achieved following "long-term or intense association with others involving personal communication" (p. 18). Student engagement is even more intense as students are focusing, sharing, and working on projects, presentations, and course capstone experiences. This stage may or not happen with every course. Stage 3 does happen frequently with cohorts that stay together through the twelve to eighteen months of completing a master's degree.

Strategies for Shaping and Evolving Community

Faculty behaviors for shaping and helping learners develop a stage 3 community are very similar to the behaviors that help develop the stage 2 community of mutual acceptance and effective communication. Review this list of faculty behaviors for building community, and put a check next to or circle behaviors that you use consistently. Then select one of the behaviors that you would like to use more frequently in these closing weeks:

- Supporting and encouraging peer-to-peer discussion and collaborations
- Posing open-ended questions about what students think and think they know or would like to know
- Making positive observations about students' participation in the learning experiences
- Encouraging connection making and linking of ideas among the learners
- Encouraging the linking of course content to current events and problems, with links to learners' personal work and career environments as appropriate
- Challenging students to share questions, strategies, and insights about the course content

Faculty Behaviors That Support Stage 3 Community

Faculty behaviors that help a class move beyond the mutual acceptance and effective communication of stage 2 to the commitment and support of stage 3 include variations of the following behaviors, which also support the integration of knowledge into a learner's knowledge. Pick one of these behaviors to focus on in the last one or two discussions:

- Grappling with issues and problems together, including problems for which the answers are unknown
- Encouraging learners to brainstorm and challenge each other about innovative strategies and solutions
- Communicating with learners on the intersection of interests and core concepts in the course content

- Sharing relevant experiences that support future networking and professional collaboration

Your students' postings will likely show evidence of developing personal and professional relationships. Obviously one of the lasting outcomes of learning and sharing discoveries together is the development of these longer-lasting relationships. When we ask our students what they take with them from a course, professional and personal friendships for the future are usually mentioned.

Intervening Conditions That Can Hinder Community Development

In striving to achieve a stage 3 of community that is evidenced by stimulating and comfortable camaraderie, are we aiming so high that we set ourselves up for disappointment? Here is a reality check.

In her study on building community, Brown (2001) identified fifteen lifestyle conditions that might hinder a group of learners from developing into a vibrant learning community. She called these "intervening conditions," and they include many of the familiar lifestyle and commitment issues, such as health, work, family, logistics, and technology. Some of the conditions that she included might not readily come to mind:

- Personalities and how they manifest themselves online.
- Interaction of learner and faculty teaching and learning styles.
- Varying expectations and needs from a course. Some students really just want the credit and the grade and have no interest in networking. For working professionals, this needs to be an acceptable option.

What does this reality check suggest? Be patient and understanding with yourself and your students. Review the list of faculty behaviors for building community. If you are doing many of them, the community that is evolving in your course may be what makes sense for a particular group of students. Be sure that you are enjoying the discussions and learning that are happening, and then relax.

CW Tip 4: Learners as Leaders

This tip answers questions such as these:

- Why empower learners as leaders of course experiences?
- What are some of the ways to do this without appearing as if I am not doing "my" job of teaching?

Part of our challenge as instructors is managing the delicate balance between directed and self-directed learning in a set of course experiences. One instructional strategy that can help this balance is to include learner-as-leader experiences.

Providing opportunities for learners to take the lead in learning experiences for a group or the course community can provide a sense of empowerment that is both a critical element and a desired outcome of participation in an online learning community (Palloff & Pratt, 1999).

Learners-as-leaders experiences shift the learner's mind-set from viewing the instructor as the primary content authority to developing a mind-set of himself or herself as a valuable contributor to the learning experience and the development of content. Learners then can see themselves as knowledge generators and connectors. Having learners lead activities also supports Vygotsky's theory of the zone of proximal development. As learners develop expertise, their zones shift and expand. Ideally course experiences are designed with flexibility to be reshaped by and for learners to adapt to these shifting zones.

As the shifts occur in the learner's mind-sets and zones, the role of the instructor also shifts, from directing and telling to supporting, clarifying, critiquing, coaching, and shaping. Simultaneously with this shift, the instructor also learns more from the students. This tip provides a few hints on designing and implementing learner-as-leader activities.

Learners-as-Leaders Experiences: Orientation and Planning Time

Learner-led activities generally succeed when learners are prepared, expectations are clear and purposeful, processes and procedures are explicit, and the activities fit learners' state of readiness and personal goals. Here are some steps to include in your planning:

- Many learners may need to be oriented to the idea of leading a group or class activity, such as a forum, discussion, role-play, debate, or project. Start talking about the concept of learner-led activities from the beginning of the course.

- Provide learners with a detailed description of the activity and the expected outcomes and responsibilities for them. An overview of the activity with a link to the detailed directions often works well.

- Encourage learners to begin making choices about their planned learner-led activity after the first phase of the course has been completed.

- Provide time in the course calendar for learners to begin planning the activities around the middle of the term.

- Schedule instructor-team discussion time for the activities before the team is scheduled to lead an activity. Depending on the scope and complexity of the activity, this discussion could be one week or many weeks before the activity. The instructor serves as counselor and consultant in this discussion, keeping the focus on the outcomes and clear expectations.

Individual Versus Team-Led Activities

The phrase "safety in numbers" is often true for learner-led activities. Learner-as-leader activities can often be very effective as team-based activities. The teams should be small, to minimize the likelihood of learners' opting out of an activity. Larger groups of three to five students can work well for more complex projects, but experience suggests that smaller teams work better and encourage more activity on the part of each learner. Each member's voice is heard more often with smaller groups too. There should also be intragroup accountability, which means that peers evaluate the participation quality of their fellow team members.

Making Outcomes Explicit

In addition to knowing the purpose and outcomes of the activity, it is helpful if students know how the outcomes fit into the larger context of the overall course plan. Once the outcomes from the instructor are clear and learners embrace them, they can also develop additional goals or outcomes for the activity. The expected outcomes of an activity should be stated in the syllabus so that learners know from the beginning of the course what they will be expected to accomplish through their learner-led activity.

Choosing the Type of Activity

Gagné, Briggs, and Wager (1992) describe five kinds of learning outcomes: intellectual skills, verbal information, cognitive strategy, attitude, and motor skill. Of these five, the first four lend themselves best to learner-led activities because the activities easily can be accomplished in an online learning environment. Achieving the outcomes of motor skill proficiency in an online course is still in the future for most current learning environments.

Some of the most common learner-led activities are to lead a group in a discussion, forum, or research topic. Other good activities are to work in

---

TABLE 11.1

Checklist for a Learner-Led Activity

	Yes	No	Comments
1. Are the learning outcomes for the activity clearly stated in the activity description or syllabus?			
2. Is the learner-led activity introduced with sufficient time for learners to begin planning it?			
3. Is the activity fully described with clear expectations, options, and directions, including a rubric for grading the activity?			
4. Are learners provided several weeks to plan the activity?			
5. Does the topic activity provide enough range of choice so that learners can be creative in their choice and implementation of the activity?			
6. Does the participation grade include participation in the learner-led activities?			

Source: Conrad and Donaldson (2004, p. 108).

---

teams on complex problems or projects, prepare and conduct debates, and role-play key concepts or games. Again the keys to success are preparation, consultation, and clear expectations.

It should always be assumed that learners are novice activity leaders and therefore should be encouraged to keep their activity simple both from a pedagogical and technological perspective.

The process of designing and implementing a learner-led activity can be challenging, but it is possible to start simply by increasing the expectations for the usual roles in group work. Another satisfying practice of learner-led activities is work on current professional projects (see Table 11.1).

CW Tip 5: Course Wrapping with Concept Mapping: A Strategy for Capturing Course Content Meaningfully

This tip answers questions such as these:

- What is concept mapping?

- What benefits come with concept mapping? How can it help with capturing and representing course content?

- Are there any free software tools for concept mapping or its cousin, mind mapping?

With so many priorities competing for attention in the closing weeks of a course, great learning opportunities can get lost in the shuffle. When the frantic feelings are over, our learners may be tempted to wonder, *What was that all about, and how am I and my brain different?*

This tip describes concept mapping, a tool that can assist learners in framing their course knowledge for future use and in pruning and focusing on core concepts. This strategy can be a powerful tool for knowledge creation and consolidation.

Concept Mapping

Concept mapping requires thinking structurally about concepts. When we consider the question of what we want our learners to take with them from a course, it is usually a rich set of concepts integrated into their knowledge base that we want most to encourage. Learners also value a set of concepts that they can talk about because it can be helpful in sharing with family and friends what their course work means to them.

This tip provides a definition of concept mapping and a description of concept mapping software. Concept mapping is a good choice for course wrapping.

A Bit of Background on Concept Mapping

The development of concept mapping is generally attributed to the work of Joseph Novak at Cornell University as part of a 1972 research program seeking to follow and understand changes in children's knowledge of science (Novak & Cañas, 2007). Concept mapping is rooted in the theories of cognitive restructuring, going back even further to the work of Ausubel in the 1960s, who stressed the importance of prior knowledge in learning new knowledge. Meaningful learning, according to Ausubel, occurs with only three conditions: conceptually clear resources, a learner's prior knowledge, and the learner's active choice to learn (Novak & Cañas, 2007).

Concept mapping is generally considered to be a tool for these types of cognitive processes:

- Integrating old and new knowledge
- Assessing understanding or diagnosing misunderstanding
- Brainstorming
- Problem solving

In other words, it is a useful tool for meaningful learning. And similar to the context in which it was developed, concept mapping can be used to follow how knowledge changes and evolves.

Core Concepts About Concept Mapping

Very briefly, "concept maps are graphical tools for organizing and representing knowledge" (Novak & Cañas, 2008, p. 1). Figure 11.1 shows a concept map that answers the question, "What is a concept map?" Note that concept maps are generally read from top to bottom.

This map on concepts includes a definition of a concept, which can be seen on the low middle left. Novak and Cañas define a concept as a "perceived regularity in events or objects, or a records of events or objects" (p. 10). The concept map also provides characteristics of concepts, such as, concepts are hierarchically structured; are labeled with symbols or words; and can be combined to form propositions.

We can talk about concepts only with words, but as the concept map shows, concepts are much more than just words. They are really a cluster of related ideas. Single words are often used as labels for complex ideas, and we can readily think that students own a concept when in reality they own only the word. For example, leadership is a concept and works relatively well as a simple label, but many concepts are clearer when stated as propositions containing multiple concepts. Think about the number of concepts in your course and how you might represent them graphically.

Concept maps are organized hierarchically; however, the hierarchy of complex concepts is not always clear. The structuring of concept maps requires identifying the components of concepts, relationships, and dependencies. By identifying cross-links, new patterns and relationships among the knowledge concepts often reveal themselves. Nursing students using mind mapping in a clinical practicum made comments such as, "I'm finally able to make sense of all the pieces of the puzzle, and to form relationships among the pieces of data" (Cahill & Fonteyn, 2000, p. 220).

Integrating Concept Mapping into a Course

To start using concept mapping in a course experience, Novak and Cañas (2008) recommend starting with a focus question—one that clearly specifies the problem or issue the concept map should help to resolve. This question helps to frame the particular domain of knowledge for a learner to map. Creating concept maps requires learners to use both their generalized available body of knowledge as well as the course content knowledge. In other words, part of any learning activity is relating new knowledge to existing knowledge, and the process of concept mapping helps this,

FIGURE 11.1

Concept Map Showing Key Features of Concept Maps

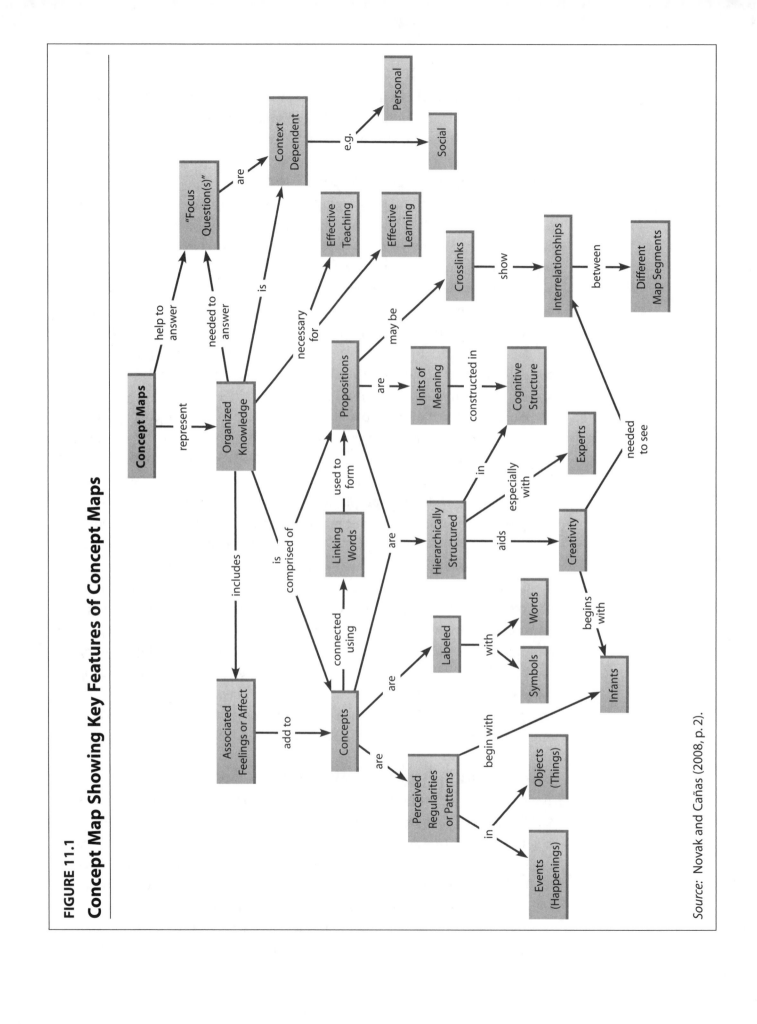

Source: Novak and Cañas (2008, p. 2).

highlighting the fact that the course knowledge is not independent or wholly separate from what students already know.

Developing a good focus question for a concept map is itself a useful collaborative instructional experience. Particularly toward the end of a course, you want the learners to think about what they knew about the course knowledge at the beginning of the course, what they think they know now, and what they wish they knew more about or how to do something. What students wish they knew can be a rich source of focus questions. Another good end-of-course activity is to modify the concept map they may have initiated at the beginning of the course.

Is There a Good Tool for Concept Mapping?

One possible reason that concept mapping hasn't been more generally used in instruction or even in general problem solving is that the software to support this type of thinking and analysis has been somewhat clunky, nonshareable, or not readily available. Novak and others are now offering a tool for concept mapping that looks promising and is free for higher education: CmapTools (v. 5.03); it is available from the Institute of Human and Machine Cognition (http://cmap.ihmc.us/conceptmap.html). Another reason for the slow adoption of concept mapping is that it requires instructors to think differently about what they know, and it requires a shift from a linear approach to acquiring knowledge to a more networked and web-like approach. In some ways, concept mapping requires even more knowledge and expertise because it requires propositional knowledge and knowledge of patterns and relationships. An example of the steps in building a concept map on answering the focus question, "How are emotions and reason balanced in organizational management," is available at http://www.informationtamers.com/WikIT/index.php?title=How_to_make_a_concept_map.

Concept mapping can be an effective strategy at many levels. It requires thinking, analysis, weighing of ideas, and identifying relationships and patterns. It's worth turning to as a way of wrapping up a course. It also reminds us how important it is to design into the course strategies that require learners to pay attention to what they think they may know and not know.

Other sources of tools for concept mapping are the tools for mind mapping, a related and similar approach to graphically representing knowledge. One of the better-known mind-mapping software is the iMind-Map (http://www.imindmap.com/) by Tony Buzan, an author and consultant on maximizing one's brainpower, and his colleague entrepreneur Chris Griffiths. A good starting place for checking out the world of mind-mapping tools is the Mind-Mapping Software Blog by Chuck Frey (http://mindmappingsoftwareblog.com). Or research YouTube for some demonstrations of the various tools. Some of the more popular mind-mapping tools are providing versions of their software for iPhone and iPod Touch.

PREPARING FOR THE COURSE WRAP

This set of tips has suggestions for preparing you and your students for the closing weeks of the course and focusing on meaningful experiences to wrap up the larger course experience.

CW Tip 6: Pausing, Reflecting, and Pruning Strategies

This tip answers questions such as these:

- Why is pausing and reflecting so important? How can we integrate these processes into course designs?
- What are some techniques for pruning and reflecting on content?
- What do researchers say about how memory works?

Now is a good time to return to a focus on cognitive presence. As you will recall, cognitive presence means that you and your students explicitly and publicly construct and confirm meaning through sustained discourse. A simpler mantra that you might use with your students is "constructing and confirming meaning." This affirms that learning is about the community's actively creating its individual and collective knowledge. And this knowledge is unique to this group of learners.

This tip on pausing, reflecting, and pruning focuses on an element of the learning process that is often neglected: that of the processes of reflection and pruning. Our brains and memories are simply not designed for remembering everything. Daniel Schacter (2001), a professor and chair of Harvard University's Department of Psychology, has identified "seven sins of memory," which include one that is well-known to all of us: the "sin" of transience, or the tendency to forget things over time. While at first glance this memory trait is a negative, Schacter suggests that we view transience and other memory traits of omission, such as blocking and absent-mindedness, not as flaws in the architecture of memory but as costs we pay for benefits in memory that make it work as well as it does most of the time.

To help us remember, many of our new technologies, such as smart phones, cameras, recorders, and GPS trackers, are going beyond capturing key life moments to support "life-logging," a term used to describe systems that document every conversation and movement. Twitter services, for example, enable us to share what we are doing each moment in messages to all our "followers." Just as we may cringe at the thought of every moment of our lives being captured and recorded, we may well cringe at every moment of our teaching and learning processes being recorded as well. Learning, like life, can be messy. And a large percentage of the activities of learning are best left behind.

Similarly, in the online environment, where so much is being captured, discussed, and archived, it is good to focus on strategies that encourage the elaborate encoding processes for integrating concepts that are important to remember and use. Pause-and-reflect learning strategies encourage time for students to identify and encode the core concepts and skills that are the foundation for subsequent learning:

- Plan pausing, reflecting, and summarizing times into your course on an ongoing basis. This type of design helps students organize and integrate knowledge and develop confidence in what they know and avoid being overwhelmed. It is a way to move content elements from short-term memory into longer-term memory. One technique useful for this reflection strategy is the discussion-wrapping tip referred to EM 12. You will recall that discussion wrapping is something that you do or that individual students or small teams of two do to summarize the key points of a discussion topic. When directing students to prepare summaries of the discussion, one technique is to use terms such as the *bottom line*, *core concepts*, and *implications for next steps*.

- Hold synchronous sessions in a live online classroom that are open question-and-answer sessions or concept summary sessions. Again, you can lead these sessions or students can lead them and prepare the questions. With live classrooms, you can hear in real time what students are thinking and understanding about the course. Faculty who have started using this technology report that it is their and their students' favorite way of gathering and thinking out loud together.

- Ask your students to focus on what questions they have at this point in the course. Have them write down, speak about, or think out loud about what is confusing them. The practical inquiry model (Garrison, Anderson, & Archer, 2000) affirms that two processes in developing useful knowledge are integration and resolution. Integration refers to reaching some group or team convergences by connecting ideas, identifying relationships and patterns, and proposing solutions. With resolution, the group or larger community applies and tests solutions in the real-world scenarios.

- Plan other activities that provide time and opportunity for students to describe, define, and use the core concepts in various contexts. These can be compare-and-contrast activities and challenges for how the core concepts are expressed in classic and current scenarios.

- Plan a lessons-learned paper or discussion by asking learners to discuss what they learned and why it was important to them. This technique is sometimes termed a reverse exam.

The reasons that pause-and-reflect activities are so important is that they encourage the encoding of knowledge by noting relationships, categories, and unique application examples.

Here are the seven sins of memory—and their surprising virtues—identified by Schacter. More about each of these seven sins of memory is available at the Web site of the American Psychological Association: http://www.apa.org/monitor/oct03/sins.html.

1. Transience—forgetting that occurs with the passage of time

2. Absent-mindedness—forgetting probably caused by lack of attention or divided attention and preoccupation

3. Blocking—unable to recall a bit of information that we know we know

4. Misattribution—errors in recall; we remember events that never happened, attribute features of an event itself to a different time or place, and remember events, but find they happened to someone else

5. Suggestibility—a tendency to incorporate misleading information from external sources into personal recollections

6. Bias—the tendency to be influenced by factors, such as consistency, change, the present, role of the self, generic stereotype

7. Persistence—tendency to remember those things you would rather forget

CW Tip 7: Creating a Closing Experience: Wrapping Up a Course with Style

This tip answers questions such as these:

- What techniques help with reducing the stress and panic often induced by end-of-course projects and requirements?

- What techniques can reinforce the most important of the core concepts?

The closing weeks of a course are usually busy and can often be quite stressful. In such times, planning and list making, along with deep-breathing exercises, can be helpful for reducing stress and calming us. A favorite image that comes to mind is from productivity consultant David Allen's book (2002), *Getting Things Done*. Allen notes that making a list helps us to clear the "psychic RAM" of our brain, and we feel more relaxed and in control. Once we have made our list and schedule, we don't have to continually remind ourselves of what needs to be done and when. In fact, some users of mind-mapping tools find that these tools work better than lists for them in keeping track of the whole picture of what they have to do.

Here are a few hints for closing out a course experience with style, panache, and pleasure.

Remind Students of What's Next and When Assignments and Readings Are Due

This hint places the burden of creating a master "Things to Do to Complete a Course" list on the instructor. Some faculty may think this falls under the category of helping students too much. We like to think that making such a master list benefits the instructor as much as the student because it is a chance to ensure that the deadlines and assessment tasks that an instructor must do needs to be in sync with learner deadlines. Such a master list also helps to keep students focused on learning the course knowledge and completing their projects.

Just as each module has an overview of the module requirements, the instructor in the role of coach provides a to-do list and schedule for the remaining tasks for the learners that is useful for the coach as well.

As always, post such teaching direction in a prominent place on the course site, and then make references to the list in other places and possibly with your voice or text announcements every few days. Another way of doing this is to set up a community forum and have a community to-do list with room for hints, suggestions, and reminders.

Plan a Celebration Session to End the Course

A course is composed of a series of structured learning experiences and merits from an ending experience. A well-designed course ending provides opportunities for reflection and integration of useful knowledge. It is also a time to wrap up positive social and cognitive experiences.

When we get together for family and holiday time, we often do a lot of hugging as we disperse and return to our usual daily responsibilities. The end of a course can be closed with cognitive hugging and concept pruning, reflecting explicitly on the knowledge and skills students look forward to using in the future.

End-of-course experiences can focus on one or all of these areas: content, interaction and community, and the full course experience.

End-of-Course Content Experiences

Both faculty and learners benefit from end-of-course content experiences. For faculty it is an opportunity to summarize and affirm the core concepts of a course. One way of doing this is to state somewhere, "If you remember nothing else, remember 'THIS' or 'THESE'" (fill in your favorite mantra for what you consider the most foundational core concepts). Many faculty like to prepare or use a course summary that includes trends and encourages the development of lifelong discipline habits, particularly for graduate students. For example, an obvious goal for many graduate students is to develop the habit of reading a specific journal or other publication in their discipline or tracking a particular expert as a way of integrating the course content over time.

For learners, the end of the course is a time to tie up loose ends and put the finishing touches on new perspectives. Recall that as we develop concepts, it is often necessary to identify and build relationships among ideas and concepts within our existing body of knowledge. This also requires pruning what we have learned so that we can readily access and use essential and useful concepts.

A strategy that promotes end-of-course reflection is to ask the learners to identify and share one of their most meaningful insights from the course. Another is to have them identify an object that symbolizes one of their meaningful learning experiences that they are taking away from the class and talk about their symbolic object and their experiences (Schmier, 2006). The end of course is also a time for discussing what learners will be doing next. What courses are next on their schedule, or what learning tasks are they going to turn to next?

End-of-Course Interaction Experiences

Learners often create a helpful, supportive, and dynamic learning community over eight to fourteen weeks. Closing out such an experience can sometimes be wrenching; other times it is much easier. Providing a time and "place" for saying good-bye, just as we provide a time and place for learners to introduce themselves at the beginning of a course, is a good thing to do. A simple way to do it is to provide a "closing forum" where students share a closing comment, such as the end-of-course content insight that they will take with them that they gleaned from a collaborative experience.

One of the most valuable parts of a successful learning experience is expanding our network of colleagues, so providing a way for students to stay in touch is also helpful. This can happen naturally in a cohort-based program. Another technique might be to encourage them to share where and when they might meet again, such as which other courses they might be in again. Other times, "until we meet again" works just fine. One faculty shared that one of the most heart-warming comments that he remembers is a student saying that he disliked "seeing the class come to an end!"

This wrap-up forum can be a good activity for the end of the last week. It might be combined with a debriefing on the projects. If you are using an online classroom or other virtual space, the last synchronous meeting can be combined with a discussion of a few closing thoughts.

End-of-Course Full Course Experience

The end of a course also brings the time for students to complete course evaluations. This is an important feedback mechanism for the institution, but is often less useful for faculty. So ask the learners for feedback about particular elements of the course experience while it is fresh in their minds:

- What was the most useful resource or assignment for the course, and why?

- What problems, if any, did they have with the use of the online learning tools—either "operator error" or "designer error"?

- What did they notice about the course that you think might be changed in some way? You can add your own comment here to get them started: "Here is one thing I noticed …"

- Were they ready for the course content? What might have helped if they were not?

- Open question for other suggestions or recommendations

This informal feedback can be in a separate place on the course site and be quite unstructured and anonymous. The goal is for ongoing updating and quality enhancement of the course experiences for faculty and learners. Of course, you can remind the students that you would like ideas that will improve the course for others, keeping the focus on constructive feedback.

Closing Thought

Designing the end-of-course experiences at this time can also bring into relief all the tasks that you have planned for your learners during these final weeks. If need be, you can choose to modify the requirements. The last few weeks of a course can be some of the most stimulating and creative learning time as learners are putting it all together. So prepare a special coffee or other favorite beverage or music and enjoy your students and their dialogue at this time.

CW Tip 8: Real-Time Gatherings: Stories and Suggestions for Closing Experiences

This tip answers questions such as these:

- What are online classrooms, and what are they good for?

- I am clueless and intimidated and too busy to use the online synchronous classrooms. How can I possibly get started?

- What about the students? Are they ready to use these tools?

- Do real-time gatherings help build community?

Online classrooms have arrived. Online applications are finally easy enough to use that they are becoming a standard teaching and learning tool for online courses. Some uses of online classrooms for demonstration, problem solving, and question-and-answer and review sessions were discussed in one of the early middle tips (EM Tip 9). Online classrooms have even more potential for teaching and learning activities during the closing weeks. Recall that these classrooms provide a place where we can talk interactively in real time. This means that they are useful for all the types of dialogue and discussion and presentations that are common in the latter part of a course. Online classrooms provide a venue for question-and-answer sessions, presentations, and project summaries and demonstrations.

Getting Used to Online Classrooms

Three of the leading online classrooms are Elluminate, Wimba, and Adobe Connect. Online classrooms represent a complex technology where things can go wrong on a regular basis. Moreover, they require headphones and recommended microphones for full participation, although effective participation is possible without headphones. In addition, they require some time and energy in developing new habits of communicating and sharing, and remembering to press a button to talk can feel strange at first. But once an instructor and students use an online classroom, they rarely want to teach and learn online without it. Live classrooms make it possible to interact in real time from wherever you might be as long as you have a good network connection.

One of the most enthusiastic faculty that I talked to about the online classroom taught business writing. She held twice-weekly sessions in which she and her learners collaboratively analyzed business writing samples and student work pieces for effectiveness and construction. Together they developed a comfort level with the technology that really worked for them. So how might you use the online classroom? Here are some ideas.

Using the Online Classroom: Faculty Stories

Some faculty become passionate about using the online classroom. While teaching a graduate course focused on leadership in the virtual workplace with sixteen students, faculty member Debra Dinnocenzo at Duquesne University used it for gathering her students together in real time, both as a full class and as smaller teams for content and project discussions. The students often used the environment by themselves for team meetings and for project work, bypassing the challenges of setting up conference calls, and using the archiving feature to capture their work. Debra also highly recommends using the live real-time environment to invite experts to her class.

Getting Started with Online Classrooms

Debra had a definite advantage in getting started: she is currently the president of Virtual Works! a small company located in Wexford, Pennsylvania (www.VirtualWorksWell.com). She does describe herself as "over the top" in her use of virtual collaborative tools, and of course, this makes sense, given her company and what she does on a daily basis, which is helping people to be more connected, effective, and productive in the virtual workplace. So when Debra learned that online classrooms were available for use with her online class, she wasted no time in getting the tools activated for her class. Depending on your own institution and resources, you may need to become certified in the use of this tool. In any case, many free online live and archived tutorials and quick guides are readily available.

The other part of getting started was the question of how well prepared her students were for these real-time environments. Although Debra herself may have been perfectly comfortable with collaborative software, her students were not. So she set up a Virtual Happy Hour: a live open classroom "space"—and one of eight classrooms she set up for her class. This Happy Hour classroom was a place for students to go and just explore in a hands-on, no-pressure way with how the technology worked. There was no learning goal or purpose other than getting comfortable with the tool and with how to talk and interact within the live classroom.

Once five or six students expressed comfort and delight with the live classroom, Debra held an optional discussion session and then archived it for the other students. Gradually the effects rippled out, and Debra expanded the use of the classroom by inviting a psychology professor from a nearby university to address her students. Thirteen of her sixteen students participated in the interactive discussion and seminar. Most submitted questions ahead of time for the guest lecturer, using a special discussion forum established just for the "virtual visitor."

Why Eight Classrooms?

You may be wondering why Debra set up eight classrooms. Four of them were set up for four teams of four students each. This classroom served as a gathering place for these students to meet whenever they needed or wanted to. The teams used the classrooms as dedicated meeting rooms for working on projects, sharing ideas, and simply getting together. Two of the classrooms were set up for virtual visitors: one was set up as a place for general classroom activities, and the other was the Happy Hour Room. Another way of thinking about these virtual spaces is that it is almost as if the class has its own conference center, for its own purposes for the duration of the course. Consider the many possibilities that lie therein.

Using Live Classroom for a Course Closing Experience

If we extend the concept of the online classrooms as a conference center for the course, many possible uses for closing experiences become apparent. Debra used the general course classroom for having a course celebration closing party, complete with course trinkets, beverages, and special closing discussions. This may be more that what you want to do, but it tickles the imagination. Students sent company-logoed cups or hats to Debra, who then mailed a "party package" to all her students. Alternatives to this approach might be to simply determine the "party menu" and everyone bring their own beverage or treat to the event at their computer.

The closing weeks of a course almost always include project demonstrations, presentations, and group activities. The online classroom is ideal for these types of closing activities. And as discussed in another tip, including assessment and review activities makes the evaluation of student learning transparent and collaborative as well as fun.

Likely Questions

One question you may have is whether all this synchronous activity reduces the number of postings on discussion boards. This particular class averaged a bit over two hundred messages a week, so, if anything, the community that develops with the real-time gatherings may be prompting even greater asynchronous interaction.

Another question you may have is about how students respond to online courses using synchronous places when online courses are designed primarily as asynchronous and independent of time and place requirements. Informal feedback from faculty and students suggests that these gatherings work if they are optional rather than required and if the gatherings are captured and archived so that students who are unable to participate in real time can still access the experience asynchronously.

Depending on the infrastructure for your online course, creating online classrooms can be very easy or a little more difficult. Some questions that you will want to ask of your contact at your institution include the following:

- *How do I create and set up online classrooms for my course?* In some CMS systems, the online classroom appears as an option under a Communications tab. If so, click on it and create a classroom just as you might create a forum or discussion board.

- *How do I record and archive the online classroom sessions?* Press the archive button at the beginning of the session and again at the close of it. Once the session is archived, you can post the link to the recording anywhere it is convenient in your course.

- *How do I prepare technically for an online session?* Most online classroom systems have prerecorded or live tutorials available on their Web sites. Or you can prepare by attending sessions offered by your institution.

- *How do I prepare the content for an online session?* Preparing well for the content of online sessions is extremely important. The goals for everyone need to be clear, and everyone who is a leader for the session needs to be prepared—either with questions, demonstrations, or polls to make it useful and engaging.

CW Tip 9: Debriefing Techniques with Students: What One Change Would They Recommend?

This tip answers questions such as these:

- How can I know which course experiences really make a difference in learning; alternatively, how can I know which course experiences are duds?

- What are some strategies for encouraging students to help improve future courses?

Wouldn't you like to know specifically which of the course activities and experiences really worked for your students' learning? Which activities had an impact on their knowledge, skills, and ways of thinking? The best way to do this is to ask.

Create a special "place" for the course debriefing—as simple as a new discussion forum, as quick as a survey, or as complex as a wiki that you have developed with all the course readings and resources. Once you have selected the particular place or tool, ask your students after their final projects are completed one or more of these questions:

- What was the best, or a very good, course experience—reading, activity, project, and discussion—for you personally? And why?

- What would you have liked to have studied in more detail or explored more widely?

- What course activity do you strongly recommend to keep for the next offering of this course? Why?

- What one change would you recommend?

You might focus questions on a new activity that you introduced this term or imagine that a new learner about to enroll in the course wanted advice about how to succeed in the course. Students do have a soft place in their hearts generally for students who might be taking the course after them. For example, you might ask one of these questions:

- What did you enjoy or not enjoy about [a new resource, the use of new audio or video resources, or a new two-person team assignment, for example]?

- If you had one piece of advice for a student about to start this course, what would it be?

A simple debriefing of this sort is valuable for students as they focus on what specific assignments, readings, and experiences worked for them. This debriefing gives immediate and specific feedback that can quickly be applied to the new course offering. Students then also feel as if they are contributing to the program quality and feeling that their comments make a difference. Students are often asked or required to complete other questionnaires regarding their learning experiences, but these tools are most helpful to administrators. The feedback is often too delayed or too generic to be of much use to faculty in helping with course design.

When faculty use this debriefing activity, they are often pleasantly surprised. Students often respond that the best parts of the course are those that are the least work for the faculty, and that activities on which you might spend a great deal of time are not that important after all.

Conclusion—and What's Next?

If you have been using this book as a guide to teaching your first online course, you are likely ready to take a deep breath, celebrate, and give yourself a few pats on the back. Completing a new task that is as complex and challenging as teaching and coaching students in a new environment is very satisfying. By now you probably have developed a feeling of competence in at least a few areas. Be sure to take time to acknowledge your success at whatever level you are. Stop and write a note to yourself or a short note to a colleague, and share what you feel very good about and what your top priorities are for when you teach a course for the second time.

In the final chapter of this book, we'll look at some issues you might have faced and how to improve your next offering of this course or your next online course.

Part Three

What's Next

Chapter 12

Reflecting and Looking Forward

Chapter Overview

Congratulations on completing your first (or second or more) online course. By now you've completed your review and grading of all the students' work, turned in the grades, and are probably ready for a day or two off. Do take the time to reward yourself for taking on a new challenge and making it work.

The best time to reflect and debrief yourself about the experience, either by yourself or with one of your mentors, colleagues, or department chair, is while the experience is still fresh. So don't wait too long before doing this debriefing. Review what worked well, what may not have worked so well, and any possible surprises that you encountered. If you will be teaching this course again, now is also the time to plan revisions. If you will be teaching a different online course, make a record of the general insights you have developed.

Reflecting and Looking Forward Using the Four Course Phases

Reflecting on a course and planning for the next offering of a course can be a joy and a struggle. Very probably, there were successful moments as well as tough ones. Developing a "lessons learned" summary for yourself and revising the course to be more effective takes time and a bit of practice. However, just as time-on-task is an essential part of learning; time-on-task is part of the process of becoming an expert online faculty.

Here are sets of questions and descriptions of common problems for the four phases of a course. You can use these to guide the reflection of course you have just completed and to guide the planning and revisions for your next course.

Design and Preparation Phase

Start your reflection by reviewing the course from the beginning: the design and preparation phase. Check yourself with these questions:

- What did you not have prepared as well as you thought you had? One area that usually takes more practice is creating the discussion forum postings and the directions for those postings. You can never be too clear and explicit.

- Was your syllabus clear enough on the policies?

- Did your syllabus clearly map out the week-by-week view of readings, assignments, and expectations?

- In the assignments, did you talk to the students as if you were talking to them face-to-face in a classroom? Many syllabi state, "the students will do this" or "the students will do that." That format is appropriate for curriculum review but not for instructions to the students.

- What about your assessment plan and the rubrics for each of the components of the plan? Did you and your students use the rubrics well? Or would you like to refine and adapt them more to the particular content?

Common Problem Area: Learners Were Confused About Activities

You no doubt realize that some of your instructions may need to be clarified if learners were confused. So one step is to review and clarify your instructions on readings, assignments, and postings. However, it may also be that learners are not reading your instructions. If that is the case, you might want to set up a self-quiz about the syllabus and other major directions in the course. The automated quiz functions available in most systems are a good tool for this. Another useful strategy is to create a student forum for students to talk with each other about instructions. Of course, you can also use this place to respond and clarify as well.

Common Problem Area: Some Students Can Be Bullies or Simply Have Bad Manners

Online courses are not exempt from the challenge of difficult students. Students can be difficult by acting or speaking inappropriately in the discussion forum, for example. Susan Ko, director of the Teaching and Learning Center at the University of Maryland, University College, describes a couple of undesirable behaviors: "Such [difficult] students often create new topic threads when only a reply is really called for and pepper existing discussion threads with inane comments."

Students who behave this way sometimes are just looking for more personal attention, and a personal e-mail can sometimes help this. A good general rule is to handle difficult students online in the same way that you would handle them in a face-to-face class: take them to one side and in a personal and confidential way provide some counsel. (For more ideas go to http://deoracle.org/online-pedagogy/.)

Reflecting on Phase One, Course Beginnings

The themes for the course beginnings focused on social presence, getting acquainted, launching the community, and ensuring that all the content and tools for teaching and learning were in place. These questions will get you started:

- How did the initial getting-acquainted experiences work? Did all your students respond in a timely and appropriate manner? Did you share enough of yourself and help to make social connections as the base for the cognitive connections?

- Did you follow up with all students to ensure that everyone was engaged in the course in the first few days of the course? If you lost any of your students, this can often be the place you can ensure that students feel welcome and are in the right course at the right time.

- Launching of the learning community is often linked to course goals and objectives. Did you have a forum that focused on the learners' setting personalized and customized goals? How did it work? Did you feel that the students made a connection between themselves and the goals of the course?

- Did the students acquire the core required content resources in a timely manner? Did getting the materials pose any difficulties? Do you want to make changes in the sets of content resources for the next course?

- Did the students—or you—have any unresolved technical issues regarding the tools used in the course? Was the needed technical support in place and responsive?

- Were there other administrative issues that created difficulties that need to be reported to administrators?

Common Problem Area: Discussions Were Flat or Never Got Going

If you felt as if your discussions did not take off or were generally flat without passion or energy, review the discussion questions. Did you tend to use one-answer questions or those that called for a yes or no and nothing more? If so, be sure to develop open-ended questions by using such phrases as, "In what way...," or "Based on your own experiences...," or "Using data from your particular region or discipline perspective..." Another question to ask yourself is whether you were too involved too early in the discussions. Did learners wait to read what you wrote or ask you what you thought before posting their own response? If so, make it clearer in the instructions that you will guide discussion and will comment primarily to encourage and facilitate and to help craft a discussion summary.

Common Problem Area: You Are Not Feeling Comfortable with the Course Management System

If there were activities that you wanted to design for students using the course management system but didn't quite know how to, plan to get those questions answered before teaching another online course. For example, you may have questions about setting up groups, using some audio tools, or using the synchronous online classroom. The best way to ensure that you will be ready and able to use these features in your next course is to create a "Top Three Things That I Want to Know How to Do" list and then write out the steps to make that happen. You may want to take a refresher course with your institution to expand your knowledge about the system. The second time around it will all make more sense, and you will get even more ideas about how to make better use of the tools.

Reflecting on Phase Two, Early Middle

One of the most important tasks for keeping the ball rolling in the early middle is the nurturing of a learning community for your students. This is accomplished with a strong teaching and cognitive presence. Here are some of the questions to reflect on:

- How did you feel about the process of building the learning community?

- Did you see the learners getting engaged with the content?

- Did you keep cycling back to the core concepts and linking those concepts to the learning outcomes? Or did you not review, summarize, or link back well enough?

- Did you focus time on getting to know the individual learners? Did you know where they were coming from and what they hoped to learn so that you could help them discern patterns and relationships?

Common Problem Area: A Learning Community Never Formed

If a learning community never really came together, this might be a response to your teaching presence. In some cases, you may need to revise your rubrics to place more emphasis on students' continuing the flow of a discussion and responding to other students' comments and responding to the ideas and assertions in the readings. Community forms only when learners do more than simply taking turns in response to a question. Recall that community depends on "long, thoughtful, threaded discussion on a subject of importance after which participants felt both personal satisfaction and kinship" (Brown, 2001, p. 18). A greater focus on core required readings and case studies can provide the basis of shared experiences and a deeper connection to the content and to the other learners.

Another aspect of community is equality. This means that your role as an expert can overpower the learners, so you may need to be more in the background in the discussions and reserve your more expansive expertise for the summaries, mini-introductions, and concept demonstrations and for facilitating and drawing out from the learners what they know. Another design strategy to build into your course is to assign one or two learners as a team to lead a forum discussion for a week. Review the many tips on community building as well.

Reflecting on Phase Three, Late Middle

The late middle is a time of increased exploration and engagement with the content while also shifting into a content resolution and focus stage. Here are some questions to reflect on:

- How were the students doing midway through the course? Were they engaged and working well?
- Had the students identified their course projects? Did you help to ensure that the projects were a good match for the students and the course goals?
- Were the students actively supporting and helping each other?
- How were you feeling about the course at this point? Did you feel as if you wanted to adapt some of the course readings or requirements?

Common Problem Area: Assignments Were Consistently Late

If learners were consistently turning in assignments a day or more late, you may wish to deduct points or use a clever ticket system devised by one of our colleagues. He gave each student a "one late assignment free" ticket that the learner could use when an emergency arose and he or she needed to turn in an assignment late. In other cases, you may decide on a policy of subtracting points for each day that an assignment is late. You may also want to review your assessment plan and see if you have too many assignments, making it difficult for learners to complete them all. When you review your assessment plan, consider how directly the assessment plan supports the learning of the course objectives. Some faculty also use the announcement feature and remind students two or three days before an assignment is due.

Reflecting on Phase Four, Closing Weeks

In the closing weeks of a course, you are guiding and mentoring the students in their projects. You are also finding ways to affirm and confirm the learners' understanding of the core concepts in the course and mentor the learners in achieving the learning outcomes. Here are a few questions to check how the teaching and learning in this part of the course worked:

- Were students involved in peer review of project work?

- Were the students collaborating with and challenging their colleagues?

- Were the teams working well? Or were any adjustments you had to make working?

- Did you help the learners organize themselves for the last part of the course, making sure that the goals, outcomes, and expectations all were still making sense?

Common Problem Area: The Course Could Use More "Pizzazz"

If you are feeling comfortable in your course system and would like to add more media or more variety to your course, you may want to consider using one or two of the technology tools described in earlier chapters. A good place to start is adding audio to your welcome message. This could be done with a simple slide presentation—perhaps two or three slides with audio. Or you could make a video welcome message if you feel ready for that. You might also want to add two or three podcasts, either audio or video, with short concept introductions or reviews of one or two course modules. As always, keep it simple, move slowly, and don't feel that you have to revolutionize your course all at once.

Common Problem Area: Final Course Evaluation Responses Unpleasantly Surprised You

If learners are feeling unhappy or experiencing dissatisfaction with your course, it's a good idea to know this before the end-of-course evaluations.

As recommended in one of the tips on feedback, ask for feedback early in the course and, depending on circumstances, at other points as well, such as feedback on a project assignment or unusual resources. If you did not ask for feedback early in your first course, be sure to design in a couple of feedback points for your next course.

Common Problem Area: Something Is Not Quite Right, But You're Not Sure What

If you're feeling uncomfortable about how the course went, this is a good time to evaluate the alignment of your learning outcomes, assessments, and activities. Do they all relate to one another, or is there an objective that didn't make sense for these students? Or is there a learning outcome that should be added? If the course elements are not aligned, the course can easily go off-track without anyone noticing until a major assessment occurs. One of the tips suggested asking your students for specific feedback on a new assignment, reading, or activity. If you did that, then be sure to use that feedback as you revise your course.

Reflecting and Looking Forward with the Learning Experiences Framework

Another way of reviewing your course is to use the learning experiences framework described in Chapter Two. You'll recall that this framework has four elements: the learner, the faculty mentor, the content, and the context or environment. Here are a few questions for each of the four elements.

Learner

- What did you learn about the learners in your course?
- Did anything about the learners in your course surprise you? The amount of time they spent on the course? How they wanted to interact?
- Were the learners who you thought they would be? Were they interested in achieving the designated learning outcomes that you had planned or were they interested in refreshing or developing a different area of expertise?
- Did they have the appropriate prerequisite skills?
- Did they interact and collaborate as expected?
- Did they successfully complete the course?
- If a learner was unsuccessful, why did that happen?

If your learners did not have the prerequisite skills that you thought they would have, you may want to develop a precourse unit, that is, a review of what learners need to be able to do or know before beginning the course. This could be a self-paced unit that includes self-tests. If a high percentage of learners were unsuccessful, reexamine the alignment of objectives, activities, and assessment. The course might have gotten off-track in some way, and assessment did not match the content or activities. If interaction and collaboration did not take off and blossom, review the expectations stated about collaboration. Make sure that at least 20 to 30 percent of the course points were allocated to participation so as to send the message that interaction is important.

Faculty Mentor

- Were you adequately present in the course?

- Did you guide and not dominate the discussions?

- In what ways could you have helped learners be more successful?

- How do you think your instruction could be improved? Think about all the areas you are responsible for: instruction, design, implementation, teaching presence, and learner response. How would you improve each of these?

If you did not develop a satisfactory relationship with the students individually or as a group, review your social, teaching, and cognitive presence in the course. Maybe you remained aloof from the students and didn't give them a chance to get to know you. Maybe your teaching direction at the general course level was effective, but you did not shift and provide any personal or customized mentoring or guidance. And review your cognitive presence. Did you help the students become knowledgeable and comfortable with the core concepts and regularly review, facilitate, and challenge the students?

Content and Knowledge Resources and Goals

- Did your choice of required, recommended resources work for the students? Were the resources at the right level of difficulty?

- Did the resources provide enough variety in terms of media? Did you have a set of text, audio, video, and current resources?

- Were the materials in a mobile and digital format that made it easy for the students to access and use?

- Were the content resources effective at helping the students achieve the course learning outcomes?

- Did you build in opportunities for learners to add to the content you had planned?

In the first cycle of a course, the resources may or may not be effective at engaging the students in the way you would like. The resources might not be a good fit, or there may not be a rich enough set to challenge, assist, or engage the students. Be sure to review the resources and add or delete, and perhaps annotate, recommended sources.

Copyright issues might also need to be addressed. Most institutions have policies and staff people to help if you need to address issues of fair use and appropriate use.

Environment and Context

- Where did the students do their best work at learning: individually, in small teams, or in larger groups?

- Which tools and resources were the best fit for the content and your students?

- Did technical issues detract from the course?

- Did the students use many of the new Web applications to do their teamwork and their collaborative or synchronous work? Which of these tools might you want to build into your next course?

- What information might learners need for resolving problems more effectively in future offerings of the course?

These questions are a combination of pedagogical strategy, student preferences, and the particular demands of the content and the performance goals of the course, so answering the questions might be difficult after your first course. But you may want to be alert in future course cycles to some of these questions. As for yourself, review where you do your best teaching in an online course and record the habits, strategies, and tools that work best for you.

Advice from Fellow Online Instructors

You are not alone in the triumphs and challenges you have faced in designing and implementing your online course. Developing expertise in teaching online is a process of continuing dedication over time. Here are a few words that may resonate with you from those who have made similar journeys.

Advice 1: Just Do Your Best

Almost every objection raised by faculty who imagine what online teaching "must" be like has been answered by the actual experience of doing it and searching for ways to make an online course the best it can be. I still tell my students, "This is a class with no back seats," and do everything I can, whether high tech or low tech, to make it so. Nobody has it all figured out, but just do your best to be better at it tomorrow than you were yesterday, and you'll make it fine!
—David W. Forman, Ed.D., Graduate Education, Georgetown College, Georgetown, Kentucky

Advice 2: It's Kind of Fun to Do the Impossible!

The reason I love teaching online is the challenges of working with incredibly unique individuals with highly diverse backgrounds. When computers began to be used in teaching, I heard a lot of negative predictions about them: "They will take away the human touch." "They will be cold and impersonal." "They just won't work." I'm the type of individual who says, "Show me!" Instead of accepting such negative predictions at face value, I look for the silver lining. What someone else sees as impossible, I learn to welcome as a challenge! This is what drew me to exploring the positive possibilities of teaching by computer in 1994 when a senior faculty member said, "Why not try this? And I think you should be the one to do it!!"

I was delighted by the students' positive response to the two online courses I developed and taught that summer. They were far from cold and impersonal, and the students sang the praises of its flexibility and the individual attention that they got from me. I'll never forget how one of them, a student who had been somewhat fearful of statistics, excitedly printed out all of her study notes and went to show our depart-ment chair what she was learning. You'd think she was showing him a stash of gifts from the genuine joy and excitement in her voice.

These successes fueled my passion to keep it going. Keep peeking outside the box. Keep pushing the boundaries of what can be done in online teaching and learning. So from that humble beginning, I developed more courses ... that led to more student demand for them ... that in turn led to other faculty members wanting to get in on a very good thing! As Walt Disney once said: "It's kind of fun to do the impossible!"
—Mary I. Dereshiwsky, Ph.D, Professor, College of Education, Northern Arizona University, Flagstaff, Arizona

Advice 3: Begin with the End in Mind

In my first semester as an assistant professor, I was given an online course, developed by another instructor to teach. The course was Instructional Systems Design, a project-based course for graduate students. As a new professor with three new preps, I tried to make minor changes to the course rather than starting with the learning objectives I had developed. First lesson learned: modifying someone else's course to your objectives is almost harder than starting from scratch.

Because I thought the course would be "reusable" as it was, I did not plan enough time for review and revision and consequently made adjustments on the fly. The lack of congruence between my learning objectives and the existing instructional materials caused difficulty for the students' ability to readily grasp and apply the concepts. I learned that designing quality online courses must begin with the end in mind: what your learners will be able to do! Determine the learning objectives for your course first, and then choose the content, assessments, and technologies! Backward planning will also help provide an overall temporal time line for your course.

Adequate time to align the instructional materials with the learning objectives is interrelated with what I believe is the second best practice: an online course must be fully designed and developed before the first learner accesses the course. I have worked with many instructors who did not fully grasp the concept of what a complete online course entails until after they had invested an exorbitant amount of time teaching and developing concurrently!

The dual role of developer and instructor left little time for comprehensive feedback on the discussion boards or assignments, much less for teachable moments! The experience was painful for both the instructor and the students. So be sure to give yourself enough time to completely design and develop an online course. Depending on the content, support, and technology, the time required could range from six months for a new course to six weeks to revise a course. When is your course complete? When another instructor is able to teach your online course with little or no prep!

—Kathy Ingram, Ph.D., Jacksonville University, Jacksonville, Florida

Rubrics and Best Practices for Quality Online Courses

In Chapter Four on getting your online course ready, we referred to a Quality Matters Rubric from the Quality Matters Institute. This rubric is a tool that you can use to help you evaluate the quality of your online course. There are other checklists that you might want to refer to as well. One of the most recognized set of guidelines is *Best Practices for Electronically Offered Degree and Certificate Programs* developed by the eight regional accrediting commissions in response to the emergence of technologically mediated instruction offered at a distance as an important component of higher education (http://www.ncahlc.org/download/Best_Pract_DEd.pdf).

Two other monographs on ensuring quality in distance learning are available from the Council for Higher Education:

- Accreditation and Assuring Quality in Distance Learning. CHEA Monograph Series 2002, No. 1. http://www.chea.org/pdf/mono_1_accred_distance_02.pdf (2002a).

- Specialized Accreditation and Assuring Quality in Distance Learning. CHEA Monograph Series 2002, Number 2. http://www.chea.org/pdf/mono_2_spec-accred_02.pdf (2002b).

Conclusion: Innovation as a Three-Phase Process

A business innovation professor at Harvard describes the cycle of innovation as a three-phase process: imitation, incremental improvements, followed by transformational processes (Rosenbloom, 1999). These phases can guide our innovation journey in online teaching and learning as well. The first time you design and teach a course, you tend to do things in much the same way you've always done them but using the new technology, the new online space, the new course management system. In your next two or three cycles of teaching, you'll become comfortable with the base set of tools, add new tools, refine your use of the base set of tools, and refine your teaching strategies and content resources. By the third and later cycles, you venture forth and create a new course maximizing the new environment and testing innovative new strategies.

Of course, with the ever-increasing rate of change, we don't see an end to innovation. We just start the three cycles again. What doesn't change is the fundamental relationship of a teacher to student or mentor to learner. That is our treasure and one we always will have.

Resources for Learning More About the Research and Theory of Teaching Online

BECOMING A MASTER in the art and skill of teaching and learning online is a journey. Here are some resources to help you along the way. Becoming an expert is a matter of years and dedication, not just months. Be patient with yourself, enjoy the process, and invite your colleagues and students to share and enjoy the journey with you.

As you are learning how to teach online, watch for excellent resources on topics such as research on learning, memory, and brain development. These are all areas that are changing how we think about teaching and learning. It is also useful to be alert to how your learners, and people in general, are using new technologies. This will have an impact on our teaching and learning environments, and probably sooner rather than later.

The resources listed here are just some of our favorites. In these days of the Internet, it is not possible to be comprehensive. Thus, these are just starting points.

Books

Teaching and Learning Online

Anderson, T., & Elloumi, F. (2008). *The theory and practice of online learning* (2nd ed.). Alberta, Canada: Athabasca University.

Bender, T. (2003). *Discussion-based online teaching to enhance student learning: Theory, practice and assessment.* Sterling, VA: Stylus Publishing.

Boettcher, J. V., & Conrad, R. M. (2004). *Faculty guide for moving teaching and learning to the Web* (2nd ed.). Phoenix, AZ: League for Innovation.

Bonk, C. J., & Zhang, K. (2008). *Empowering online learning.* Jossey-Bass, San Francisco.

Brookfield, S. D., & Preskill, S. N. (2005). *Discussion as a way of teaching: Tools and techniques for democratic classrooms* (2nd ed.). San Francisco: Jossey-Bass.

Conrad, R. M., & Donaldson, J. A. (2004). *Engaging the online learner: Activities and resources for creative instruction.* San Francisco: Jossey-Bass.

Draves, W. A. (2000). *Teaching online.* River Falls, WI: Lern Books.

Garrison, D. R., & Vaughan, N. D. (2008). *Blended learning in higher education: Framework, principles, and guidelines.* San Francisco: Jossey-Bass.

Hyman, R. T. (1980). *Improving discussion leadership.* New York: Teachers College Press.

Palloff, R., & Pratt, K. (2003). *The virtual student.* San Francisco: Jossey-Bass.

Palloff, R., & Pratt, K. (2007). *Building online learning communities: Effective strategies for the virtual classroom* (2nd ed.). San Francisco: Jossey-Bass.

Palloff, R., & Pratt, K. (2009). *Assessing the online learner.* San Francisco: Jossey-Bass.

Brain, Cognition, Learning, and Memory

Bohm, D. (1996). *On dialogue.* New York: Routledge.

Bloom, B. S. (Ed.). (1956). *Taxonomy of educational objectives, Handbook 1: Cognitive domain.* Reading, MA: Addison-Wesley.

Bransford, J. D., Brown, A. L., & Cocking, R. R. (Eds.). (2000). *How people learn. Brain, mind, experience, and school* (Exp. ed.). Washington, DC: National Academies Press.

Daniels, H., Cole, M., & Wertsch, J.V. (2007). *The Cambridge companion to Vygotsky.* Cambridge: Cambridge University Press.

Kandel, E. (2006). *In search of memory: The emergence of a new science of mind.* New York Norton.

Moll, L. C. (Ed.). (1990/2004). *Vygotsky and education: Instructional implications and applications of sociohistorical psychology.* Cambridge: Cambridge University Press.

Pink, D. H. (2005). *A whole new mind.* New York: Penguin.

Roediger, H. L., Dudai, Y., & Fitzpatrick, S. M. (Eds.). (2007). *Science of memory: Concepts.* New York: Oxford University Press.

Schacter, D. L. (2001). *The seven sins of memory: How the mind forgets and remembers.* Boston: Houghton Mifflin.

Zull, J. E. (2002). *The art of changing the brain: Enriching teaching by exploring the biology of learning*. Sterling, VA: Stylus Publishing.

Journals

Campus Technology, http://www.campustechnology.com

eLearning Reviews, http://www.elearning-reviews.org

Innovate: A Journal of Online Education, http://innovateonline.info/

International Review of Research in Open and Distance Learning, http://www.irrodl.org/index.php/irrodl

Journal for Asynchronous Learning Networks, http://www.aln.org/publications/jaln/index.asp

Journal of Interactive Online Learning, http://www.ncolr.org/

Journal of Online Learning and Teaching, http://jolt.merlot.org

National Teaching and Learning Forum, http://www.ntlf.com/

Organizations, Conferences, and Certifications

EDUCAUSE Learning Initiative, http://www.educause.edu/eli

Faculty Development Institute sponsored by the Learning Resources Network, www.lern.org

International Council on Open and Distance Education, http://www.icde.org/

Sloan-C International Conference on Online Learning, http://www.sloanconsortium.org/aln

University of Wisconsin's Annual Conference on Distance Teaching and Learning Conference, http://www.uwex.edu/disted/conference/

Communities and Listservs

OL Daily and OL Weekly by Stephen Downes, Stephen's Web, http://www.downes.ca/about.htm

Online Faculty Club, www.lern.org

Online Learning Update, Ray Schroeder, ed., OTEL, Online@ Illinois Springfield http://people.uis.edu/rschr1/onlinelearning/blogger.html

Professional and Organization Development Network in Higher Education https://listserv.nd.edu/

SL Educators (The SLED List\), https://lists.secondlife.com/cgi-bin/mailman/listinfo/educators

Other Teaching and Learning Resources

Adjunct Success, Richard Lyons, http://www.developfaculty.com; mix of free and subscription resources

Assessing group work and projects, University College/Dublin Centre for Teaching and Learning, http://www.ucd.ie/teaching/goodPracticeAssessment_sub/groupWork.html

Canadian Institute of Distance Education Research at Athabasca University, http://cider.athabascau.ca/Distance Education Clearinghouse

DE Oracle @ UMUC, http://deoracle.org/

Illinois Online Network Online Education Resources, http://www.ion.uillinois.edu/resources/tutorials/

Instructional Design for Online Courses, http://www.ibritt.com/resources/dc_instructionaldesign.htm

iTunes University, http://www.apple.com/education/mobile-learning/

Library of E-coaching Tips for Teaching Online by Designing for Learning, http://www.designingforlearning.info/services/writing/ecoach/index.htm

MIT OpenCourseWare, http://ocw.mit.edu/OcwWeb/web/home/home/index.htm

Multimedia Educational Resource for Learning and Online Teaching (MERLOT), http://www.merlot.org/merlot/index.htm

Penn State University Hot Teams for Technology White Papers, http://tlt.its.psu.edu/hot-team

Penn State University Schreyer Institute for Teaching Excellence, http://www.schreyerinstitute.psu.edu/Tools/

Theory into Practice database, http://tip.psychology.org/

Top 100 Tools for Learning 2009, http://www.c4lpt.co.uk/recommended/

University of Wisconsin's Annual Conference on Distance Teaching and Learning Conference, http://www.uwex.edu/disted/conference/

Other Books and Articles of Interest

Batson, T. (2009). Why is Web 2.0 important to higher education? *Campus Technology*. Retrieved April 17, 2009, from http://campustechnology.com/Articles/2009.

Boettcher, J. V. (2003). Course management systems and learning principles—Getting to know each other. *Syllabus, 16*(12), 33–36. Retrieved October 4, 2009, from http://campustechnology.com/Articles/2003/06/Course-Management-Systems-and-Learning-Principles-Getting-to-Know-Each-Other.aspx.

Boettcher, J. V. (2004). Design levels for distance and online learning. In R. Discenza, C. Howard, & K. Schenk (Eds.), *Distance learning and university effectiveness: Changing educational paradigms for online learning*. Hershey, PA: Idea Group.

Borthick, A. F., Jones, D. R., & Wakai, S. (2003). Designing learning experiences within learners' zones of proximal development (ZPDs): Enabling collaborative learning on-site and online. *Journal of Information Systems, 17*(1), 107–134. Retrieved December 15, 2009, from http://www2.gsu.edu/%7Eaccafb/pubs/JISBorthickJonesWakai2003.pdf.

Brown, M. (2007). Mashing up the once and future CMS. *EDUCAUSE Review, 42*(2), 8–9. Retrieved April 3, 2007, from http://www.educause.edu/ir/library/pdf/erm0725.pdf.

Coates, J. (2007). *Generational learning styles*. River Falls, WI: Learning Resources Network.

Gould, M., & Padavano, D. (2006, May). Seven ways to improve student satisfaction in online courses. *OnlineClassroom*, pp. 1–2.

Hayles, K. N. (2007). Hyper and deep attention: The generational divide in cognitive modes. *Profession, 13*, 187–199.

Knowles, M. (1980). *The modern practice of adult education: From pedagogy to andragogy* (2nd ed.). New York: Association Press.

Mabrito, M. (2004). Guidelines for establishing interactivity in online courses. *Innovate, 1*(2). Retrieved November 12, 2008, from http://www.innovateonline.info/index.php?view=article&id=12.

Moskal, B. M. (2000). Scoring rubrics: What, when and how? *Practical Assessment, Research & Evaluation, 7*(3). Retrieved April 26, 2009, from http://pareonline.net/getvn.asp?v=7&n=3.

Muirhead, B. (2006, January). Creating concept maps: Integrating constructivism principles into online classes. Article 2. *International Journal of Instructional Technology and Distance Learning, 3*(1). Retrieved April 11, 2009, from http://www.itdl.org/Journal/jan_06/article02.htm.

Palloff, R., & Pratt, K. (2007). *Building online learning communities: Effective strategies for the virtual classroom* (2nd ed.). San Francisco: Jossey-Bass.

Paul, R., & Elder, L. (2008). *The analysis and assessment of thinking*. Retrieved April 11, 2009, from http://www.criticalthinking.org/page.cfm?PageID=497&CategoryID=68.

Paul, R., & Elder, L. (2008). *The miniature guide to critical thinking: Concepts and tools*. Dillon Beach, CA: Foundation for Critical Thinking.

Pelz, B. (2004). (My) three principles of effective online pedagogy. *Journal of Asynchronous Learning Networks, 8*(3). Retrieved November

12, 2008, from www.sloan-c.org/publications/jaln/v8n3/v8n3_pelz.asp.

Roediger, H. L., Dudai, Y., & Fitzpatrick, S. M. (Ed.). (2007). *Science of memory: Concepts*. New York: Oxford University Press.

Shieh, D. (2009, March 6). These lectures are gone in 60 seconds. *Chronicle of Higher Education*. Retrieved April 17, 2009, from http://chronicle.com/free/v55/i26/26a00102.htm.

Svinicki, M. (2006). *The discussion class: Interaction functions*. Retrieved April 27, 2009, from www.utexas.edu/academic/diia/gsi/coursedesign/interaction.php.

Vesely, P., Bloom, L., & Sherlock, J. (2007). Key elements of building online community: Comparing faculty and student perceptions. *Journal of Online Learning and Teaching, 3*(3). Retrieved January 9, 2009, from jolt.merlot.org/vol3no3/vesely.htm.

Weiman, C. (2007, September–October). Why not try a scientific approach to science education? *Change*, pp. 9–15. Retrieved September 28, 2009, from http://www.changemag.org/Archives/Back%20Issues/September-October%202007/full-scientific-approach.html.

Weimer, M. (2002). *Learner-centered teaching*. San Francisco: Jossey-Bass.

References

Abramson, L. (2007). Online courses catch on in U.S. colleges. *NPR Morning Edition*. Retrieved April 15, 2009, from http://www.npr.org/templates/story/story.php?storyId=16638700.

Akyol, Z., & Garrison, D. R. (2008). The development of a community of inquiry over time in an online course: Understanding the progression and integration of social, cognitive and teaching presence. *Journal of Asynchronous Learning Networks, 12*(3), 322.

Allen, D. (2002). *Getting things done: The art of stress-free productivity.* New York: New York Penguin.

Allen, I. E., & Seaman, J. (2008). *Staying the course: Online education in the United States.* Needham, MA: Sloan-C. Retrieved April 9, 2009, from http://www.sloan-c.org/publications/survey/index.asp.

Anderson, C. (2006). *The long tail: Why the future of business is selling less of more.* New York: Hyperion Books.

Bartoletti, R. (2007). *Discussion board assignment.* Texas Woman's University. Retrieved April 24, 2009, from http://www.twu.edu/downloads/de/discussion_rubric.pdf.

Bennett, D. (2009). *Trends in the higher education labor force: Identifying changes in worker composition and productivity.* Center for College Affordability and Productivity. Retrieved September 17, 2009, from http://www.centerforcollegeaffordability.org/uploads/Labor_Force.pdf.

Bloom, B. S. (Ed.). (1956). *Taxonomy of educational objectives, Handbook 1: Cognitive domain.* Reading, MA: Addison-Wesley.

Boettcher, J. V. (1998). Let's boldly go . . . to the education Holodeck. *Syllabus, 11*(10), 18–22. Retrieved April 23, 2009, from http://www.designingforlearning.info/articles/holodeck.html.

Boettcher, J. V. (2003). Course management systems and learning principles—Getting to know each other. *Syllabus, 16*(12), 33–36. Retrieved October 4, 2009, from http://campustechnology.com/Articles/2003/06/Course-Management-Systems-and-Learning-Principles-Getting-to-Know-Each-Other.aspx.

Boettcher, J. (2007). Ten core principles for designing effective learning environments: Insights from brain research and pedagogical theory. *Innovate Journal of Online Education, 3*(3). Retrieved April 24, 2009, from http://innovateonline.info/index.php?view=article&id=54.

Boettcher, J. V. (2009, April). Have we arrived? *Campus Technology.* Retrieved October 4, 2009, from http://campustechnology.com/articles/2009/04/01/elearning.aspx?sc_lang=en.

Boettcher, J. V., & Conrad, R. M. (2004). *Faculty guide for moving teaching and learning to the Web* (2nd ed.). Phoenix, AZ: League for Innovation.

Bohm, D. (1996). *On dialogue.* New York: Routledge.

Bok, D. (2005, December 18). Are colleges failing? Higher ed needs new lesson plans. *Boston Globe.* Retrieved April 24, 2009, from http://www.boston.com/news/education/higher/articles/2005/12/18/are_colleges_failing?mode=PF.

Bok, D. (2007). *Our underachieving colleges: A candid look at how much students learn and why they should be learning more.* Princeton, NJ: Princeton University Press.

Bonk, C. J., & Zhang, K. (2008). *Empowering online learning. 100+ activities for reading, reflecting, displaying, and doing.* San Francisco: Jossey-Bass.

Bransford, J. D., Brown, A. L., & Cocking, R. R. (Eds.). (2000). *How people learn: Brain, mind, experience, and school* (Exp. ed.). Washington, DC: National Academies Press. Retrieved April 24, 2009, from http://www.nap.edu/books/0309070368/html/.

Briskin, L. (2005). *Assigning grades and feedback policies.* Retrieved February 4, 2009, from www.arts.yorku.ca/sosc/Foundations/documents/EXAMPLEOFACHECKLIST.pdf.

Brookfield, S. D., & Preskill, S. N. (2005). *Discussion as a way of teaching: Tools and techniques for democratic classrooms* (2nd ed.). San Francisco: Jossey-Bass.

Brown, J. S. (1997). Research that reinvents the corporation. In J. Brown (Ed.), *Seeing differently: Insights on innovation.* Cambridge, MA: Harvard Business Press.

Brown, J. S. (2006). New learning environments for the 21st century: Exploring the edge. *Change.* Retrieved December 9, 2009, from http://www.johnseelybrown.com/Change%20article.pdf

Brown, J. S., Collins, A., & Duguid, P. (1989, January–February). Situated cognition and the culture of learning. *Educational Researcher,* pp. 32–42.

Brown, J. S., & Duguid, P. A. (2000). *The social life of information.* Cambridge, MA: Harvard Business Press.

Brown, R. E. (2001). The process of community-building in distance learning classes. *Journal of Asynchronous Learning Networks, 5*(2), 18–35. Retrieved January 15, 2007, from www.sloan-c.org/publications/JALN/v5n2/pdf/v5n2_brown.pdf.

Bruckman, A. S. (2005). Student research and the Internet. *Communications of the ACM, 4812,* 35–37.

Bruner, J. S. (1963). *The process of education.* New York: Vintage Books.

Byrnes, J. P. (1996). *Cognitive development and learning in instructional contexts.* Boston: Allyn & Bacon.

Burge, E. (2008). Online issues carrying ethical implications. Closing Session, 14th Sloan-C International Conference on Online Learning, Orlando, FL, November 5–7.

Burnett, K., Bonnici, L. J., Miksa, S. D., & Joonmin, K. (2007). Frequency, intensity and topicality in online learning: An exploration of the interaction dimensions that contribute to student satisfaction in online learning. *Journal of Education for Library and Information Science, 48*(1), 21–35.

Business-Higher Education Forum. (2003). *Building a nation of learners: The need for changes in teaching and learning to meet global challenges.* American Council on Education. Retrieved April 24, 2009, from http://www.bhef.com/publications/documents/building_nation_03.pdf.

Cahill, M., & Fonteyn, M. (2000). Using mind mapping to improve students' metacognition. In J. Higgs & M. Jones (Eds.), *Clinical reasoning in the health professions* (pp. 214–221). Burlington, MA: Butterworth-Heinemann.

Carlson, A. (2001). *Authentic learning: What does it really mean?* Innovative Teaching Showcase from Western Washington University. Retrieved April 27, 2009, from pandora.cii.wwu.edu/showcase2001/authentic_learning.htm.

Chang, R. Y., & Kelly, P. K. (1999). *Step-by-step problem solving: A practical guide to ensure problems get (and stay) solved.* San Francisco: Jossey-Bass/Pfeiffer.

Characteristics of a quality online discussion posting or message. St. John's University. Retrieved April 27, 2009, from www.stjohns.edu/faculty/portable_old/portable1/tools/messages.sju.

Clabaugh, G. K. (Ed.). (2009). *Jerome Bruner's educational theory.* Retrieved September 29, 2009, from http://www.newfoundations.com/GALLERY/Bruner.html.

Collins, A., Brown, J. S., & Holum, A. (1991). Cognitive apprenticeship: Making thinking visible. *American Educator.* Retrieved April 24, 2009, from http://www.21learn.org/archive/articles/brown_seely.php.

Conrad, R. M., & Donaldson, J. A. (2004). *Engaging the online learner: Activities and resources for creative instruction.* San Francisco: Jossey-Bass.

Coppola, N. W., Hiltz, S. R., & Rotter, N. G. (2004). Building trust in virtual teams. *IEEE Transactions on Professional Communication, 47*(2), 95–104.

Cooper, S. T., Tyser, R. W., & Sandheinrich, M. B. (2007, September). The benefits of linking assignments to online quizzes in introductory biology courses. *MERLOT Journal of Online Learning and Teaching*, 3(3). Retrieved December 15, 2009, from http://jolt.merlot.org/vol3no3/cooper.pdf.

Council for Higher Education. (2002a). *Accreditation and assuring quality in distance learning*. Washington, DC: Author. Retrieved December 15, 2009, from http://www.chea.org/pdf/mono_1_accred_distance_02.pdf?pubID=246.

Council for Higher Education. (2002b). *Specialized accreditation and assuring quality in distance learning*. Washington, DC: Author. Retrieved December 15, 2009, from http://www.chea.org/pdf/mono_2_spec-accred_02.pdf.

Cross, K. P., & Angelo, T. A. (1993). *Classroom assessment techniques: A handbook for college teachers*. San Francisco: Jossey-Bass.

Damasio, A. (1999). *The feeling of what happens: Body and emotion in the making of consciousness*. New York: Harcourt.

Daniels, H. (2001). *Vygotsky and pedagogy*. New York: RoutledgeFalmer.

Daniels, H. (2007). Pedagogy. In H. Daniels, M. Cole, & J. V. Wertsch (Eds.), *The Cambridge companion to Vygotsky* (pp. 307–331). Cambridge: Cambridge University Press.

Del Rio, P., & Alvarez, A. (2007). Inside and outside the zone of proximal development: An ecofunctional reading of Vygotsky. In H. Daniels, M. Cole, & J. V. Wertsch (Eds.), *The Cambridge companion to Vygotsky* (pp. 276–303). Cambridge: Cambridge University Press.

Dewey, J. (1916). *Democracy and education: An introduction to the philosophy of education*. New York: Macmillan.

Dewey, J. (1933). *How we think*. Boston: Houghton Mifflin.

EDUCAUSE. (2009). 7 Things you should know about Google Wave. Retrieved December 12, 2009, from http://net.educause.edu/ir/library/pdf/ELI7055.pdf.

Freeman, W. J. (2000). *How brains make up their mind*. New York: Columbia University Press.

Gagné, R. M. (1965). *The conditions of learning*. New York: Holt.

Gagné, R. M., Briggs, L. J., & Wager, W. W. (1992). *Principles of instructional design* (4th ed.). Fort Worth, TX: Harcourt Brace.

Garrison, D. R. (2006). Online collaboration principles. *Journal of Asynchronous Learning Networks*, 10(1). Retrieved April 7, 2009, from http://www.sloan-c.org/publications/jaln/v10n1/v10n1_3garrison_member.asp.

Garrison, D. R. (2009, August 4–7). Collaborative constructivism and community inquiry. Forum presentation at the Annual Conference on Distance Teaching and Learning, Madison, WI. Retrieved December 12, 2009, from http://mediasite.ics.uwex.edu/mediasite5/Viewer/?peid=4cb54f8a57cb41b99186c9db49e761a3.

Garrison, D. R., Anderson, T., & Archer, W. (2000). Critical inquiry in a text-based environment. Computer conferencing in higher education. *Internet in Higher Education, 2*(2), 87–105. Retrieved April 7, 2009, from http://auspace.athabascau.ca:8080/dspace/bitstream/2149/739/1/critical_inquiry_in_a_text.pdf.

Garrison, D. R., Anderson, T., & Archer, W. (2001). Critical thinking, cognitive presence, and computer conferencing in distance education. *American Journal of Distance Education, 15*(1), 7–23.

Garrison, D. R., Anderson, T., & Archer, W. (2004). *Critical thinking and computer conferencing: A model and tool to assess cognitive presence.* Retrieved April 18, 2009, from http://communitiesofinquiry.com/files/CogPres_Final.pdf.

Garrison, D. R., & Vaughan, N. D. (2008). *Blended learning in higher education: Framework, principles, and guidelines.* San Francisco: Jossey-Bass.

George, B. (2007, May 25). The authentic leader: An interview with Bill George. *Harvard Business School Podcast Archives.* Retrieved April 24, 2009, from http://www.hbs.edu/mba/admissions/podcasts-all.html.

Gibson, D. (2003). Network-based assessment in education. *Contemporary Issues in Technology and Teacher Education* [Online serial], *3*(3).

Gibson, D. (2006). *The global challenge.* Retrieved April 23, 2009, from http://www.globalchallengeaward.org/.

Gibson, D., & Swan, K. (2006). *How to know what your students know!* 12th Annual ALN International Conference on Asynchronous Learning, Orlando, FL.

Goodyear, P., Jones, C., Asensio, M., Hodgson, V., & Steeples, C. (2003). Constructing the "good" e-learner. Proceedings of the 10th Biennial European Association for Research on Learning and Instruction (EARLI) Conference, Padova, Italy.

Gould, M., & Padavano, D. (2006, May). Seven ways to improve student satisfaction in online courses. *Online Classroom,* pp. 1–2.

Grinter, R., & Palen, L. (2002). Instant messaging in teen life. In *Proceedings of the 2002 ACM Conference on Computer Supported Cooperative Work.* Retrieved December 15, 2009, from http://www.cs.colorado.edu/~palen/Papers/grinter-palen-IM.pdf.

Grogan, G. (2005). *The design of online discussions to achieve good learning results.* Retrieved November 12, 2008, from www.elearningeuropa.info/index.php?page=doc&doc_id=6713&doclng=6&menuzone=1.

Gunawardena, C. N., Lowe, C. A., & Anderson, T. (1997). Analysis of a global online debate and the development of an interaction analysis model for examining social construction of knowledge in computer conferencing. *Journal of Educational Computing Research, 17*(4), 397–431.

Hake, R. R. (1998). Interactive-engagement vs. traditional methods: A six-thousand-student survey of mechanics test data for introductory physics courses. *American Journal of Physics, 66,* 64–74. Retrieved February 4, 2010, from http://www.physics.indiana.edu/~sdi.ajpv31.pdf.

Hanson, V. D. (2002). Socrates dies at Delium, 424 B.C. In R. Cowley (Ed.), *What if? 2: Eminent historians imagine what might have been.* New York: Berkley.

Haskell, R. E. (2000). *Transfer of learning: Cognition, instruction, and reasoning.* Orlando, FL: Academic Press.

Hayles, N. K. (2007). Hyper and deep attention: The generational divide in cognitive modes. *Profession 2007,* MLA, pp. 187–199.

Heckman, R., & Annabi, H. (2005). A content analytic comparison of learning processes in online and face-to-face case study discussions. *Journal of Computer-Mediated Communication, 10*(2), article 7. Retrieved April 24, 2009, from http://jcmc.indiana.edu/vol10/issue2/heckman.html

Institute of Human and Machine Cognition. *CmapTools (v. 5.03).* Retrieved April 18, 2009, from http://cmap.ihmc.us/conceptmap.html.

Internet Resources for Higher Education Outcomes Assessment. (2009). North Carolina State University. Retrieved April 17, 2009, from http://www2.acs.ncsu.edu/UPA/assmt/resource.htm#about.

Isaacs, G. (2002). *Assessing group tasks.* University of Queensland. Retrieved April 17, 2009, from www.tedi.uq.edu.au/teaching/assessment/groupass.html.

Kandel, E. (2006). *In search of memory: The emergence of a new science of mind.* New York: Norton.

Kearsley, G. (2003–2009). Theory into practice database. Retrieved December 9, 2009, from http://tip.psychology.org/.

Kim, K–S., & Moore, J. L. (2005). Web–based learning: Factors affecting students' satisfaction and learning experience. *First Monday, 10*(11). Retrieved April 27, 2009, from http://firstmonday.org/htbin/cgiwrap/bin/ojs/index.php/fm/article/view/1294/1214.

Krathwohl, D. R. (2002). A revision of Bloom's taxonomy: An overview. *Theory into Practice, 41*(4), 212–218.

Legon, R. (2006, September). *Comparison of the Quality Matters Rubric to accreditation standards for distance learning.* Retrieved December 15, 2009, from http://www.qualitymatters.org/Documents/Comparison%20of%20the%20Quality%20Matters%20Rubric%20-%20Summary.pdf.

Lenhart, A. (2009, August). Teen and mobile phones over the past five years: Pew Internet look back. Retrieved September 26, 2009, from http://www.authoring.pewinternet.org/Reports/2009/14—Teens-and-Mobile-Phones-Data-Memoaspx.

Lenhart, A., & Madden, M. (2007). *Teens, privacy, and online social networks.* Pew Internet & American Life Project. Retrieved April 7, 2009, from http://www.pewinternet.org/~/media//Files/Reports/2007/PIP_Teens_Privacy_SNS_Report_Final.pdf.

Lenhart, A. M., Madden, M., Macgill, A. R., & Smith, A. (2007). *Teens and social media*. Washington DC: Pew Internet & American Life Project. http://www. pewinternet.org/~/media//Files/Reports/2007/PIP_Teens_Social_Media_ Final.pdf.pdf.

Maisie, E. (2001). *Steps to instant collaboration*. Retrieved April 15, 2009, from http://trends.masie.com/archives.

Mayer, R. E., Bove, W., Bryman, A., Mars, R., & Tapangco, L. (1996). When less is more: Meaningful learning from visual and verbal summaries of science text-book lessons. *Journal of Educational Psychology, 88,* 64–73.

McKeachie, W. J., Pintrich, P. R., Lin, Y. G., & Smith, D.A.F. (1986). *Teaching and learning in the college classroom: A review of the research literature*. Ann Arbor: Regents of the University of Michigan.

McTighe, J., & Wiggins, G. (1999). *The understanding by design handbook*. Alexandria, VA: Association for Supervision and Curriculum Development.

Moallem, M. (2005). Designing and managing student assessment in an online learning environment. In P. Comeaux (Ed.), *Assessing online learning* (pp. 18–33). San Francisco: Jossey-Bass/Anker.

Moore, M. (1997). Theory of transactional distance. In D. Keegan (Ed.), *Theoretical principles of distance education* (pp. 22–38). New York: Routledge.

Muirhead, B. (2006). Creating concept maps: Integrating constructivism principles into online classes. Article 2. *International Journal of Instructional Technology and Distance Learning, 3*(1). Retrieved December 11, 2009, from http://www.itdl. org/Journal/jan_06/article02.htm.

Murphy, E., & Manzanares, M.A.R. (2006). Profiling individual discussants' behaviours in online asynchronous discussions. *Canadian Journal of Learning and Technology, 32*(2). Retrieved April 27, 2009, from http://www.cjlt.ca/ index.php/cjlt/article/view/55/52.

Murphy, G. L. (2004). *The big book of concepts*. Cambridge, MA: MIT Press.

Newberry, R. (2008). *Duquesne's faculty resources: Blogs*. Retrieved October 4, 2009, from http://www.edtech.duq.edu/facultyresources/blogs.cfm.

Novak, J. D., & Cañas, A. J. (2007). Theoretical origins of concept maps, how to construct them and their uses in education. *Reflecting Education, 3*(1), 29–42. Retrieved April 24, 2009, from http://www.reflectingeducation.net/ index.php?journal=reflecting&page=article&op=viewFile&path[]=41& path[]=43.

Novak, J. D., & Cañas, A. J. (2008). *The theory underlying concept maps and how to construct and use them* (Tech. Rep. IHMC CmapTools 2006–01 Rev 01–2008). Florida Institute for Human and Machine Cognition. Retrieved September 24, 2009, from http://cmap.ihmc.us/Publications/ .ResearchPapers/TheoryUnderlyingConceptMaps.pdf.

O'Banion, T. (1999). *Launching a learning-centered college.* Mission Viejo, CA: League for Innovation in the Community College and PeopleSoft.

Ohler, J. (2008). The semantic web in education. *EDUCAUSE Quarterly, 31*(4). Retrieved September 21, 2009, from http://net.educause.edu/ir/library/pdf/EQM0840.pdf.

Oldenburg, R. (1999). *The great good place: Cafes, coffee shops, bookstores, bars, hair salons, and other hangouts at the heart of a community* (3rd ed.). New York: Marlowe & Company.

Painter, C., Coffin C., & Hewings, A. (2003). Impacts of directed tutorial activities in computer conferencing: A case study. *Distance Education, 24*(2), 159–174.

Palloff, R., & Pratt, K. (1999). *Building online learning communities: Effective strategies for the virtual classroom.* San Francisco: Jossey-Bass.

Palloff, R., & Pratt, K. (2003). *The virtual student.* San Francisco: Jossey-Bass.

Paul, R., & Elder, L. (2002). *Thinking with concepts.* Foundation for Critical Thinking. Retrieved April 15, 2009, from http://www.criticalthinking.org/articles/thinking-with-concepts.cfm.

Paul, R., & Elder, L. (2008). *The miniature guide to critical thinking: Concepts and tools.* Dillon Beach, CA: Foundation for Critical Thinking.

Peirce, B. (2004). Strategies for teaching thinking and promoting intellectual development in online classes. *Instructional Area Newsletter, 19*(3). Retrieved April 24, 2009, from http://academic.pgcc.edu/~wpeirce/MCCCTR/.

Pelikan, J. (1992). *The idea of the university: A reexamination.* New Haven, CT: Yale University Press.

Picciano, T. (2009). *Blending with purpose: Multimodal model.* Retrieved April 23, 2009, from www.youtube.com/watch?v=jAj5uBKyqv8.

Pinker, S. (1997). *How the mind works.* New York: Norton.

Polya, G. (1957). *How to solve it* (2nd ed.). Princeton, NJ: Princeton University Press.

Reder, L. M., & Anderson, J. R. (1980). A comparison of texts and their summaries: Memorial consequences. *Journal of Verbal Learning and Verbal Behavior, 198*, 121–134. Retrieved April 27, 2009, from http://act-r.psy.cmu.edu/publications/pubinfo.php?id=285.

Richardson, J., & Swan, K. (2003). Examining social presence in online courses in relation to students' perceived learning and satisfaction. *Journal of Asynchronous Learning Networks, 7*(1), 68–88.

Roberto, M. A., & Edmondson, A. C. (2007). *New leadership and team simulation: Mount Everest.* Harvard Business for Educators. Retrieved February 21, 2009, from http://harvardbusinessonline.hbsp.harvard.edu/b02/en/common/item_detail.jhtml;jsessionid=CGJQM2HLB1TCGAKRGWDR5VQBKE0YIISW?id=2650&_requestid=41858.

Roper, A. R. (2007). How students develop online learning skills. *EDUCAUSE Quarterly, 30*(1). Retrieved September 21, 2009, from http://net.educause.edu/ir/library/pdf/EQM07110.pdf.

Rosenbloom, R. S. (1999). *Sustaining American innovation: Where will technology come from?* Paper presented at the Forum on Harnessing Science and Technology for American's Economic Future, National Academy of Sciences, Washington, DC.

Rovai, A. (2002). Building sense of community at a distance. *International Review of Research in Open and Distance Learning, 3*(1), 1–16. Retrieved January 29, 2008, from http://www.irrodl.org/index.php/irrodl/article/view/79/153.

Schacter, D. L. (2001). *The seven sins of memory: How the mind forgets and remembers.* Boston: Houghton Mifflin.

Schank, R. C., & Abelson, R. (1977). *Scripts, plans, goals, and understanding.* Mahwah, NJ: Erlbaum.

Schmier, L. (2006, October 31). *Ending the semester.* Posting to Professional & Organization Development Network in Higher Education Listserv. Retrieved April 19, 2009, from https://listserv.nd.edu.

Sellers, S. L., Roberts, J., Giovanetto, L., Friedrich, K., & Hammargren, C. (2007). *Reaching all students: A resource for teaching in science, technology, engineering & mathematics.* Madison, WI: Center for the Integration of Research, Teaching, and Learning. Retrieved December 12, 2009, from http://www.cirtl.net/DiversityResources/resources/resource-book/downloads/Reaching%20All%20Students%20Resource%20Book.pdf.

Senge, P. (1990). *The fifth discipline: The art and practice of the learning organization.* New York: Doubleday.

The seven sins of memory by Daniel Schacter. *American Psychological Association APA Online, 34*(9). Retrieved April 18, 2009, from http://www.apa.org/monitor/oct03/sins.html.

Shapiro, E. G. (1990). Effect of instructor and class characteristics on students' class evaluations. *Research in Higher Education, 31*(2), 135–148.

Shea, P. (2006). A study of students' sense of learning community in online environments. *Journal of Asynchronous Learning Networks, 10* (1), 35–44. Retrieved December 16, 2009, from http://www.sloan-c.org/publications/jaln/v10n1/pdf/v10n1_4shea.pdf.

Sorcinellini, M. D., Austin, A. E., Eddy, P. L., & Beach, A. L. (2006). *Creating the future of faculty development—Learning from the past, understanding the present.* San Francisco: Jossey-Bass/Anker.

Swan, K., & Shih, L. F. (2005). On the nature and development of social presence in online course discussions. *Journal of Asynchronous Learning Networks, 9*(3), 115–136. Retrieved April 23, 2009, from http://www.kent.edu/rcet/Publications/upload/socpresJALN.pdf.

Teaching and Learning with Technology. (2001–2005). *Building blocks for teams.* Penn State. Retrieved April 17, 2009, from http://tlt.its.psu.edu/suggestions/teams/student/.

Theroux, J. (2007). What it takes to innovate: The experience of producing an online, real-time case study [Electronic Version]. *Journal of Asynchronous Learning Networks.* Sloan Consortium 11. Retrieved September 23, 2009, from http://www.sloan-c.org/publications/jaln/v11n4/pdf/v11n4_theroux.pdf.

Thomas, D., & Brown, J. S. (2009). Why virtual worlds can matter. *International Journal of Media and Learning, 1*(1), 37–49. Retrieved December 9, 2009, from http://www.johnseelybrown.com/needvirtualworlds.pdf.

Tracy, B. (2007). *Eat that frog! 21 great ways to stop procrastinating and get more done in less time!* San Francisco: Berrett-Koehler.

University of Guelph Library Learning Services. (2009). *Fast facts: Group work.* Retrieved April 17, 2009, from http://www.lib.uoguelph.ca/assistance/learning_services/fastfacts/group_work.cfm.

Vygotsky, L. S. (1962). *Thought and language* (E. Hanfmann and G. Vakar, Trans.). Cambridge, MA: MIT Press.

Vygotsky, L. S. (1978). *Mind in society: The development of higher psychological processes.* Cambridge, MA: Harvard University Press.

Ward, G. C. (2002). The luck of Franklin Delano Roosevelt. In R. Cowley (Ed.), *What if? 2: Eminent historians imagine what might have been.* New York: Berkley.

Washington State University. (2006). *Critical and integrative thinking rubric.* Retrieved April 17, 2009, from http://wsuctproject.wsu.edu/.

Weigel, V. B. (2005). From course management to curricular capabilities: A capabilities approach for the next-generation CMS. *EDUCAUSE Review, 40*(3). Retrieved October 4, 2009, from http://net.educause.edu/ir/library/pdf/ERM0533.pdf.

Wieman, C. (2008). *Science education in the 21st century: Using the tools of science to teach science.* Forum Features 2008. EDUCAUSE. Retrieved November 3, 2008, from http://net.educause.edu/ir/library/pdf/ff0814s.pdf.

Working Group of the Indiana Partnership for Statewide Education (2008). *Guiding principles for faculty in distance learning.* Retrieved December 9, 2008, from http://www.ihets.org/archive/progserv_arc/education_arc/distance_arc/guiding_principles_arc/index.html.

Young, A., & Norgard, C. (2006). Assessing the quality of online courses from the students' perspective. *Internet & Higher Education, 9*(2), 107–115.

Index

Page references followed by *fig* indicate an illustrated figure; followed by *e* indicate an exhibit; followed by *t* indicate a table.

A

Abelson, R., 15
Abramson, L., 120, 137
Accreditation and Assuring Quality in Distance Learning, 260
Activities: addressing student confusion over, 250; assessment project, 154–156; collaborative, 41, 127–130, 136–145, 188–193, 220; corresponding to dialogues and tasks, 82, 84; group projects, 127–130; individual, 41, 219; learners-as-leaders experiences, 226–229t; project coaching of, 160–161; relevant learner projects, 153–156; sample weekly schedule for, 83t; small group, 41, 220; team, 164t, 199–200, 221, 228; wrapping course and closing, 37t, 46–47, 229–243, 236–243. *See also* Asynchronous activities; Learning experiences; Project assignments; Synchronous activities
Adobe Connect, 138, 240
Akyol, Z., 102
Allen, D., 46, 196, 237
Allen, I. E., 9
Alvarez, A., 45
Amazon.com, 202
American Psychological Association, 236
Anderson, C., 222
Anderson, J. R., 151
Anderson, T., 38, 53, 64, 81, 102, 158, 201, 235
Annabi, H., 147
Announcements tool: communicating teaching presence through, 110–113; description of, 77–78
Anonymous student feedback, 122
Apple iPod series, 45
Archer, W., 38, 53, 64, 81, 102, 158, 235
Assessing Group Tasks (Isaacs), 193
Assessing Group Work Web site, 191

Assessment: continuous nature of online course, 8; group projects, 190–193; during late middle weeks of course, 160; plan for, 154, 156; of students' zone of proximal development (ZPD), 79–81; unique characteristics of online, 74. *See also* Course evaluations; Feedback; Peer reviews
Assessment plan: online courses and, 68t; unique characteristics of online, 74
Assessment project: importance of, 154–156; three-step process for planning, 156
Assignments. *See* Project assignments
Asynchronous activities: class discussions, 7; CMS (course management system) tools for, 144, 204; description of, 42; VoiceThread used for, 29, 164t. *See also* Activities
Audacity, 58, 163, 164t
Audio lectures: effective use of resources for, 140–145; pedagogical use during phase 1, 58, 59t, 60; pedagogical use during phase 2, 108t
Audio resources: discussion feedback or announcements use of, 142; enriching and expanding course, 142–143; incorporating published, 142; online book sites offering, 144; your biography and introductory posting use of, 141–142
Ausubel, D., 230
Authentic problem solving: course content on, 217–218; definition of, 217; resources for, 221; segmenting the problems for, 220–221; steps in, 218–219; three major phases in, 219–220

B

Bartoletti, R., 125
Behaviors: difficult student, 250–251; problem formulation, 171–172; problem solution, 172
Bernstein, B., 5, 22

Best Practices for Electronically Offered Degree and Certificate Programs Best Practices, 260

Blackboard: description of, 65, 114; Performance Dashboard in, 115*fig*–116

Blended/hybrid courses, 9*t*

Blogs: CMS (course management system), 204; course beginnings use of, 59*t*, 60–61; faculty, 37; as learning tool, 28–29; Mind-Mapping Software Blog, 234; pedagogical use during phase 1, 59*t*; pedagogical use during phase 2, 107*t*; pedagogical use during phase 3, 163*t*, 164*t*; pedagogical use during phase 4, 214*t*; used for project planning, 203

Bloom's Taxonomy, 89, 160

Boettcher, J. V., 9, 22, 24, 27, 137, 182

Bohm, D., 148

Bok, D., 172

Bonk, C. J., 85

Bonnici, L. J., 75

Bransford, J. D., 16, 19, 34, 86, 170, 172

Briggs, L. J., 228

Briskin, L., 179

Brookfield, S. D., 92

Brown, A. L., 16, 19, 86, 170

Brown, J. S., 15, 46

Brown, R. E., 39, 105, 200, 224, 226, 253

Bruckman, A. S., 168, 201

Bruner, J., 14, 14–15, 19

Building Blocks for Teams (Teaching and Learning with Technology Group), 189

Building a Nation of Learners: The Need for Changes in Teaching and Learning to Meet Global Challenges (2003 report), 159

Burge, E., 182

Burnett, K., 75

Business-Higher Education Forum, 159, 172

Buzan, T., 233

Byrnes, J. P., 86

C

Cahill, M., 231

Cañas, A. J., 230, 231, 232

Car Talk (NPR radio program), 200

Carlson, A., 217

Celebration session, 237–240

Center for Critical Thinking and Moral Critique, 91, 195

Center for the Study of Higher Education (University of Melbourne), 191

Centre for Learning and Performance Technologies, 121

Chang, R. Y., 218

Chunking, 33

Clabaugh, G. K., 14

Clarity of expectations, 55

Classrooms. *See* Online classrooms

Closing activities. *See* Online course wrapping activities

Closing weeks. *See* Online course (phase 4)

Cmap Tools, 214*t*, 233

Coaching: during closing weeks, 212–213; learners on personalizing their projects, 197–198; online course role of, 7; project, 160–161. *See also* Faculty

Cocking, R. R., 16, 19, 86, 170

Coffin, C., 43

Cognitive apprenticeships, 15

Cognitive presence: description of, 54, 81, 151–152; practical inquiry model for building, 152*fig*, 159–160; tips for building, 104–106, 145–153; tools and behaviors used to build, 153

Cognitive restructuring theories, 230

Cognitive structures, 14

Collaborative activities: group projects, 127–130, 188–193; problem-solving, 220; small group, 41, 220; synchronous, 136–145. *See also* Team activities

Collins, A., 15, 46

Committee on Developments in the Science of Learning, 16

Communication: peer-to-peer, 39–40, 84, 112–113, 133–136, 182; related to availability of help on projects, 198; strong learning communities fostered by, 79; teaching presence through, 103, 110–114. *See also* Dialogues

Communication patterns, 73

Communication tools: Announcements tool, 77–78, 110–113; e-mail, 59*t*, 107*t*, 110–114; group projects and related, 188–189; instant messaging, 59*t*, 61, 107*t*, 113; selecting the appropriate, 113–114; Skype, 107*t*, 112, 163, 164*t*, 188; Twitter, 28–29, 59*t*, 76, 113. *See also* Discussion boards; Social networking

Community of inquiry, 76, 81. *See also* Learning community; Online course community

Concept mapping: concept maps of key features of, 232*fig*; core concepts about, 231; description of, 230; integrating into a course, 231, 233; learning opportunities of, 229–230; origins and development of, 230–231

Concept mapping tools, 214*t*, 233–234

Concepts: combining personalized learning with core, 37*t*, 45–46; identifying patterns, relationships, and linkages of, 170; learner need to learn core, 26–29; as organized knowledge clusters, 31–32, 46; pruning and reflecting on learned, 211–212; Vygotsky on process of forming, 31

The Conditions of Learning (Gagné), 32

Conferencing tools, during phase 1, 61

Conrad, R. M., 9, 78, 97, 101, 229

Constructivism learning theory, 14–15

Constructivism philosophy, 12–13, 89

Content: authentic problem solving, 217–218; customizing resources of, 27*fig*; using digital format resources for, 37*t*, 44–45; end-of-course experiences on, 238; expert events focusing on, 206–207; learner need for concepts versus, 26–29; learning experience framework reflections on, 256–257; matching practice to, 33; nurturing of the, 104

Content resources, 27*fig*, 68*t*

Context: learning experiences, 29–30; reflections on, 257

Cooper, S. T., 176

Coppola, N. W., 75

Cordell, S., 137, 138

The Core Rules of Netiquette (Shea), 73

Council for Higher Education Accreditation, 69

Course beginnings. *See* Online course (phase 1)

Course community. *See* Online course community

Course evaluations: as end-of-course experience, 239; peer reviews, 107*t*, 126–127, 191–193; preventing unpleasant surprises from, 254–255; research on, 123; Team Member Evaluation Form, 192*e*. *See also* Assessment; Feedback

Course expectations: clarity of learner, 55; developing teacher and learner, 37*t*, 40–41; on response time to questions/assignments, 74; strategies for managing learner, 181–182

Course management system (CMS): asynchronous tools in your, 144, 204; course management and learning role of, 110–114; description of, 65; using forum to receive feedback, 121–122; pedagogical use during phase 1, 59*t*; pedagogical use during phase 2, 107*t*; performance tracking in, 114; problem of not feeling comfortable with, 252. *See also* Online classrooms; Online course management strategies

Courses: comparing online and campus, 7–8, 9*t*; definition of a, 6; faculty concern over workload of, 6; introducing four stages of, 9–12*t*. *See also* Online courses

Critical thinking: development of, 172–173; emerging, developing, and mastering, 195; examples of criterion for, 195*t*; rubric for analyzing, 194–195

The Cyber Café, 181

Cyberbits, 71

Cybercafé, 71

D

Damasio, A., 19, 24, 34, 149

Daniels, H., 5, 34

Debriefing students, 244–245

Del Rio, P., 45

Dereshiwsky, M. I., 258

"Designing by threes" principle, 182

Dewey, J., 13–14, 19, 34, 171, 220

Dialogues: "designing by threes" principle on, 182; 80/20 rule on, 182–183; F-L (faculty to learner), 39, 84, 182; L-L (learner to learner), 39–40, 84, 133–136, 182; L-R (learner to resource), 39, 84, 182; promoting peer interaction through meaningful, 135–136; sample weekly schedule for, 83*t*; tasks and activities corresponding to, 82, 84; teaming students for one discussion week, 199–200. *See also* Communication

Difficult students, 250–251

Dinnocenzo, D., 241–242

Discussion board postings: allocating points and using rubrics for, 95*t*–96; characteristics of a quality, 146–147; importance of regular, 78; managing and evaluating, 93–94; preparing engaging, 37*t*, 43–44; requirements for student responses, 86–88; simple rules about feedback on, 173–174; three parts of a good, 145–146

Discussion board question types: factual, 90; problem-solving, 91; Socratic, 44, 90–91, 160, 195

Discussion board questions: additional resources on, 92–93; characteristics of good, 88–93; core assumption of constructivism on, 89; on core concepts in course, 91–92; developing great and effective, 88; providing rapid response to students, 175–176; requirements for student responses to, 86–88; rule of thumb for length of discussion, 88; types of, 89–91; weekly number of, 86. *See also* Questioning

Discussion board threads: characteristics of a quality posting to start, 146–147; discussion wrap of a, 148–151; moving to reflective and developed conversation, 147–148; three parts of a good posting to initiate, 145–146

Discussion boards: best learning goals for, 85–86; communicating teacher presence through, 110–114; description of, 65, 69*t*; ensuring lively participation in, 94–95; faculty role in, 96–99; monitoring, 94; pedagogical use during phase 3, 163*t*; pedagogical use during phase 4, 214*t*; regularly posted comments on the, 78; scoring rubrics for, 65; as student questioning format, 167–169; why and how of, 84–85. *See also* Communication tools; Online class discussions

Discussion lists: managing and evaluating postings on, 93–96; preparing engaging posts for, 37*t*, 43–44

Discussion as a Way of Teaching (Brookfield and Preskill), 92

Discussion wrap: benefits of using a, 148–149; involving students in, 150; suggested strategies and resources for, 151; summarizing the discussion in, 149–150

Distance Education Teaching and Learning Resources Web site, 108

Donaldson, J. A., 78, 97, 101, 229

Dublin Centre for Teaching and Learning (University College), 193

Duguid, P., 15

Duquesne University, 241

E

E-mail: communicating teacher presence through, 110–114; pedagogical use during phase 1, 59*t*; pedagogical use during phase 2, 107*t*

Early middle. *See* Online course (phase 2)

Early Warning System tool, 114

Eat That Frog! 21 Great Ways to Stop Procrastinating and Get More Done in Less Time! (Tracy), 196

eBay.com, 202

Edmondson, A. C., 221
EDUCAUSE, 139
80/20 rule, 182–183
Elder, L., 90
Elluminate, 138, 240
Emoticons, 73
Empowerment: during late middle weeks of course, 161; social networking for community, 199–208
End-of-course experiences: on content, 238; interaction, 238–239; student evaluation of course, 239
Evaluations. *See* Course evaluations
Expectations. *See* Course expectations
Experiential learning, 13–14
Expert events: online classroom guest lecturer, 242; preferred time to include, 206; setting up, 207
Experts: benefits of inviting course participation by, 204–205; locating appropriate, 206; resources on online course use of, 207–208; types of content good for an, 206–207

F

F-L (faculty to learner) dialogue, 39, 84, 182
Facebook, 59*t*, 61, 76, 164*t*, 201
Factual questions, 90
Faculty: advice from fellow online instructors to, 257–259; concerns and questions about online classrooms by, 243; course workload issue for, 6; discussion board role of, 96–99; getting-acquainted posting sent by, 75–76; getting-acquainted-cognitively posting by, 77; learning experience framework reflections by, 256; as learning experiences framework element, 21*fig*, 22; major categories teaching online, 5; monitoring by, 94, 114–116, 187–188; online versus campus course responsibilities of, 7; project coaching by, 160–161; reassessing course for improvements, 255; setting explicit expectations for, 40–41; stories on using online classroom by, 241–242; strategies for shaping learning community, 225–226; weekly rhythm challenged by personal schedule of, 118. *See also* Coaching; Teaching online
Faculty advice: 1: just do your best, 258; 2: it's kind of fun to do the impossible!, 258; 3: begin with the end in mind, 259
Fast Facts: Group Work, 189–190
Feedback: addressing content issue, 178–179; anonymous student, 122; asking for early informal student, 42–43; checklist for short written assignment, 179–180; using CMS forum to receive, 121–122; debriefing students, 244–245; developing loop of learner, 120–123; providing early and often, 174–175; providing formative for learning and personal, 176; providing time for weekly, 118–119; rubric for written assignment, 179; rubrics, quizzes, and peer review as, 123–127; simple rules about online learning, 173–174; timely and efficient assignment, 175, 176–180. *See also* Assessment; Course evaluations; Rubrics

Flickr, 164*t*, 200, 202
Flip Video, 28
Fonteyn, M., 231
Forman, D. W., 258
Freeman, W. J., 31
Frey, C., 234
FY 05/06 Quality Matters rubric, 69

G

Gagné, R. M., 32, 228
Garrison, D. R., 38, 53, 54, 55, 56, 64, 81, 102, 103, 147, 151, 152, 158, 171, 235
Genetic epistemology, 14
George, B., 143
Getting Things Done (Allen), 46, 237
Getting-acquainted posting, 75–76
Getting-acquainted-cognitively posting, 77
Gibson, D., 19, 155, 186
Global Challenge, 155
Goodyear, P., 434
Google Apps for Education, 139
Google Docs, 108*t*, 164*t*, 188
Google Gmail video chat, 188
Google Gmail voice, 188
Google Wave, 139
Gore, A., 223
Gould, M., 75
Grading. *See* Rubrics
Griffiths, C., 233
Grinter, R., 113
Grisham, J., 144
Grogan, G., 43
Group projects: additional thoughts on managing, 189–190; additional thoughts on, 129–130; assessing, 190–193; communication and presentation tools for, 188–189; managing and facilitating, 186–190; sample form for availability and contact information, 129*e*; small groups used for, 41, 220; steps for setting up, 127–129. *See also* Project assignments; Synchronous collaborative activities; Team activities
"Guest Lecturers in the Online Environment" (Varvel), 207, 208
Guide to Rating Critical and Integrative Thinking (Washington State University), 96, 194
Gunawardena, C. N., 201

H

Hake, R. R., 167
Hanson, V. D., 222
Happy Hour classroom, 242
Harvard Business Online, 221
Harvard Business Review, 15, 143
Haskell, R. E., 86
Hayles, N. K., 116
Heckman, R., 147
Hewings, A., 43
Hiltz, S. R., 75
Holum, A., 46
Hosseini, K., 144

How People Learn research, 170
How People Learn—Brain, Mind, Experience, and School (Bransford, Brown, and Cocking), 16
How We Think (Dewey), 13
Hurricane Katrina, 206

I

Ideacasts series (*Harvard Business Review*), 143
Illinois Online Network, 207, 208
iMindmap, 214*t*, 233
Individual work: learning experiences of, 41; problem-solving process, 219
Ingram, K., 259
Innovation three-phase process, 260
Instant messaging: pedagogical use during phase 1, 59*t*, 61; pedagogical use during phase 2, 107*t*; teacher presence through, 113
Institute of Human and Machine Cognition, 233
Instruction strategies: different learning outcomes of different, 32–33; refocusing on the learner, 47
Interaction end-of-course experience, 238–239
Internet Resources for Higher Education Outcomes Assessment Web site, 193
Interviewer-expert modeling, 169–170
iPhone, 214*t*
iPod Touch, 214*t*
Isaacs, G., 193
iTunes store, 143
iTunes University, 143

J

Joonmin, K., 75

K

Kandel, E., 24
Kearsley, G., 13, 14
Kelly, P. K., 218
Kim, K.-S., 183
Kindle, 45
King, M. L., Jr., 222
King, S., 144
Kite Runner (Hosseini), 144
Knauff, B., 115
Knowledge: concept mapping of, 214*t*, 229–234; concepts organized as clusters of, 31–32; identifying insights to reveal, 170; identifying patterns and linkages to reveal, 170; interviewer-expert modeling to reveal, 169–170; learners' personalized, 23–24; as learning experiences framework element, 21*fig*, 22–23; practical inquiry model on integrating useful, 235–236; student inquiry as reflection of knowledge, 167; usefulness of, 14–15; ZPD (zone of proximal development) readiness for, 13, 24, 30–31. *See also* Learning
Knowledge construction tasks, 201
Knowledge-integration processes, 170
Ko, S., 250
Krathwohl, D. R., 89, 160

L

L-L (learner to learner) dialogue: description of, 39–40, 84; designing by threes principle on, 182; promoting peer interaction with, 133–136
L-R (learner to resource) dialogue, 39, 84, 182
Large group work experiences, 41
"Late assignment free" ticket, 253–254
Late middle weeks. *See* Online course (phase 3)
Launching a Learning-Centered College (O'Banion), 47
Leadership and Team Simulation: Everest, 221
Learner Corner, 71
Learner expectations: clarity of, 55; developing teacher and, 37*t*, 40–41; setting explicit, 40–41; strategies for managing, 181–182. *See also* Students
Learner independence, 211
Learner projects. *See* Learning experiences
Learners: campus versus online, 7–8; encouraging tough questions asked by, 200–201; every structured learning experience is centered around, 21–23; facilitating project assignment learning for, 196–198; knowledge, skills, attitudes of, 23–24; as leaders, 226–229*t*; learning experience framework reflections by, 255–256; need to learn core concepts by, 26–29; observations on learning community and, 147; refocusing instruction on, 47; setting explicit expectations for, 40–41. *See also* Students
Learners-as-leaders experiences: checklist for, 229*t*; choosing the type of, 228–229; individual versus team-led activities, 228; making outcomes explicit, 228; orientation and planning time for, 227–228; providing opportunities for, 226–227
Learning: Ausubel's three conditions for meaningful, 230; customizing project assignment, 183–186; experiential, 13–14; landscape for online teaching and, 16*fig*; learning tools shape, 34–35; more practice equals more, 33; questioning as core of, 160; ten core principles of, 19–35; usefulness of knowledge and, 14–15; zone of proximal development on readiness for, 13, 24, 30–31. *See also* Knowledge
Learning community: faculty behaviors supporting, 225–226; focus on building, 112; intervening conditions hindering, 226; nurturing the, 104; observations on learner and, 147; problem of undeveloped, 253; social networking for empowering, 199–208; strategies for shaping and evolving, 225; strategies and tools for building, 133–145; three stages of building, 224–225. *See also* Community of inquiry; Online course community
Learning environment: all learning experiences include the, 29–30; as learning experiences framework element, 21*fig*, 23; online, 3–5. *See also* Learning resources
Learning experience framework: different instruction produces different outcomes, 32–33; faculty mentors as directing the, 25–26; four elements of, 21*fig*–23; how learning tools shape learning, 34–35; illustrated diagram of, 21*fig*; includes the environment or context, 29–30; interaction between tools and

learning, 34–35; learner need to learn core concept, 26–29; learners' customized knowledge, skills, and attitudes, 23–24; more practice equals more learning, 33; reflecting and looking forward with the, 255–257; ZPD (zone of proximal development) readiness for, 13, 24, 30–31, 33, 79–81, 186

Learning experiences: assessment plan and, 154–156; centered around learners, 21–31; context of all, 29–30; end-of-course, 237–240; faculty mentors directing, 25–26; large group work, 41; launching relevant, 153–154; learners-as-leaders, 226–229t; learning environment component of, 29–30; stories and suggestions for, 240–243; student debriefing as faculty, 244–245; wrapping up course with closing, 37t, 46–47, 236–243. *See also* Activities; Project assignments

Learning habits, 180–181

Learning management system (LMS), 65

Learning outcomes: different instruction required for different, 32–33; learning tools as shaping, 34–35; more practice equals better, 33; setting explicit expectations for, 40–41

Learning resources: audio, 58, 59t, 60, 108t, 141–144; authentic problem solving, 221; campus versus online, 8; content, 27fig, 68t; customizing content, 27fig; digital format, 37t, 44–45; using digital format content, 37t, 44–45; discussion board questions, 92–93; discussion wrap, 151; on using experts, 207–208; L-R (learner to resource) dialogue, 39, 84, 182; learning experience framework reflections on, 256–257; learning shaped by, 34–35; reflections on content and knowledge, 256–257; teaching presence through course materials and, 102–103; video, 58, 59t, 60, 64, 108t, 140–145, 164t, 202, 214t. *See also* Learning environment; Technology tools; Web sites

Learning theories: Brown's cognitive apprenticeship, 15; Bruner's constructivism, 14–15; constructivism philosophy and use of, 12–13; Dewey's experiential learning, 13–14; five areas of research in, 16; Piaget's genetic epistemology, 14; Schank's schema theory, 15; Theories of Practice database on, 12–13; Vygotsky's theory of social development, 13

Legon, R., 69

Lenhart, A. M., 113, 136

Lin, Y. G., 7

LinkedIn, 59t, 61, 76, 164t, 202

Live collaborative time, 78

The Long Tail: Why the Future of Business Is Selling Less of More (Anderson), 222

Lowe, C. A., 201

M

Madden, M., 113, 136

Maise, E., 140

McCain, J., 223

Macgill, A. R., 136

McKeachie, W. J., 7

McTighe, J., 156

Management strategies. *See* Online course management strategies

Managing Learner-Instructor Interaction and Feedback, 96

Manzanares, M.A.R., 171, 172

Materials. *See* Learning resources

Mayer, R. E, 151

Memory: "seven sins of," 234, 236; strategies to help with, 234–236

Mentors: learning experience framework reflections by, 256; online course role of, 7; teaching presence by, 103

Mercy College, 147

Miksa, S. D., 75

Mind mapping tools, 214t

Mind in Society: The Development of Higher Psychology Processes (Vygotsky), 19

Mind-Mapping Software Blog, 234

Moallem, M., 8, 160, 191

Monitoring: discussion boards, 94; group projects, 187–188; Performance Dashboard for student, 114–116

Moodle, 65

Moore, J. L., 183

Moore, M., 82, 93

Muirhead, B., 89

Murphy, E., 171, 172

MySpace, 59t, 61, 76

N

Netiquette guidelines, 72–73

New Deloitte Research Center, 15

New Media Consortium, 205

Newberry, R., 94

Nings, 59t, 61, 76

The NMC Campus Observer, 205

Norgard, C., 75

North Carolina State University, 193

Novak, J., 230, 231, 232, 233

O

O'Banion, T., 47

Ohler, J., 204

Oldenburg, R., 29

Online class discussions: asynchronous format of most, 7; communicating teacher presence through, 110–114; ensuring lively participation in, 94–95; solving problem of flat, 251–252; teaming students for, 199–200. *See also* Discussion boards

Online classrooms: access to full-functioned open, 138–139; course closing experience in, 242–243; creating, 138; faculty concerns and questions about, 243; faculty stories on using, 241–242; getting used to, 240–241. *See also* Course management system (CMS)

Online course community: building learning focused, 112; creating supportive, 37t, 38–40, 55; established during course beginnings, 52; nurturing the, 104;

promoting peer interaction for building, 133–145; social networking for empowering the, 199–208; stimulating and comfortable camaraderie of, 224–226; strategies and tools for building, 133–136. *See also* Community of inquiry

Online course launch preparations: course site, 65–66; discussions and rubrics, 65; essential course pieces, 63–64; quality standards for online course, 67–69*t*; review of, 250; syllabus, 64, 68*t*, 72–75, 102, 154, 250; to-do list for, 66–67; weekly teaching guides, 64–65. *See also* Online course wrapping activities

Online course management strategies: audio and video resources, 140–145; building cognitive presence, 145–153; early feedback loop, 120–123; feedback tools to use as, 123–127; L-L (learner to learner), 39–40, 84, 133–136, 182; launch preparations, 63–69*t*; launching and assessing relevant learning projects, 153–156; learning through available tools, 114–117; setting up and structuring groups, 127–130; synchronous collaboration tools, 136–140; teaching assistant, 130–133; tools for communicating teaching presence, 110–114; weekly rhythm challenges to, 117–120. *See also* Course management system (CMS)

Online course (phase 1): beginnings tips for, 55–57, 62–99; course beginnings during the, 51–53; course beginnings themes during, 53–57; description of, 10*t*; reflections on, 251–252; technology tools and pedagogical uses during, 59*t*–60*t*; technology tools used during, 57*t*–61

Online course (phase 2): description of, 11*t*; early middle weeks of, 100–102; nurturing content and learning community, 104; reflections on, 252–253; teaching presence during, 102–103; technology tools used during, 106–108*t*; tips for the early middle, 104–106, 109–156

Online course (phase 3): events during late middle weeks of, 157–159; reflections on, 253–254; technology tools used during, 162–164*t*; themes, best practices, and principles of, 159–161; tips for the, 162, 165–208

Online course (phase 4): events taking place during the, 210–211; reflections on, 254–255; technology tools used during, 213–215; themes, best practices, and principles of, 211–213; tips for closing weeks of the, 213, 216–245

Online course phases: 1: beginnings—starting off on the right foot, 10*t*, 51–61, 62–99, 251–252; 2: early middle—keeping the ball rolling, 11*t*, 100–156, 252–253; 3: late middle—letting go of the power, 11*t*, 157–208, 253–254; 4: closing weeks—pruning, reflecting, and wrapping up, 11–12*t*, 209–245, 254–255; reflecting and looking forward to using, 249–255

Online course site: description of, 68*t*; management systems for, 65; social presence on the, 77–78; technology support of, 65–66

Online course tips (phase 1): 1: course launch preparations, 63–69; 2: hitting the road running: the first week, 70–71; 3: online syllabus, 72–75; 4: launching social presence, 75–79; 5: Vygotsky's zone of proximal development, 79–81; 6: getting into the swing: ideal weekly rhythm, 81–84; 7: discussion boards, 84–88; 8: characteristics of good discussion questions, 88–93; 9: managing and evaluating discussion postings, 93–96; 10: faculty role in the first weeks, 96–99; overview of, 55–57, 62–63

Online course tips (phase 2): 1: tools for communicating teaching presence, 110–114; 2: learning and course management systems, 114–117; 3: weekly rhythm challenges, 117–120; 4: early feedback loop from learners to you, 120–123; 5: early feedback tools, 123–127; 6: setting up and structuring groups, 127–130; 7: teaching assistant, 130–133; 8: promoting peer interaction, 133–136; 9: synchronous collaboration, 136–140; 10: using audio and video resources, 140–145; 11: discussion postings, 145–148; 12: discussion wraps, 148–151; 13: developing cognitive presence, 151–153; 14: launching and assessing learner projects, 153–156; overview of, 104–106

Online course tips (phase 3): 1: questions and answers, 166–169; 2: techniques for making students' knowledge visible, 169–170; 3: defining problems and finding solutions, 170–173; 4: feedback in online learning, 173–176; 5: feedback on assignments, 176–180; 6: reshaping learning habits of online students, 180–183; 7: customizing and personalizing learning, 183–186; 8: managing and facilitating group projects, 186–190; 9: assessing group projects, 190–193; 10: rubric for analyzing critical thinking, 194–195*t*; 11: four effective practices during project time, 195–198; 12: conversations that help build community, 199–201; 13: social networking to build learning community, 201–204; 14: inviting experts, 204–208; overview of, 162

Online course tips (phase 4): 1: authentic problem solving, 217–221; 2: what-if scenarios, 221–224; 3: camaraderie of learning community, 224–226; 4: learners as leaders, 226–229*t*; 5: concept mapping, 229–234; 6: pausing, reflecting, and pruning strategies, 234–236; 7: closing experience to wrap up course, 236–240; 8: closing experiences, 240–243; 9: debriefing students, 244–245; overview of, 213

Online course wrapping activities: concept mapping, 229–234; creating closing learning experience, 236–240; debriefing students, 244–245; pausing, reflecting, and pruning strategies, 234–236; planning, 37*t*, 46–47; stories and suggestions for, 240–243. *See also* Online course launch preparations

Online courses: adding "pizzazz" to, 254; blended/ hybrid, 9*t*; celebration and end-of-course experiences, 237–240; cycle of innovation and future of, 260; description of, 9*t*; elements of a, 68*t*–69*t*; phases of engagement during, 97*t*; quality standards for, 67, 69; reassessing for improvements, 255; setting explicit expectations for, 40–41; to-do list for preparing, 66–67; unique characteristics of, 7–8; Web facilitated, 9*t*. *See also* Courses; Teaching online

Online environment: major categories of faculty teaching in, 5; preparing to teach in the, 3–4; reflections on, 257

Online instructors. *See* Faculty

Online teaching tool set. *See* Technology tools

Open forum, 163*t*

P

Padavano, D., 75

Painter, C., 43

Palen, L., 113

Palloff, R., 125, 227

Palomar College, 141

PARC (Palo Alto Research Center) [Xerox], 15

Part-time adjunct faculty, 5

Patience, 55

Paul, R., 90

Pausing strategies, 234–236

Pedagogy: definition of, 5–6, 22; phase 1 technology tool applications to, 59*t*–60*t*; phase 2 technology tool applications to, 107*t*; phase 3 technology tool applications to, 163*t*–164*t*; phase 4 technology tool applications to, 214*t*

Peer interaction: building community by promoting, 133–136; promoting meaningful dialogue and questioning for, 135–136; strategies for promoting, 134–135

Peer reviews: assessing group projects through, 191–193; pedagogical use during phase 2, 107*t*; receiving feedback through, 126–127; Team Member Evaluation Form for, 192*e*. *See also* Assessment

Peer-to-peer communication: building community through promoting, 133–136; encouraging, 112–113; L-L (learner to learner) dialogue as, 39–40, 84, 133–136, 182. *See also* Synchronous activities

Peirce, B., 92

Pelikan, J., 39, 182

Penn State, 189

Penn State University, 96

Performance dashboard: in Blackboard, 115*fig*–116; monitoring student engagement/progress using, 114–116; pedagogical use during phase 2, 107*t*

Personalized learning: combining core concepts with, 37*t*, 45–46; learners' knowledge and, 23–24

Phase 1. *See* Online course (phase 1)

Phase 2. *See* Online course (phase 2)

Phase 3. *See* Online course (phase 3)

Phase 4. *See* Online course (phase 4)

Piaget, J., 14, 19

Picciano, T., 64

Pinker, S., 19

Pintrich, P. R., 7

"Pizzazz" adding, 254

Plagiarism detection, 75–76

Plato, 222

Podcasts: online book sites offering, 144; pedagogical use during phase 2, 108*t*; sharing, 144; starting points with specific publishers, 143; subscribing to, 143–144

PollDaddy, 121

Polya, G., 218

Polya's four-step problem solving, 218–219

Portland Community College, 108

Practical inquiry model: defining problem using, 171; on integrating useful knowledge, 235–236; overview of, 152*fig*; resolution process component of, 152*fig*, 159–160

Practice: better learning outcome with more, 33; four effective strategies for project time, 195–198; matching content to, 33

Pratt, K., 125, 227

Prerecorded tutorials, 214*t*

Presence: cognitive, 54, 81, 104–106, 145–153, 159–160; description of, 53; social, 51–52, 54, 75–78; teaching, 54–55, 102–103, 110–114

Presentation tools, 188–189

Preskill, S. N., 92

Problem formulation behaviors, 171–172

Problem solution behaviors, 172

Problem solvers: developing, 172–173; questions asked by, 91

Problem-solving process: authentic, 217–221; Polya's four-step, 218–219; problem solution behaviors leading to, 172; questions for, 91; seven-step, 218; what-if scenarios, 221–224

Problems: defining, 171; formulation of, 171–172; segmenting authentic, 220–221; solution of, 172

Progress reports/updates, 198

Project assignments: asking for progress reports or updates on, 198; checklist for short written, 179–180; communicating availability of help on, 198; completion of last, 212; customizing and personalizing learning during, 183–186; faculty coaching on, 160–161, 197–198; guidelines for developing requirements of, 184–186; guiding questions for, 186; helping learners get unstuck on, 196–197; problem of consistently late, 253–254; providing timely and efficient feedback, 175, 176–180; reminder to students on due dates of, 237; round-robin of knowledge construction tasks, 201; rubric for written, 179; rubrics for easy grading of, 177–178; social networking pedagogical strategy for, 202–203; task model of, 185–186; ZPD (zone of proximal development) guiding the, 13, 24, 30–31, 33, 79–81, 186. *See also* Activities; Group projects; Learning experiences; Quizzes; Tasks

Pruning strategies, 234–236

"Psychic RAM," 46, 237

Q

Quality Matters Institute, 67, 260
Quality Matters (QM) project, 69
Quality Online Messages (St. John's University), 147
The Question Place, 181
Questioning: as core of teaching and learning, 160; encouraging students to develop tough, 200–201; leveraging the power of, 166–173; providing rapid response to students', 175–176; Socratic, 44, 90–91, 160, 195; tips on effective use of, 166–169; types of discussion, 90–91. *See also* Discussion board questions
Quizzes: pedagogical use during phase 1, 60*t*; pedagogical use during phase 2, 107*t*; receiving feedback through, 126; syllabus self-quiz, 250. *See also* Project assignments

R

Reasoning Across the Curriculum, 92
Reder, L. M., 151
Reflections: on the learning experiences framework, 255–257; learning strategies using, 234–236; on using online course four phases, 249–255
Resolution process: description of, 159–160; as practical inquiry model stage, 152*fig*
Resources. *See* Learning resources
Richardson, J., 19, 75
Roberto, M. A., 221
Roper, A. R., 181
Rosenbloom, R. S., 260
Rotter, N. G., 75
Rovai, A., 39
Rubrics: for analyzing critical thinking, 194–195*t*; assignment, 177–178; best practices for online course, 260; discussion board, 65; discussion postings, 95*t*–96; feedback using, 123–126; FY 05/06 Quality Matters, 69; group project, 127–128; for participation and levels of thinking, 125*t*; pedagogical use during phase 2, 107*t*; Quality Matters Institute, 67, 69, 260; sample three-point, 125*t*; for written assignment, 179. *See also* Feedback

S

St. John's University, 147
Sakai, 65
Sandheinrich, M. B., 176
Schacter, D., 234, 236
Schallert, D., 151
Schank, R., 15
Schema theory, 15
Schmier, L., 238
Seaman, J., 9
Second Life, 33, 61, 72, 205
Sellers, S. L., 97
"Semantic Web" (Web 3.0), 204
Senge, P., 88
"Seven sins of memory," 234, 236
Shapiro, E. G., 123

Shea, P., 39
Shea, V., 73
SimCity, 33
Simulations: Leadership and Team Simulation: Everest, 221; pedagogical uses during closing weeks, 214*t*; Second Life, 33, 61, 72, 205; SimCity, 33
Skype: group projects using, 188; pedagogical use during phase 2, 107*t*; pedagogical use during phase 3, 163, 164*t*; teaching presence built through, 112
Small groups: problem-solving process by, 220; work experiences of, 41
Smith, A., 136
Smith, D.A.F., 7
The Social Life of Information (Brown), 15
Social networking: community empowerment through, 199–208; encouraging an environment of, 203–204; pedagogical strategy with individual course projects using, 202–203; pedagogical use during phase 1, 59*t*, 61, 76; pedagogical use during phase 3, 164*t*. *See also* Communication tools; *specific Web applications*; Web 2.0
Social presence: Announcements tools and course site, 77–78; description of, 51–52, 54; getting-acquainted posting to establish, 75–76; getting-acquainted-cognitively posting to establish, 77; learner satisfaction related to, 75
Socrates, 222
Socratic questions, 44, 90–91, 160, 195
Specialized Accreditation and Assuring Quality in Distance Learning, 260
Stage theory of child development, 14
Standards (online course), 67, 69
Stanford University, 218
Star Trek Holodeck, 22
Steps to Instant Collaboration metric, 140
Students: addressing bad behavior by, 250–251; assessing their zone of proximal development, 79–81; debriefing, 244–245; discussion wrap participation by, 150; evaluations by, 123, 192*e*, 239; getting acquainted with, 80–81; learning habits of, 180–181; reshaping learning habits of, 180–181; three techniques for revealing knowledge of, 169–170; weekly rhythm challenges of, 119–120. *See also* Learner expectations; Learners
"Stump the Chump" challenge (*Car Talk*), 200
Survey Monkey, 121
Survey tools, 121
Swan, K., 19, 75
Syllabus: assessment plan included in the, 154; characteristics of online, 72–75; description of, 64, 68*t*; design and preparation of, 250; self-quiz about, 250; teaching presence through, 102
Synchronous activities: challenges of scheduling, 120; communication tools for, 188; description of, 42; pedagogical use during phase 2, 107*t*; pedagogical use during phase 4, 214*t*; Web conferencing tools for, 61. *See also* Activities; Peer-to-peer communication

Synchronous collaborative activities: access to full-functioned open live classrooms for, 138–139; choices in collaborative, 137–138; informal and free options for instant, 139; mixing and matching for spontaneous and customizable, 139–140; online classrooms and tools for, 136–140, 136–145. *See also* Group projects

T

Task model: be explicit about project, 185; complement process guidelines with guidelines of, 185–186

Tasks: corresponding to dialogues and activities, 82, 84; during early middle period of course, 101–102; round-robin of knowledge construction, 201; sample weekly schedule for, 83*t*. *See also* Project assignments

Teaching assistants: benefits of using, 130; job description for, 131–132; win-win of working with, 132–133

Teaching guides: description of, 68*t*; weekly, 64–65

Teaching and Learning Center (University of Maryland), 250

Teaching and Learning with Technology Group, 189

Teaching and Learning Technology group (Penn State University), 96

Teaching online: expanding your teaching tool set for, 103; guiding principles for distance learning and, 78–79; landscape for online learning and, 16*fig*; preparing for online environment and, 3–4; questioning as core of, 160; strategies for managing learner expectations, 181–182; ten best practices for, 36–47; traditional approach to teaching versus, 4. *See also* Faculty; Online courses

Teaching online best practices: 1: be present at the course site, 37*t*–38; 2: create supportive online course community, 37*t*, 38–40; 3: develop teacher/learner expectations, 37*t*, 40–41; 4: use large group, small group, and individual experiences, 37*t*, 41; 5: use synchronous and asynchronous activities, 37*t*, 42; 6: ask for informal feedback, 37*t*, 42–43; 7: prepare engaging discussion posts, 37*t*, 43–44; 8: use content resources available in digital format, 37*t*, 44–45; 9: combining concept and personalized learning, 37*t*, 45–46; 10: plan good closing and wrap activity, 37*t*, 46–47

Teaching presence: establishment of, 54–55; three categories of, 102–103; tools for communicating, 103, 110–114

Team activities: Leadership and Team Simulation: Everest, 221; learners-as-leaders experiences, 228; partnering students for one discussion week, 199–200; pedagogical use team wikis, 164*t*. *See also* Collaborative activities; Group projects

Team Member Evaluation Form, 192*e*

Technology tool applications: pedagogical uses of phase 1, 59*t*–60*t*; suggested pedagogical uses of phase 2, 107*t*; suggested pedagogical uses of phase 3, 163*t*–164*t*; suggested pedagogical uses of phase 4, 214*t*

Technology tools: expanding your teaching tool set, 103; group project communication and presentation, 188–189; used during phase 1, 57*t*–61; used during phase 2, 106–108; used during phase 3, 162–164*t*; used during phase 4, 213–215. *See also* Learning resources

Ten core learning principles: 1: every structured experience has four elements, 21–23; 2: on learners' knowledge, skills, attitudes, 23–24; 3: faculty mentors direct the learning experience, 25–26; 4: learner need to learn core concepts, 26–29; 5: learning experience includes environment or context, 29–30; 6: ZPD (zone of proximal development), 13, 24, 30–31; 7: concepts are organized knowledge clusters, 31–32; 8: different instruction required for different outcomes, 32–33; 9: more practice equals more learning, 33; 10: interaction between tools and learning, 34–35; listed, 20–35; origins of the, 19–20

Tenured faculty, 5

Testing. *See* Quizzes

Texas Woman's University, 124

Text messaging: pedagogical use during phase 1, 59*t*; pedagogical use during phase 2, 107*t*

Theories of Practice database, 12–13

Theory of cognitive structures, 14

Theory of social development, 13

Theroux, J., 221

Thought and Language (Vygotsky), 19

A Thousand Splendid Suns (Hosseini), 144

Top 26 Most Important Rules of Email Etiquette, 73

Tracy, B., 196, 197

Traditional face-to-face courses, 9*t*

Troubleshooting, 74

True North: Discovery Your Authentic Leadership (George), 143

Twitter: description of, 28–29, 76; pedagogical use during phase 1, 59*t*; teacher presence through, 113

Tyser, R. W., 176

U

UMassOnline, 221

University of Calgary, 53

University College, 193

University of Guelph Learning Services, 189

University of Illinois-Springfield, 137

University of Maryland, 92, 250

University of Melbourne, 191

University of Queensland, 193

University of Texas, 151

Untenured faculty, 5

V

Varvel, V., 207

Vaughan, N. D., 151, 152, 171

Video lectures: effective use of resources for, 140–145; pedagogical use during phase 1, 58, 59*t*, 60; pedagogical use during phase 2, 108*t*

Video resources: enriching and expanding course, 142–143; incorporating published, 142; podcasts, 108*t*, 143–144; YouTube, 60, 64, 164*t*, 202, 214*t*

Virtual Resource Site for Teaching with Technology (University of Maryland), 92

The Virtual Student (Palloff and Pratt), 125

Virtual Works!, 241

Virtual worlds: pedagogical uses during closing weeks, 214*t*; Second Life, 33, 61, 72, 205; SimCity, 33

VoiceThread, 29, 164*t*, 200

Vygotsky, L.: on balanced dialogue, 183; on concepts as knowledge clusters, 46; on learning being a sociocultural activity, 23; on learning tools, 34; *Mind in Society: The Development of Higher Psychological Processes* by, 19; on process of concept formation, 31; as social constructivist, 20; theory of social development by, 13; *Thought and Language* by, 19; ZPD (zone of proximal development), of, 13, 24, 30–31, 33, 79–81, 186

W

Wager, W. W., 228

Ward, G. C., 222

Washington State University, 96, 194, 195

The Water Cooler, 181

Web 2.0: description of, 202; interconnectivity and interactivity features of, 204. *See also* Social networking

Web 3.0, 204

Web facilitated online courses, 9*t*

Web sites: American Psychological Association, 236; Assessing Group Work, 191; *Best Practices for Electronically Offered Degree and Certificate Programs Best Practices*, 260; Blackboard's Performance dashboard, 116; Center for Critical Thinking and Moral Critique, 195; Centre for Learning and Performance Technologies, 121; CmapTools, 233; CMS (course management system), 114; community of inquiry, 76; concept mapping resources, 233–234; discussion wrap summaries, 151; Distance Education Teaching and Learning Resources, 108; Dublin Centre for Teaching and Learning (University College), 193; emoticons, 73; global business solution for mitigating climate change, 155; Google Apps for Education, 139; Google Docs, 188; Google Gmail voice and video chat, 188; Guest Lecturers in the Online Environment, 208; Guide to Rating Critical and Integrative Thinking, 194; handling difficult students, 251; Harvard Business

Online, 221; Illinois Online Network, 208; *Internet Resources for Higher Education Outcomes Assessment*, 193; iTunes store, 143; iTunes University, 143; Managing Learner-Instructor Interaction and Feedback, 96; Mind-Mapping Software Blog, 234; monographs on ensuring quality distance learning, 260; *The NMC Campus Observer*, 205; plagiarism detection, 75–76; Polya's four-step problem-solving process, 218; practical inquiry model, 152; Quality Online Messages, 147; Second Life, 205; seven-step problem-solving process, 218; subscribing to podcasts, 143; Theories of Practice database, 12–13; *Top 26 Most Important Rules of Email Etiquette*, 73; Virtual Resource Site for Teaching with Technology (University of Maryland), 92; Virtual Works!, 241; Wimba Voice Board instructions, 141–142; Zoho Office Suite, 139. *See also* Learning resources

WebStudy, 117

Weekly schedule: challenges to the rhythm of, 117–120; example of, 83*t*; getting a regular rhythm, 81–82, 84

Weekly teaching guides, 64–65

Weigel, V. B., 186

Wieman, C., 7, 167

What-if scenarios: description of, 222; four reasons for course use of, 223; getting started and challenges of, 223; learning through, 221–222

Wiggins, G., 156

Wikis: CMS (course management system), 204; pedagogical use during phase 1, 59*t*, 60–61; pedagogical use during phase 2, 107*t*; pedagogical use during phase 3 of team, 164*t*

Wimba Collaborative Suite, 141–142, 240

Wimba Voice Board, 108*t*, 138, 141

Wired magazine, 222

Working Group of the Indiana Partnership for Statewide Education, 78

Wrapping up. *See* Online course wrapping activities

X

Xerox Corporation, 15

Y

Young, A., 75

YouTube: as course technology tool, 60, 164*t*; pedagogical use during phase 4, 214*t*; posting faculty mini-lectures, 64; social networking through, 202

Z

Zhang, K., 85

Zoho Office Suite, 139

Zone of proximal development (ZPD): assessing students', 79–81; description of, 13, 24, 30–31; designing course projects around, 186; matching content and practice to, 33

The following constitutes a continuation of the copyright page.

• • •

Table 1.1: From Boettcher, J. V., & Conrad, R. M. (2004). *Faculty guide for moving teaching and learning to the Web* (2nd ed.). Phoenix, AZ: League for Innovation in the Community College. Allen, I. E., & Seaman, J. (2008). *Staying the course: Online education in the United States, 2008.* http://www. sloan-c.org/publications/survey/index.asp.

Figure 2.2: From Boettcher, J. V., & Conrad, R. M. (2004). *Faculty guide for moving teaching and learning to the Web* (2nd ed.). Phoenix, AZ: League for Innovation in the Community College.

Table 2.1: From Boettcher, J. (2007). Ten core principles for designing effective learning environments: Insights from brain research and pedagogical theory. *Innovate, 3*(3). Retrieved October 21, 2009, from http://www.innovateonline.info/index.php?view=article&id=54. Reprinted with permission of the Fischler School of Education and Human Services, Nova Southeastern University.

Chapter Five: Peirce, B. (2004). Strategies for teaching thinking and promoting intellectual development in online classes. *Instructional Area Newsletter, 19*(3). Retrieved April 24, 2009, from http://academic.pgcc. edu/~wpeirce/MCCCTR/ttol.html.

Table 5.4: From Conrad, R. M., & Donaldson, J. A. (2004). *Engaging the online learner: Activities and resources for creative instruction.* San Francisco: Jossey-Bass, p. 11. Reproduced with permission of John Wiley & Sons, Inc.

Table 7.2: From Palloff, R., & Pratt, K. (2003). *The virtual student.* San Francisco: Jossey-Bass, p. 91. Reproduced with permission of John Wiley & Sons, Inc.

Figure 7.2: Garrison, D. R., & Vaughan, N. D. (2008). *Blended learning in higher education: Framework, principles and guidelines.* Hoboken, NJ: Wiley. Reproduced with permission of John Wiley & Sons, Inc.

Chapter Nine: Briskin, L. (2005). *Assigning grades and feedback policies.* Retrieved February 4, 2009, from www.arts.yorku.ca/sosc/Foundations/ documents/EXAMPLEOFACHECKLIST.pdf.

Table 11.1: From Conrad, R. M., & Donaldson, J. A. (2004). *Engaging the online learner: Activities and resources for creative instruction.* San Francisco: Jossey-Bass, p. 108. Reproduced with permission of John Wiley & Sons, Inc.